Radical Discipleship

Radical Discipleship

Following Jesus in the Twenty-First Century

ROBERT P. VANDE KAPPELLE

WIPF & STOCK · Eugene, Oregon

RADICAL DISCIPLESHIP
Following Jesus in the Twenty-First Century

Copyright © 2022 Robert P. Vande Kappelle. All rights reserved. Except for brief quotations in critical publications or reviews, no part of this book may be reproduced in any manner without prior written permission from the publisher. Write: Permissions, Wipf and Stock Publishers, 199 W. 8th Ave., Suite 3, Eugene, OR 97401.

Wipf & Stock
An Imprint of Wipf and Stock Publishers
199 W. 8th Ave., Suite 3
Eugene, OR 97401

www.wipfandstock.com

PAPERBACK ISBN: 978-1-6667-5273-1
HARDCOVER ISBN: 978-1-6667-5274-8
EBOOK ISBN: 978-1-6667-5275-5

Unless otherwise noted, Bible quotations are from the *New Revised Standard Version of the Bible*, copyright © 1989 by the Division of Christian Education of the National Council of the Churches of Christ in the United States of America. Used by permission.

To my granddaughter Katherine:
in the sure conviction
that her youthful love of God and others
will culminate in radical discipleship.

Contents

Preface ix

Chapter 1 Sharing the Toolkit 1

Chapter 2 An Elegant Christology 14

Chapter 3 Temperament, Personality, and Discipleship 25

Chapter 4 The Centrality of Discipleship in the Bible, Part I 39

Chapter 5 The Centrality of Discipleship in the Bible, Part II 55

Chapter 6 Jesus as Archetype of the Self 69

Chapter 7 What Would Jesus Want Modern Disciples to Know 83

Chapter 8 What Would Jesus Want Modern Disciples to Know and Do 105

Chapter 9 Radical Discipleship Illustrated, Part I 124

Chapter 10 Radical Discipleship Illustrated, Part II 140

Chapter 11 Radical Discipleship Illustrated, Part III 155

Chapter 12 Following Jesus: Then and Now 167

Appendix: "Called to Discipleship": A Sermon 187

Bibliography 193

Index 197

Preface

NEARING MY EIGHTH DECADE, I am aware that my driving passion is to understand and implement adequately the core principles that informed the beliefs and practices of Jesus of Nazareth, and to attain—if only partially and imperfectly—the status of faithful disciple.

If discipleship means apprenticeship, then modern disciples of Jesus are called to live radically as "little Christs," modeling their life and character on Jesus, their Master and Mentor. If apprenticeship to Jesus is the basic form of God's presence with us, then discipleship entails ongoing openness to God's radical agenda to love and renew the world and all its inhabitants by challenging the status quo, beginning with oneself. In a word, discipleship is "Christlikeness."

In this respect, discipleship is incarnational at all times, not just in religious moments. Inner Christlikeness includes religious rituals and moral character, but radical discipleship makes every act of family, business, and community a time of learning how to live as Jesus would live. Being faithful in "little things" is a good place to start, for such faithfulness trains us for being faithful "in much," which occurs when we are ready (Luke 16:10). As we note in chapters 4 and 5 below, in the gospels Jesus works with disciples both individually and as a team, whereas in Acts and the epistles God uses an all-inclusive community of loving persons to change the world. Viewed from this perspective, the Bible demonstrates how early communities based on discipleship are established, and how they nurture communion with God and fellowship with one another.

Through the ages there have been many brilliant examples of what discipleship can be, but presently what we see and what nonbelievers see, especially in the West, is a Christian culture devoid of discipleship to Jesus. Many Christians still worship Jesus, but they have failed to fall in love with his humanity and humility. For them, Jesus is not someone to imitate but only someone to worship as divine. Unlike *The Scandal of Divine*

Love, my 2017 study that uses biblical titles to explain why Christians believe that Jesus holds the key to the nature of God and human destiny, this volume focuses on the "historical Jesus" to explore the meaning of the message and ministry of this "man from Galilee" for twenty-first century disciples.

When we examine Christianity today, we must acknowledge that it is not working well as a transformative agent in society: suffering, fear, violence, injustice, greed, and meaninglessness abound. While modern men and women still find meaning in the ministry and teachings of Jesus, the majority of Christians, at least in their behavior and impact upon the world, are not much different than non-Christians.

Let's be honest: many Christians are not highly transformed people. Instead, they tend to reflect their own culture more than operating as any kind of leaven within it. With regards to religion in general, we must admit that it has probably never had such a bad name. Christianity is considered "irrelevant" by many and "toxic" by others, viewed more often as a part of the problem rather than as any kind of solution. Young people in particular are turned off by how judgmental, exclusionary, impractical, and ineffective Christian culture seems to be.

Many Christians have not been taught how to plug into the nondualist mindset of Jesus. Rather, they often reflect the predominant values of power, greed, and war. The dualistic mind reads reality in simple binaries—good and bad, right and wrong—and thinks itself smart because it chooses one side. This approach gets us nowhere. In the past, those who understood Jesus' teaching best seem to have been those who experienced great suffering or surrendered to great love. Could this be the core of the gospel, that people experience God through unconditional love rather than through disconnected ideas about God? What we need today is a practice-based faith that teaches us how to connect with the Infinite in ways that actually transform our finite priorities and perspectives, enabling us to live out of the resources of our True Self (our infinite self made in the "image of God") rather than out of the resources of our False Self (what we call our ego or finite self).

We must rediscover what Francis of Assisi (1182–1226) called the "marrow of the gospel." It is time for Christians to transform their sense of self, rebuilding from the bottom up. If the church's theological foundation is not solid and sure, everything we build on it is weak and ineffective. Perhaps questioning religious baggage is a blessing, for it is time to begin anew. In the year 1205, Francis heard Jesus saying, "Francis, rebuild my church, for you see it is falling into ruin." If that was the case then, it is doubly true today. If Jesus tells us the church is falling into ruin, I trust we too can admit it without being accused of negative thinking or unbelief. For something new and good to happen, something false and ineffectual must be set aside.

For modern Christians dissatisfied with the religiosity, dogmatism, supremacy, and negativity present in Christendom, the good news is that there are options regarding Christianity. As theologian Brian McLaren reminds us, we don't have to choose between staying compliantly or leaving defiantly; we can stay, but do so defiantly, by modeling a different way of being Christian, that is, by remaining faithful to radical discipleship rather than faithful to forms of Christendom that long ago abandoned such discipleship in favor of institutionalized and dogmatized ecclesiology. To remain defiantly is to imitate Jesus, who stayed within Judaism while wrestling with his Jewish identity. He decided that the legacy of his parents, ancestors, and of the prophets was worth staying for, particularly if it meant saving that legacy from corruption by the religious gatekeepers of his day, naming their corruption and toxicity with words such as "whitewashed tombs" and "brood of vipers" (Matt 23:27, 33). Would he have been wiser to have left quietly for some other country or religion, instead of challenging the status quo of his own faith tradition? Jesus stayed, and counted the cost, for it led him to the cross. Was he a fool to think that the tiny handful of people who understood a sliver of his message and saw a glimmer of what he saw could outlive him and do greater things than he had done? Are we willing to be that kind of radical disciple?

As you honor your personal story, I invite you to reflect on how your spirituality is intertwined within the larger human story of abundance and need, security and anxiety, acceptance and betrayal, love and rejection, gain and loss, faith and despair, certainty and doubt, belief and disbelief, justice and injustice, privilege and prejudice, all entangled with racism, sexism, classism, and other systems of oppression.

Together, let us dare to imagine a world we believe is possible, a thriving mindset rooted in the values of freedom, dignity, and compassion, where every person, family, and community flourishes fully. Let us be "Jesus people," followers and imitators of the one who lived life fully and authentically, exemplifying what Jesus meant when he told his followers, "I come that you may have life, and have it abundantly" (John 10:10). The mark of the follower of Jesus is not to be "a religious person" but a full person—open, free, whole, outgoing, compassionate, and a friend to those in need. Followers of Jesus are the ones who can escape the bondage of sin and share life and love unconditionally. They are the ones who have been set free by love. They see this love in the life of the human Jesus and so they call him "Lord" and his way of life "godlike" and "divine."

Note for Leaders and Participants

Radical Discipleship is useful for individual or group study. As you read this book, consider journaling as a way to grow spiritually. A good place to start is with your hopes and dreams. As you reflect and write, be honest with your thoughts and feelings, without ignoring your fears. Transparency facilitates the process of becoming healthy and whole.

Each chapter concludes with questions for discussion or reflection. Write the answers to each question in your journal. If you are reading this book in a group setting, be prepared to share your answers with others in the group. If your study is private, I encourage you to write answers to each question in your journal for review and further reflection. Leaders may select questions from these lists (or add their own questions to each list) that they deem most helpful to group discussion.

Chapter 1

Sharing the Toolkit

To paraphrase Charles Dickens, we live in the best of times, yet also in the worst of times. While it is easy to go low, that is, to focus on the negative in our society, in our assessment of things, I wish to go high. Despite political and social climates bordering on frustration and despair, there are opportunities of great promise today, of collaboration between science and religion and philosophy and theology, disciplines occasionally hostile and suspicious of the other. In an age of globalism, multiculturalism, and ecumenism, courageous institutions and individuals are learning to think and live more holistically than ever before, embracing the new while exposing themselves to uncertainty and the unknown.

This book is written in the spirit of openness and inquiry, with the understanding that each generation of thinkers and believers is required to examine anew the relationship between theology and anthropology, how views of God impact what it means to be human. The bridge, it seems, is Jesus Christ.

It is no secret that we are living in a time of major change, resulting in monumental religious conflict, chiefly in North American mainline denominations. While there are many ways of being Christian in our day, two paradigms—two overarching interpretive frameworks—may be helpful to describe the current conflict in Christianity. The first, the Precritical Paradigm, has been a common form of Christianity for the past several hundred years. This approach should not be associated with Christianity as a whole, though it remains a major voice, perhaps the majority voice in global Christianity. Its adherents

1. view the Bible as a divine product, as the unique revelation of God;
2. interpret the Bible literally;
3. equate faith with belief; the Christian life centered in believing now for the sake of salvation;
4. view the afterlife as central; the Christian life being about requirements and rewards, with the main reward a blessed afterlife;
5. view Christianity as the only true religion, and belief in God, the Bible, and Jesus as the way to heaven.

This paradigm should not be equated with "the Christian tradition," as though it were the dominant or only way of being Christian throughout history. In actuality it is the product of modernity, shaped by the birth of modern science and scientific ways of knowing. Since the Enlightenment of the seventeenth century, modernity has questioned both the divine origin and the literal-factual truth of many parts of the Bible, and the Precritical Paradigm is a response to that modern critique.

A second way of seeing Christianity, the Postcritical Paradigm, has been in existence for over a hundred years and has become an increasingly attractive movement within mainline Protestant denominations and in the Catholic Church. Like the earlier paradigm, its central features are a response to the Enlightenment, only in this case it embraces many Enlightenment ideals, including an appreciation of science, historical scholarship, religious pluralism, and cultural diversity. It is also compelling to many today who continue that form of traditional Christianity that contributed to racism, sexism, nationalism, exclusivism, and other harmful ideologies. Its adherents

1. view the Bible as a human response to God;
2. interpret the Bible historically and metaphorically;
3. view faith relationally rather than dogmatically—faith being the way of the heart, not the way of the head;
4. view the Christian life as one of relationship and transformation. Being Christian is not about meeting requirements for a future reward in an afterlife, and not very much about believing. Rather, the Christian life is about a relationship with God that transforms life in the present;

5. affirm religious pluralism. This paradigm considers Christianity as one of the world's great enduring religions, as a particular response to the experience of God in our Western cultural stream.

From the perspective of the Postcritical Paradigm, the Precritical Paradigm seems anti-intellectual and rigidly (but selectively) moralistic. Its insistence on biblical literalism seems inadequate, as does its rejection of science whenever it conflicts with literalism. It seems to emphasize individual purity more than compassion and justice. And its exclusivism, its rejection of other religions as inadequate or worse, is objectionable. Can it be that God is known in only one religion—and perhaps only in the "right" form of that religion?[1]

Science and Religion: Three Options

About a century and a half ago Charles Darwin's remarkable theory of evolution came into the Western world, says Andrew Dickson White, "like a plough into an anthill."[2] The religious and intellectual worlds of the nineteenth century, not prepared for Darwin, went scurrying in a variety of directions. Even in the twenty-first century, religious believers are still reeling from the shock Darwin apparently delivered to many traditional beliefs.

Thoughtful, modern Christians find themselves caught in a web of questions, affected by the findings of contemporary science, many of them without adequate resolution. What is the place of religion in an age of science? Has science made religion intellectually implausible? Can one believe in God today? If so, what views of God are consistent with the scientific understanding of the world? Need we any longer hold that the world is created by God? Are humans really intended to be here? Has biology shown that life and mind are reducible to chemistry, thus rendering illusory the notions of soul and spirit? How can the search for meaning and purpose in life be fulfilled in the kind of world disclosed by science? These questions make up the so-called "problem of science and religion," one of the most fascinating, important, and challenging controversies of our time. They remain very much alive in our society and continue to evoke an interesting range of responses.

---

1. Borg, *Heart of Christianity*, 16.
2. Cited by Haught in *Responses to 101 Questions*, 5.

What philosopher Alfred North Whitehead stated in 1925 still holds true today: "When we consider what religion is for mankind, and what science is, it is no exaggeration to say that the future course of history depends upon the decision of this generation as to the relations between them. We have here the two strongest general forces . . . which influence human beings, and they seem to be set one against the other—the force of our religious institutions, and the force of our own impulse to accurate observation and logical deduction."[3]

Examining the spectrum of contemporary views, Roman Catholic theologian John Haught identifies three distinct ways in which science and religion can be related to each other:[4]

1. Opposition—the conviction that science and religion are fundamentally irreconcilable.
2. Separation—the claim that there can be no genuine conflict since religion and science are each responding to radically different questions.
3. Engagement—an approach that affirms interaction and looks for possible "consonance" between the disciplines, especially for ways in which science shapes religious and theological understanding.

Prior to the great theological debates that culminated in the councils of Nicaea and Chalcedon, the early Christian theologian Tertullian (c. 160–c.230) articulated the notion of God's "Two Books," the Book of Nature and the Book of Scripture. It was this influential notion that Galileo cited approvingly in his 1615 treatise on the use of biblical quotations in matters of science. Galileo agreed with Tertullian that both nature and scripture proceed alike from the creative Word of God. Therefore, when properly read and interpreted, the truths revealed at each level cannot contradict one another. Sir Francis Bacon (1561–1626), who promoted the scientific method of induction, agreed with Galileo that if one establishes by assured empirical and logical processes the truth of something in nature that appears to be in conflict with a biblical passage, then the problem is not with what the biblical text *says* but with the *interpretation* placed upon its words.

The notion of God's "Two Books" became a commonplace in Christian thought and is still cited by those writing about the relationship

---

3. Whitehead, *Science and the Modern World*, 181–82.
4. Haught, *God After Darwin*, 24.

between religion and science. Even the great nineteenth-century champion of biblical inerrancy, Charles Hodge, agreed with Galileo and Bacon, but he put the matter more bluntly. He insisted "in common with the whole Church, that this infallible Bible must be interpreted by science," a proposition he considered "all but self-evident." Hodge used the Copernican revolution as the classic example of this view: "For five thousand years [sic] the Church understood the Bible to teach that the earth stood still in space, and that the sun and stars revolved around it. Science has demonstrated that this is not true. Shall we go on to interpret the Bible so as to make it teach the falsehood that the sun moves round the earth, or shall we interpret it by science and make the two harmonize?"[5]

Throughout history, those who promoted the "Two Books" concept were concerned to defend the integrity of both the study of nature and the study of scripture, but when the language of the latter seems to contradict the former, as in the classic example Hodge used, they encouraged readers of scripture to invoke another important element in their interpretive framework, the principle of accommodation. Accommodation is the notion that the biblical writers describe phenomena of nature in a way that was understandable and accessible to ordinary and unlearned people.

Augustine utilized the principle of accommodation in his interpretation of the "six days" of Genesis; Thomas Aquinas likewise used it when he interpreted Genesis 1 in light of Aristotelian science. John Calvin, in his commentaries on Genesis and Psalms, was quite clear in stating that the sacred writers described nature simply as it appeared to their senses: "The Holy Spirit," he wrote, "had no intention to teach astronomy; and in proposing instruction meant to be common to the simplest and most uneducated person he made use by Moses and other prophets of the popular language."[6] Noting that the author of Genesis 1 "did not treat scientifically of the stars" but referred to them "in a popular manner," he invited readers interested in learning science to come not to Genesis 1, but "to go elsewhere." Galileo was thoroughly orthodox when he wrote: "These propositions [regarding the phenomena of the heavens] uttered by the Holy Ghost were set down in that manner by the sacred scribes in order to accommodate them to the capacities of the common people."[7] Thanks to this widely accepted principle, theologians could hold that the biblical

---

5. Cited by Schneider, *Science and Faith*.
6. Cited by Schneider, *Science and Faith*.
7. Cited by Schneider, *Science and Faith*.

writers accurately and truthfully described the creation as they perceived and understood it. But they were describing natural phenomena within their ordinary human understanding, using the common language of everyday speech; they were not being guided to make revelatory statements about the nature of the universe. The "Two Books" concept remains for many theologians and scientists a fruitful metaphor for understanding the relationship between biblical and scientific knowledge.

One insight that historians and philosophers of science have given to our generation is that the theories and models that scientists construct to make sense of natural phenomena are always provisional. Such are true so long as scholars continue to offer the best account of the operations of nature; their superior explanatory power and the fruitful results of scientific research make them convincing. Yet, even though these theories may be so compelling as to be accepted as true for hundreds of years, they may still be replaced or modified whenever new knowledge provides the impetus and necessity to construct new theories to explain nature and its operations. Our knowledge of the universe remains incomplete, for the sum of human knowledge about the natural world is always increasing. The final description of the universe has yet to be devised, the full potential of science yet to be realized.

In 1998, in an article in *The American Scholar*, William Cronon listed ten qualities he most admired in people he knew who seemed to embody the values of a liberal education.[8] The first nine—listening, reading, talking, writing, problem solving, truth seeking, tolerance, leadership, collegiality—lead to the tenth: the ability to connect with others in authentic community. A liberal education is about gaining the power, the wisdom, the generosity, and the freedom to connect.

A Common Quest for Truth

Inspired by the unfathomable nature of reality and the plurality of ways by which it can be experienced and expressed, I have identified seven qualities that religiously minded and scientifically guided individuals might share in their common quest for truth. Some were suggested by the late Carl Sagan in his moving personal work, *The Demon-Haunted World: Science as a Candle in the Dark*. In chapter two he writes of his lifelong love affair with science. Science, he affirms, is more than a body

---

8. Cronon, "Only Connect."

of knowledge; it is a way of thinking and, we might add, a way of connecting. Religion is also a way of thinking and of connecting. Religion and science are less than perfect instruments of knowing, but they are the best we have, and it's important that they find ways to complement one another. My list of personal qualities for liberally educated scientists and people of faith include the following aptitudes:

1. *Intuition.* The role of intuition in scientific discovery is virtually universally acknowledged. Intuition and imagination are rarely part of a scientist's education, but they have been essential to some of science's greatest achievements. They are regarded as a gift of birth endowing some more than others with superior intuition. Furthermore, intuitive insight comes at unexpected moments—in the bath for the physicist Archimedes, when getting onto a tram car in Paris for the mathematician/physicist Poincare, or while looking into the fire after an excessive amount of drink one evening for the chemist Kekule. The history of science is filled with these anecdotes, which are qualities of experience that regularly accompany scientific insight.

Scientists are often confronted with problems not solvable by logical deduction from basic principles. For instance, how is it possible to reconcile the observations that electrons or photons can behave as particles and as waves? How are we to understand the loss of weight of a body immersed in a liquid? Again, how can the strange properties of a molecule such as benzene be reconciled with its chemical formula? Solutions to such problems are arrived at by the creative human process that involves intuition. Models may be guided by observation and by logical constraint, but the underlying principle is often an insight, a hunch, or simply by thinking "outside the box." While science is committed to facts, it remains open to new ideas, even when they don't conform to preconceptions. Science counsels adherents to entertain alternative hypotheses and see which best fit the facts.

Likewise, liberally educated religious practitioners, while committed to scriptures, traditions, theological principles, and other tenets of their faith tradition, remain open to new understandings and interpretations, even when they don't conform to presuppositions.

2. *Self-criticism.* The scientific way of thinking, like the liberally religious way, is at once imaginative and modest. It urges on us a delicate balance between no-hold-barred openness to new ideas, however heretical, and the most rigorous skeptical scrutiny of everything—new ideas and established wisdom. This kind of thinking is also an essential

tool for a democracy in an age of change. One of the reasons for the success of science is that it has built-in, error-correcting machinery at its very heart. There are no forbidden questions in science, no matters too sensitive or delicate to be probed, no sacred truths. That openness to new ideas, combined with the most rigorous, skeptical scrutiny of all ideas, sifts the wheat from the chaff. It makes no difference how smart, sincere, or beloved you are. In the realm of science, one must prove one's case in the face of determined, expert criticism. Valid criticism is expected, and debate is valued. Opinions are encouraged to contend, but they must be substantiated.

Though this may be an overly broad characterization for science, as certainly for religion at its best, every time we exercise self-criticism, every time we test our ideas against the outside world, we are doing science. When we are self-indulgent and uncritical, when we confuse hopes and facts, we slide into pseudoscience and superstition. Humans may crave absolute certainty; they may aspire to it or pretend, as partisans of certain religions do, to have attained it. But the history of science teaches that the most we can hope for is successive improvement in our understanding, learning from our mistakes, but always with the proviso that absolute certainty is elusive. One of the great commandments of science is, "Mistrust arguments from authority." Too many such arguments, in science and religion, have proved painfully wrong. Authorities, like everybody else, must support their contentions. This independence of science, its occasional unwillingness to accept conventional wisdom, makes it dangerous to doctrines less self-critical, or with pretensions to certitude.

3. *Reverence and awe.* In its encounter with nature, science and religion invariably elicit a sense of awe. The very act of understanding is a celebration of joining, merging, even if on a very modest scale, with the magnificence of the cosmos. Recognizing our place in the immensity of space and in the passage of time; grasping the intricacy, beauty, and subtlety of life—that soaring feeling, that sense of elation and humility combined—these are surely spiritual. So are our emotions in the presence of great art, music, literature, or acts of exemplary selfless courage such as those of Mohandas Gandhi or Martin Luther King Jr. "Spirit" comes from the Latin word "to breathe." What we breathe is air, which is certainly matter, however thin. Science is not only compatible with spirituality; it is also a profound source of spirituality. The notion that science and spirituality are somehow mutually exclusive does a disservice to both.

4. *Humility*. Science understands human imperfection. All humans, including revered scientists and theologians, have been wrong. Some people consider religion arrogant, especially when it resists change or forbids questioning self-imposed ecclesiastical authority. Science, too, appears arrogant, especially when it purports to contradict beliefs of long standing or when it introduces bizarre concepts that seem contradictory to common sense. While this can be profoundly disturbing, like an earthquake that rattles our faith in the very ground upon which we stand, science is displaying humility. Scientists do not seek to impose their needs and wants on nature, but instead humbly interrogate nature and take seriously what they find.

Like scientists, religionists should value independent verification of proposed tenets of belief. Science is constantly prodding, challenging, seeking contradictions or persistent residual errors, proposing alternative explanations, encouraging heresy. Science gives its highest rewards to those who convincingly disprove established beliefs. Whenever possible, religion should follow suit. In religion there should be something comparable to scientific humility.

5. *Experimentation*. Science may be hard to understand. It may challenge cherished beliefs. And when its products are placed at the disposal of politicians or industrialists, they may lead to weapons of mass destruction and grave threats to the environment. But one thing can be said about science: it delivers the goods. Though no branch of science can foretell historical events, some natural phenomena can be predicted with stunning accuracy. To know when the next eclipse of the sun will be, one might try magic or mysticism, but will do much better with science, which can routinely predict a solar eclipse, to the minute, a millennium in advance. If interested in the sex of your unborn child, you can consult a medium, who may be right, on average, only one time in two, or you can try amniocentesis and sonograms. Every religion on the planet yearns for such precision—repeatedly demonstrated before committed skeptics. No other human institution, not even religious prophecy, comes close.

Whenever possible, scientists experiment. Which experiments they conduct often depend on which theories currently prevail. Scientists are intent on testing theories to the breaking point, not trusting what is intuitively obvious. That the earth is flat was once obvious. That heavy bodies fall faster than light ones was once obvious. That some people are naturally and by divine decree slaves was once obvious. That there is such a place as the center of the universe, and that the earth sits in that exalted spot, was once obvious. The truth may be puzzling or counterintuitive. It may contradict deeply held beliefs. Experimentation is how one gets a handle on it.

While religion and science differ in subject matter, lack of experimentation is one of the reasons that the organized religions fail to inspire confidence. Which leaders of the major faiths acknowledge that their beliefs might be incomplete or erroneous and establish institutes to uncover possible doctrinal deficiencies? Beyond the test of everyday living, who is systematically testing the circumstances in which traditional religious teachings may no longer apply? Scripture is said to be divinely inspired—a phrase with many possible meanings. But what if it's simply made up by fallible humans? Miracles are attested, but what if they're a mix of charlatanry, unfamiliar states of consciousness, misapprehensions of natural phenomena, and mental illness?

At dinner some years ago the physicist Robert W. Wood was asked to respond to the toast, "To physics and metaphysics" (by "metaphysics" people then meant something like philosophy or truths one could recognize intuitively). Wood answered along these lines: The physicist has an idea. The more he thinks it through, the more sense it seems to make. He consults the scientific literature. The more he reads, the more promising the idea becomes. Thus prepared, he goes to the laboratory and devises an experiment to test it. The experiment is painstaking. Many possibilities are checked. The accuracy of measurement is refined, the error bars reduced. The physicist is devoted only to what the experiment teaches. At the end of careful experimentation, the idea is found to be worthless. So the physicist discards it, frees his mind from the clutter of error, and moves on to something else. The difference between physics and metaphysics, Wood concluded, is not that the practitioners of one are smarter than the practitioners of the other. The difference is that the metaphysicist has no laboratory.

6. *Democracy*. The values of science and the values of democracy are concordant, in many cases indistinguishable. Science thrives on, indeed requires, the free exchange of ideas, its values being antithetical to secrecy. Individual insights are never simply accepted, the status of the insight as objective truth depending upon intersubjective consensus between practicing scientists. If there is no consensus, there is no truth. This is the democratic aspect of scientific discovery, which depends upon a community of individuals who practice a shared methodology of investigation. Science holds to no special vantage points or privileged positions. Both

science and democracy encourage unconventional opinions and vigorous debate. Both demand adequate reason, coherent argument, rigorous standards of evidence and honesty. Science is a way to call the bluff of those who only pretend to knowledge. It is a bulwark against superstition and against religion misapplied. If we are true to its values, it can tell us when we are being deceived. It provides a mid-course correction to our mistakes. If we don't practice these tough habits of thought, we cannot hope to solve truly serious problems—and we risk becoming a nation of pushovers, up for grabs by the next charlatan who comes along.

7. *Elegance.* Because science carries us toward an understanding of the actual world, rather than as we would wish it to be, its findings may not in all cases be immediately comprehensible or satisfying. A little work may be needed to restructure our mindsets. Some of science is very simple. When it becomes complicated, that's usually because the world is complicated—or because we're complicated. Here the concept of "elegance" comes into play, elegance being essential to scientists working in all fields. While we usually associate a sense of elegance with art or fashion design, poetry or dance, the idea of elegance is surprisingly important in science as well.[9] The initial insight that leads a scientist to a consistent description of a set of observations, gathering them into a coherent whole, involves both subjective experience and qualitative evaluation: elegance, simplicity, beauty, truth, are the most common descriptors. The resulting theory is often parsimonious, suggesting that the simpler the theory, the closer to the truth the assumption. The implication is that truth, like nature, should be parsimonious.

In his famous book, *The Structure of Scientific Revolutions*, Thomas Kuhn argued that when scientists decide which of several alternative paradigms should be adopted, their selection would be based on, among other things, arbitrary considerations, some of which are aesthetic. The most frequently cited aesthetic qualities on the basis of which some ideas in science may be accepted are simplicity, symmetry, and elegance. Scientists often share a sense of admiration and excitement on hearing of an elegant solution to a problem, a theory, or an experiment. For scientists, as for artists and theologians, elegance implies beauty, simplicity, clarity,

---

9. As the scientist and philosopher Stephen Hawking stated in *The Grand Design*, 5, a scientific model is a good model if it: (1) is elegant; (2) contains few arbitrary or adjustable elements; (3) agrees with and explains all existing observations; (4) and makes detailed predictions about future observations that could disprove or falsify the model if they are not borne out.

and proportion; the elegant solution has a kind of stunning and unalterable rightness that inspires wonder and awe. The idea of elegance may seem strange in a discipline that prides itself on objectivity, but only so if science is regarded as a dull activity of counting and measuring. It is, of course, far more than that, making elegance a fundamental aspect of the beauty and imagination involved in religious and scientific activity.

In the pages that follow, we will explore the meaning and message of the historical Jesus, emphasizing the humanity of Jesus rather than his divinity, using physical rather than metaphysical categories, for these are the only ones accessible to us as human beings. This is not to deny the dimensions of transcendence or the supernatural, but it does mean starting where twenty-first century seekers might have the best chance of encounter with the divine. To be modern and postmodern means beginning with the familiar and the contingent. By so doing, the claims of honesty and integrity, of justice and freedom, of solidarity with universal suffering may be taken seriously and without reserve. Using this process, we may not be able to see things with finality, but in the particular concrete situation, we affirm that persons matter more than procedures, and principles more than precepts.

Today, in our cultural milieu, the place of theology in general and of Christology and soteriology in particular, is the servants' quarters, not, as in the period of Christendom, the throne. Its style will be more modest, more broken. Yet at its center is a figure, as the author of Hebrews insists he always is, who is "suited to our need" (Heb 7:26, NEB), and whom in all his humiliation Christians still rightly call "Teacher" and "Master" (John 13:13).

Questions for Discussion and Reflection

1. With respect to the Precritical and Postcritical paradigms as ways of interpreting what it means to be Christian, which do you prefer? Why? In your estimation, instead of two separate and conflicting paradigms, can some of the points in these paradigms be combined to create one holistic paradigm? Also, can you think of additional or more attractive approaches to the Christian message than these two options? Explain your answer,

2. Do you agree with the author's view that the Precritical Paradigm, when equated with traditional Christianity, is not an ancient but rather a recent product of modernity? Explain your answer.

3. In your estimation, is the theory of biological evolution compatible with Christian theology? Explain your answer.

4. In your estimation, should Christians compartmentalize science and religion into separate and distinct approaches to reality, or should they work to find consonance or harmony between them? Explain your answer.

5. In your estimation, is it more helpful to view science like mathematics, that is, as factual and objective disciplines, and theology like art, as subjective and aesthetic disciplines, or are science and theology methodologically similar in that they are both essentially interpretive in nature? Explain your answer.

6. Assess the merits and validity of the notion of God's "Two Books" as a metaphor for understanding the relationship between theological and scientific knowledge.

7. In your estimation, what can an education in the liberal arts teach us about humility, consonance, and the provisionality of our understanding and interpretation of reality?

8. Although the author suggests that science and religion potentially follow similar approaches to knowledge, including reliance on intuition, awe, and imagination, isn't his list of complementary qualities or aptitudes for practitioners of science and religion more wishful than actual, and isn't it true that these disciplines follow altogether different methods? Explain your answer.

9. Of the seven qualities listed in this chapter, which should people of religious faith aspire to adopt and follow? Explain your answer.

10. Of the seven qualities listed in this chapter, which should scientifically oriented individuals adopt and follow? Explain your answer.

11. Because the principle of elegance is central in subsequent chapters of this book, explain and assess its merits and validity for people of religious faith.

Chapter 2

An Elegant Christology

THE CHRISTIAN MOVEMENT STARTED the fourth century as a persecuted minority; it ended the century as the established religion of the Roman empire. Among the many important ecclesiastical developments and events during the fourth and fifth centuries that led to the development of Christendom, the following helped shape the church's conception of faith, vocation, and governance: (1) political events such as Constantine's contributions to Christianity, (2) the canonical process, which closed the Christian New Testament; (3) the beginnings of the papacy; and (4) doctrinal developments regarding God, the Trinity, and Jesus Christ.

The central figure in this transformation was Emperor Constantine, one of the major figures of Christian history. His embrace of Christianity is considered one of the most important events for the growth and development of Christianity in the West. As a result, the Christian church was joined to the power of the state and assumed a moral responsibility for Western society. During the fourth and fifth centuries, the church refined its doctrine and developed its structure. The church historian Eusebius saw Constantine's embrace of Christianity as its victory over the empire. Others believed culture enticed believers toward worldliness. As Søren Kierkegaard warned centuries later, when everybody is a Christian, nobody is a Christian.

During the past two centuries and continuing to our time, there has been an explosion in the scholarly investigation of Christology, the study of the person and work of Jesus Christ. (If theology is "God-talk," Christology is "Christ-talk," language about Jesus of Nazareth, his identity and significance—who he was and what he accomplished.) The word "Christology" consists of two Greek words: *logos*, meaning "talk about" or "the study of," and *Christos*, originally meaning "Messiah." For early Christians the term "Christ" quickly morphed from the narrow confines of Jesus messianism to become the Christian name of Jesus; Jesus the Christ became simply Jesus Christ.

At its inception, the Christian movement was characterized by great diversity of beliefs and practices, some Jewish, some pagan, and others uniquely Christian, but by the year 313, Christianity sought agreement and unity. Unity demanded a universal version of the church, and over time there developed a unifying conception of the church, summarized by the word "catholic," from a Greek adjective meaning "general," "whole," or "universal." Such unity required theological consensus, particularly Christological consensus.

The first Christians had a stunning array of titles, names, and expressions for Jesus, ranging from Rabbi, Messiah, and High Priest to Lord, Son of God, Word of God, Wisdom of God, and Spirit of God. In the Pauline corpus alone we find a broad range of christological titles. In addition to common titles such as God, Lord, Messiah, and Spirit we find also Angel (Gal 4:14), Rock (1 Cor 10:4), Destroyer (1 Cor 10:10); Man of Heaven (1 Cor 15:49); Power of God (1 Cor 1:18); Wisdom of God (1 Cor 1:21); the Glory (2 Cor 4:4); Image of God (2 Cor 4:4); Form of God (Phil 2:6); the Name (Phil 2:9); and the Head (1 Cor 12:12–13); and that's only a start to the Pauline list. In addition to established titles, most books of the New Testament introduce unique titles of their own. For example, Colossians speaks of Christ as Firstborn (Col 1:15); Beginning (Col 1:18); and Fullness of God (Col 1:19).

Over the next three centuries these titles would be fleshed out to incorporate a Nicene understanding: Jesus Christ was of the same substance as God the Father; he was equal with God in status, authority, and power; he was the one through whom God created all things in heaven and on earth; there never was a time when he did not exist. These were all quite exalted things to say about an apocalyptic itinerant preacher from rural Galilee crucified as a would-be messiah, a failed claimant to the vacant Jewish throne of Judea. By 381, this understanding of Jesus, recited in the Nicene Creed—or, more accurately, the Niceno-Constantinopolitan Creed—served as a benchmark of orthodoxy for all succeeding mainstream Christian churches, whether Catholic, Orthodox, or Protestant.

The classic Christian position, summarized in the "doctrine of the two natures," perfectly divine and perfectly human, was definitively stated by the Council of Chalcedon in 451. Generally stated, this position affirms the centrality of the two natures of Jesus Christ for the church, wisely noting that so long as we recognize that Jesus Christ is both truly divine and truly human, the precise manner in which this is articulated or explored is not of fundamental importance. Chalcedon defined the starting point for classical Christology to be the recognition that in the face of Christ we find the face of God.

During subsequent centuries, Christian thinkers devoted a great deal of study to Christology, speculating about the two natures of Christ while closely connecting their study to doctrines of the incarnation, the atonement, and the Trinity. Over time, two main pictures developed: of a Christ who was God in disguise and of Jesus the perfect man. Sadly, both pictures, offered as objects of devotion and belief, distanced Jesus from nonreligious individuals and led to his irrelevance for increasing numbers of people.

Dietrich Bonhoeffer spoke for many when he wrote from a Nazi prison in the 1940s: "What really bothers me incessantly is the question . . . who Christ really is for us today." For Jesus Christ to be "the same yesterday and today and forever" (Heb 13:8), he has to be a contemporary of every generation and therefore different for every generation: he must be *their* Christ, *our* Christ.

The critical question is, "How does the 'Christ for us today' relate to the Christ for other ages—whether of the first century or the sixteenth or the twentieth?" One mistake of the liberal tradition is to wish too fervently that the biblical writers might say exactly what needs to be said today. It is the same error in reverse of the traditionalists who wish too fervently that the biblical message might be the exact word we ought to pronounce now. Our exploration of the meaning of Jesus Christ—then and now—presupposes a reality there to explore. According to a Quaker observation, "we do not 'seek' the Atlantic, we explore it." The same applies to Christ, or to what Teilhard de Chardin called the Christosphere. Christians begin with a given, gracious reality. They cannot assume this dogmatically or narrowly, nor can they presuppose it of others. When Paul and other early Christians state, often uncritically, "to me, living is Christ" (Phil 1:21), or confess, "Jesus is Lord" (1 Cor 12:3), what did these mean to first-century Christians, and what do they mean to us today? The center, thankfully, is given in scripture, but the periphery is teasingly and liberatingly open.

In the words of J. M. Creed: "Christian theology need not claim that the Christian religion contains within itself all truth, or even all truth that is of religious value, but if it loses the conviction that in Jesus Christ it has found the deepest truth of God, it has lost itself."[1]

While traditionally an over-emphasis on the humanity of Jesus tended to lead to positions that the church labelled eccentric or heretical, an over-emphasis on the divinity of Jesus led to positions that the church embraced as orthodox. Today, however, the suggestion that Jesus was not completely human is actually more destructive than doubts about his divinity. To say that Jesus was not God but like God says something important. But to say that Jesus was not human but like a human is to judge his entire life a charade.

What does it mean today—post Darwin, Marx, Freud, and the deciphering of the human genome—to insist that Jesus was completely human? To say, with the ancient church theologians, that Jesus was truly man but not a man, truly human but not a human being, is nonsense to a modern person. To say that the individual personality of the man Jesus was supplied by, or included in, the hypostasis or substance of the second person of the Trinity, so that what was human was assumed by this superhuman being, strikes us as threatening the very core of Jesus' manhood, his human personhood.

While emphasis on the humanity of Jesus is central to the classic creeds of Christendom, the patristic expression of what it meant for Christ to be human—spelled out in the astonishing doctrine of *anhypostasia* or "impersonal humanity," which saw Christ not as a human person but as a divine person who assumed human nature without assuming human personality—left him aloof and alien to the human condition. Today, when we think of a human being, we think not of a solitary visitor who may have entered completely the place where we are, but only as a visitor. Rather we think of one active in the nexus of biological, historical, and social relationships with fellow human beings and with the universe as a whole. If Jesus was like us, but whose genes and chromosomes were not shaped and transmitted by millions of years of evolution, he was not a member of the species *homo sapiens*, and hence not one of us. No one can become a human unexpectedly; a genuine person can only come out of the organic human process, not into it.

As it turns out, this concern for Jesus' solidarity with the rest of creation, with the culture of Israel, the seed of David, and the rest of creation, is not only modern but also biblical. As every person participates

---

1. Creed, *Divinity of Jesus Christ*, 113.

in race, nation, or culture, Jesus was a son of Abraham. More importantly, he was a son of Adam, as all humans are, regardless of culture, nation, or race. There is no other conceivable way of being human. Not only is it impossible, by definition, that God should become human, it is also impossible, by definition, that God should "make" one so. A true human being cannot be freshly minted. Such a being might look human, but he would not be human by virtue of not belonging to the social, chemical, and biological process.

The epistle to the Hebrews speaks of Jesus as a man "who in every respect has been tested as we are" (4:15), who was "subject to weakness" (5:2), who "offered up prayers and supplications, with loud cries and tears, to the one who was able to save him from death, and he was heard because of his reverent submission" (5:7). Such language surely points to a person of common nature with ourselves. For Paul, also, the solidarity of Jesus with our present human condition is of fundamental theological importance. Without questioning the sinlessness of Jesus, Paul makes it clear that this has significance only if Jesus really did share our nature. God sent his Son "in the likeness of sinful flesh" (Rom 8:3), and "made him to be sin who knew no sin" (2 Cor 5:21). For our sake he came under the curse and custody of the law (Gal 3:13, 23), and in bearing the human likeness, he assumed the position of a slave to the powers of evil and death (Phil 2:7–8).

For Jesus to become in every respect one of us, belonging to the human race, he must have been linked through his biological tissue to the origin of life on this planet and behind that to the whole inorganic process reaching back to the star dust and the hydrogen atom. How can we judge Jesus extraordinary if we cannot first judge him ordinary? The New Testament does not seem embarrassed by Jesus' natural connection with the rest of his fellow humans: "Is not this the carpenter, the son of Mary and brother of James and Joses and Judas and Simon, and are not his sisters here with us?" (Mark 6:3; cf. 3:31; also 1 Cor 9:5; Gal. 1:19; John 2:12; Acts 1:14). This combination of witnesses is far stronger than for the virgin birth story, which on any natural reading of the words that Joseph "had no marital relations with [Mary] until she had borne a son" (Matt 1:25), implies rather than rules out subsequent relations. It asserts that Jesus was Mary's firstborn son, not her only son (Luke 2:7).

While the significance of Jesus is not understood solely from the point of view of heredity and environment, these conditions are not abrogated in Jesus, any more that they are for ordinary Christians who, as children of God, "were born, not of blood or of the will of the flesh or of the will of man, but of God" (John 1:13). However, this is not to deny that at the level of nature they are so born. The one truth does not contradict the other. As many have stated, notably Donald Baillie: "It is . . . nonsense to say that [Jesus] is 'Man' unless we mean that He is *a* man."[2]

Whatever more he is—or was—he must be one of us. If Jesus is to be our Person, our Man, he must be a human being in every sense of the word. This is what we find in the New Testament. The early Christians began with a view of Christ that was uncomplicated and relatable. They certainly did not see Jesus to be of *merely* human significance, since he embodied what God was doing in their midst. But their earliest memory was fashioned into a simplistic Christology, perhaps the earliest, of "a man," Jesus of Nazareth, singled out by God, crucified and raised from the dead, as Peter's speech on the day of Pentecost recalls (Acts 2:22–24).

Understanding Jesus and the Gospels Anew

Prior to the 1830s, practically everyone understood the gospels as either supernatural histories or natural histories. This changed in 1835 with the publication of a two-volume work entitled *Das Leben Jesu*, by the brilliant biblical scholar David Friedrich Strauss (1808–1874), then only twenty-seven years old.[3] According to Anglican bishop and biblical theologian Stephen Neil, the year 1835 and Strauss's book "marked, as few others have done, a turning-point in the history of the Christian faith."[4]

Strauss's book, an amazing work of nearly 1,500 pages containing detailed elaboration on every story in the gospels, completely restructured biblical studies. Strauss disagreed with the prevailing ways of understanding the gospels. On the one hand, he disagreed with the supernaturalists, who believed that miracles happen and that the Bible contains literal, inspired, inerrant, absolute words directly revealed by God. However, Strauss also disagreed with Enlightenment explanations that the miracle stories represented historical events that were simply misunderstood by Jesus' pre-enlightened followers. For example, in his 1827 study *The Life of Jesus*, Heinrich Paulus claimed that what really happened when Jesus

---

2. Baillie, *God Was in Christ*, 87.

3. The English translation, entitled *The Life of Jesus*, was done by Mary Ann Evans, a.k.a. the novelist George Eliot.

4. Neill, *Interpretation of the New Testament*, 12.

allegedly walked on water was that the disciples, terrified in the stormy night, thought they were in the middle of the lake, and assumed that the figure coming to them must be walking on the water. According to Paulus, a more likely explanation is that Jesus was walking in a shallow area or near the shore. However, since such explanations don't square with the account, which explicitly states that the boat was in the middle of the lake, Strauss insisted that the gospels contain neither supernatural histories nor natural histories. Instead, they contain myths.

Before we dismiss Strauss as an unbelieving skeptic, we must understand what he meant by the term "myth," and how his mythical principle of interpretation won the day, not only among critical scholars of his time, but among the vast majority of biblical scholars to this day. While the term "myth" is too loaded for many today, most scholars agree with Strauss's general principle, namely, that the stories in the gospels did not happen historically as narrated, but rather are meant to convey religious truth. To understand how the mythological principle works, let us examine Strauss's account of Jesus' walking on water.

How was it that Jesus was able to walk on top of the water? If his body didn't possess gravity (by which Strauss meant, didn't possess weight), that would mean that Jesus didn't possess a body like everyone else. However, if that was so, then Jesus was a phantom, a human in appearance only. Anyone who thinks this, Strauss pointed out, is guilty of the ancient heresy of docetism (meaning that Jesus only "seemed" or "appeared" to be human). But if Jesus wasn't really human but only "seemed" to be, how could he shed his blood? And if he wasn't a human, how could he die? And if he didn't shed his blood and die, how could he have brought salvation?

As if these concerns were not sufficient, Strauss pointed out that Jesus' body evidently had specific gravity or weight at the beginning of his ministry, when he was baptized by John. Such baptism, by immersion, could not have taken place if Jesus had been unable to get under the water then. Should we think that Jesus started out with a fleshly body but became more and more ethereal with the passing of time? Such speculation struck Strauss as absurd, and it didn't square with the notion that Jesus suffered a real, human death at the hands of the Romans.

Strauss entertained another possibility, that Jesus did have a fully human body, weight and all, only he had the ability to suspend his specific gravity at will, meaning that there were times when he weighed nothing.

This too struck Strauss as absurd. For one thing, humans can't do this, so if Jesus really was human, he would not be able to suspend gravity.

If, according to Strauss, neither supernatural interpretations nor natural explanations suggested by Enlightenment thinkers were valid, how should we read the text? In Strauss's estimation, early Christians thought metaphorically, likening the trials and tribulations of this life to a stormy sea that threatens life and limb, and the gospels invite us to think likewise. Who is able to rise above the fears, the hatreds, the enmities of this world? Who can overcome the persecutions, sufferings, and the setbacks of this life? Who can walk upright on the stormy sea? According to the gospels, Jesus can! He is the one who rises above it all, who is able to face the wind and master the waves, who can conquer all fear, dispel all doubt, and overcome all suffering. He is the one we should follow. If we do, we too can rise above it all and walk on the stormy sea of life, unhampered by the winds and waves. However, we must take care not to doubt or be fearful in our faith, lest we, like Peter, begin to sink.

According to Strauss, the story of the walking on the water was a myth. It is not something that *happened*. It is something that *happens*, then, now, and in every disciple's life. The gospels contain stories like that, stories that conveyed truths to those who told them, but they are not historically accurate.

The Influence of Jesus

After having stood at the center of Christianity for two thousand years, in recent times Jesus has been made the poster boy for all sorts of causes, from middle-class moralist to enlightened guru, from hellfire preacher to social justice warrior—and the list grows every year. The reason Jesus keeps getting a rebrand—the reason his image simple refuses to go away—is that he is without question the most influential person in history.

As the central character in the Bible, the world's best-selling book, Jesus is known the world over. In addition to being the central figure in Christianity, Jesus is also a significant figure in Islam, where he is revered as prophet. Despite having been rejected by Jews as Messiah, Jesus remains the most famous Jew of all time. Furthermore, he is admired the world over as martyr, saint, and mentor, his character revered by Hindus, Buddhists, Daoists, and Shintos alike.

Staggering inequality exists around the world today, a phenomenon that goes back into remote antiquity, when it seemed quite normal to treat people unequally. Most ancient civilizations practiced slavery, a practice defended by philosophical idealists and realists such as Plato and Aristotle. In addition, slavery, caste systems, child marriages, and honor killings continue to be tragically commonplace, perpetuated culturally as deeply held beliefs. Thankfully, such practices are countered by the ideals of equality, a mindset emphasized by Jesus and perpetuated in western cultures by Jesus-inspired followers.

By his embrace of women, children, the poor, outsiders, and other people marginalized by society, and through teachings such as his claim that God knows the number of hairs on our head and his call for shepherds to leave the ninety-nine for the one who is lost, Jesus defied the ancient world to insist that every life matters. In teaching that all people are created equal, Jesus forever offers a better way to cultural superiority and ideologies based on sexism, racism, and classism.

Because of Jesus, our definition of hero has changed. In antiquity, heroes were deeply flawed humans. Most, such as conquering emperors, samurai warriors, and knights in bright armor, were violent and necessarily partisan. On the contrary, many today esteem people who serve the needy, rescuers who sacrifice their lives for others, and leaders who relate to the humble and lowly. Once again, this extraordinary reversal is attributable to Jesus, who washed his disciples' dirty feet, who articulated claims such as the meek will inherit the earth, and who gave up his life for his friends.

Through his example, it may be said that Jesus paved the way for democracy, a form of government adopted by some 70 percent of the world's nations. Underlying democracy is the rule of law, the idea that a nation is governed by its constitution—something with higher authority than that of monarchs, presidents, senators, or mob majority. For this, followers of Jesus were inspired by the scriptures and laws of ancient Israel, which in turn were central in drafting foundation texts of modern democracy such as the Magna Carta, the English Bill of Rights, and the U.S. Declaration of Independence. These documents reasoned that if all human beings are made in God's image, a nation's citizens and not simply its elite should determine how government is formed and maintained, including responsibility to institute checks and balances to restrain its corruption. These revolutionary ideas, including human rights such as freedom of speech, press, assembly, and religion, have deeply Christian roots.

Based on the example of Jesus, his early followers proceeded to turn the world upside down, beginning with the imperial city of Rome. While early Christians were despised in the Roman empire, their programs to feed Rome's poor rivaled the city's civic guilds. Christians also scoured streets and trash heaps to rescue discarded babies—their example ultimately ending infanticide.

Christianity and compassion are deeply linked. Public healthcare, unknown in the ancient world, is largely due to the efforts of Jesus' disciples such as the Cappadocian church father Basil of Caesarea (330–379), who opened a 300-bed hospital in Cappadocia around 372. His vision gradually took hold, until medieval monks were caring for the sick in 37,000 European monasteries. As modern medicine was born, followers of Jesus led the charge again, pioneering antiseptic surgery, clinical teaching, physiology, transplant surgery, vaccines, and care for patients with contagious diseases.

The world wouldn't be the same without Christian heroes like William Carey, who ended widow burning in India, William Wilberforce, who abolished the slave trade, the British humanitarian Lord Shaftsbury, who helped abolish child labor, women working in coal mines, and treating the insane with cruelty, Martin Luther King, Jr., who transformed civil rights in the U. S., and Mother Teresa, whose name is a synonym for compassion. While Christians have no monopoly on care, it was Jesus—who gave us the parable of the Good Samaritan and backed it up with his profound love for the hungry, sick, and dying—who inspired more compassion than any single person, movement, or force in history.

Questions for Discussion and Reflection

1. In your estimation, how different would Christianity be as a religion had Constantine not been instrumental in turning it from a minority to a majority movement? Explain your answer.

2. Given the varied understandings of Jesus in early Christianity, do you believe Christianity could have grown to a world religion without a unifying Christology? Explain your answer.

3. Explain and assess the Chalcedonian doctrine of "the two natures" of Jesus Christ. Do you agree that holding such a view ultimately forces (or forced) institutional Christianity to emphasize one nature (divinity) over the other nature (humanity)?

4. To whom do you best relate, a wholly divine Christ or a fully human Jesus? Explain your answer.

5. If you consider yourself a Christian and are fully able to confess that "Jesus is Lord," how does such lordship influence, shape, or define your values, goals, and priorities?

6. In your estimation, can the humanity of Jesus serve as a bridge to God, or can only the divinity of Christ accomplish this? Explain your answer.

7. In understanding the humanity of Jesus, do you agree with the author's statement that "a true human being cannot be freshly minted"? Explain your answer.

8. If Jesus were truly human, might his sinlessness be best interpreted in relational rather than ethical ways? (NB: An affirmative answer to this question assumes a definition of "sin" as that which causes alienation from God and others, rather than a definition of "sin" as violation of religious laws or ethical standards.)

9. Explain and assess David Strauss's view that miracle stories in the Bible should be interpreted mythologically and metaphorically rather than supernaturally or naturally.

10. In your estimation, of the many ways that Jesus' life and teachings influenced modernity, which issue do you view as having been the most important or significant? Explain your answer.

Chapter 3

Temperament, Personality, and Discipleship

PEOPLE ARE NATURALLY DIFFERENT from one another in fundamental ways: they want different things, have different aims, think and learn differently, and believe differently. And of course, how they act and emote is governed by individual needs, desires, and beliefs. In many cases, differences in others trigger negative responses in others. Seeing others differing from us, it is easy to conclude that when they differ from us in behavior or response, it is due to some malady or flaw. Our job, at least for those near us, might seem to be to correct their flaws, making those near us more like us. Such a task, however, is doomed from the start. Our attempts to change others, whether spouse, sibling, lover, co-worker or friend, can produce change, but the result is likely more a distortion than a transformation. Besides, trying to change others is futile and counter-productive, in that most of the differences between human beings are essentially good.

The belief that people are fundamentally alike appears to be a twentieth century notion. The idea is probably related to the growth of democracy in the Western world. If we are equals, we must be alike. Classical psychologists such as Freud, Adler, Sullivan, Fromm, and their followers affirmed the idea of singular motivation. Whatever the drive, whether motivated by Eros, power, social solidarity, or the search after Self, each personality school made one instinct primary for everybody.

Swiss psychiatrist Carl Jung disagreed. He noted that people differ in fundamental ways, even though they all possess the same instincts to drive them from within. No instinct is more important than another; what is most significant for most individuals, however, is their preference for how they function. Because people are characterized by their preference for given functions, they may be "typed" by their preference.

The developments of psychology in the twentieth century were amazing. Behaviorists, cognitivists, constructivists and others studied the nature of human beings. Most of these theories tried to answer the question whether human personality is determined by nature (i.e. heredity) or nurture (i.e. environment or learning). Theories that claimed human personality is a function of nature (or heredity) are called temperament theories. Temperament is that aspect of our personalities that is genetically based and therefore innate. That does not mean that a temperament theory rules out the role of environment; rather, a temperament theory does not focus on environment. It should also be noted that the issue of temperament is much older than psychology itself. It has a history of at least five thousand years.

Spirituality and Personality

Spirituality and personality are deeply interrelated, so much that neither function adequately apart from the other. As I state in *Dark Splendor*, my 2015 volume on spiritual fitness for the second half of life,

> Like cyclists on a tandem, personality and spirituality travel together through the journey of life. Riding in tandem, they are deeply influenced by conditions both internal (goals, moods, desires) and external to the self. When one leans, the other leans; where one starts, the other starts; if one stops, the other stops. Though not identical, they strive to be in sync, balancing one another in profound and intimate ways. Personality takes the lead, and where personality goes, spirituality follows, though not blindly or passively. Spirituality has its own voice, and when its desires are addressed and heeded, personality thrives. When the two disagree, they must communicate, or the consequences can be disastrous. Cooperation always enhances the ride.[1]

Aware that spirituality is shaped by personality and unique to each individual, but also that "birds of a feather flock together," Urban Holmes[2] presents a helpful typology for the spiritual life revolving around four

---

1. Vande Kappelle, *Dark Splendor*, 23.
2. Holmes, *History of Christian Spirituality*.

ways that people seek to understand the experience of God and its meaning for our times:

- Type I: sacramental (an intellectual, "thinking" spirituality)
- Type II: charismatic (a heartfelt, intuitive spirituality)
- Type III: mystical (a contemplative, introspective spirituality)
- Type IV: apostolic (an active, visionary spirituality)

Likewise, Jack Haberer[3] identifies five concerns (which he calls "Godviews") that drive and divide individual Christians:

- passion about conserving truth
- passion about unity in the church
- passion about promoting intimacy with God
- passion about caring for victims
- passion about welcoming the marginalized

Huston Smith, widely regarded as the foremost authority on the history of religions, noted in his classic text, *The World's Religions*,[4] that ancient Hindu scholars identified four basic spiritual personality types: some people are primarily reflective, some are basically emotional, others are essentially active, and yet others are experimentally inclined. While the types should not be regarded inflexibly, since human beings possess all four abilities to some degree, each person prefers one style over the rest. Carl Jung seems to have built his typology of personality on this Indian model, with some modifications. For each of these personality types Hinduism prescribes a distinct yoga or spiritual path that capitalizes on the type's distinctive strength:

- Karma yoga, intended for persons of active bent, is *the path through work*. The best way for persons on this path to express their spirituality is to perform action selflessly, for the sake of God and others instead of their own. In this way tasks become sacralized; work becomes worship. The aim is to channel the love that lies at the base of one's heart through disinterested action, detached from any consequences benefitting self-interest;

3. Haberer, *Godviews*.
4. This volume was first published in 1958 as *The Religions of Man* and then revised in 1991 under its current title.

- Bhakti yoga, requiring a rare combination of rationality and spirituality, is *the path of devotion*. It is intended for those whose lives are powered primarily by emotion, the strongest of which is love. The aim is to channel the love that lies at the base of one's heart through relationship;
- Jnana yoga, intended for those who possess a strong reflective bent, is *the path of knowledge*. While thinking is important for such people, it has less to do with factual information than with insight or discernment regarding knowledge. The aim is to channel the love that lies at the base of one's heart through understanding;
- Raja yoga, intended for those who are scientifically or experimentally inclined, is *the path of liberation* (mystical union). Raja seeks freedom through self-actualization. The aim is to channel the love that lies at the base of one's heart through psychophysical (mental) experiments that culminate in harmony, freedom, and integration, leading the practitioner to direct personal experience of "the beyond that is within."

The Myers-Briggs Type Inventory

One of the most important contributions of Carl Jung to modern psychological thought is his theory of personality types. While Jung's monumental study, *Psychological Types*, requires a good deal of psychological and philosophical background to be understood, the essentials of his theory have been elaborated and developed by others, including the personality type indicator developed by Isabel Briggs-Myers and her mother Katherine Cook Briggs known as the Myers-Briggs Type Indicator (MBTI), which charts sixteen possible personality types in terms of Jungian type theory. Today, thanks to this sorting device, many Jungian concepts are widely known and accepted and millions have taken the MBTI, which is widely applied in team building, organization development, business management, education, and career and marriage counseling. Understanding one's type is making a welcome change in people's lives globally, in a wide diversity of situations.

The MBTI, now available online, is not really a test, but a sorter of preferences on four scales or categories, each consisting of two opposite poles. At the conclusion of the test you receive four letters, which comprise your personality type. They indicate the differences in people that result from

- where they prefer to focus their attention (Extraversion or Introversion) – E or I;
- the way they prefer to take in information (Sensing or Intuition) – S or N;
- the way they prefer to make decisions (Thinking or Feeling) – T or F;
- how they orient themselves to the external world (Judging or Perceiving) – J or P.

These preferences produce sixteen different kinds of people, interested in different things and drawn to different fields. Each type has its own inherent strengths as well as its likely blind spots. However, these types often blend into one another, inasmuch as each of us is a unique combination of these attitudes and functions. Discovering one's personality type is extremely beneficial, for it influences career choices, marriage choices, learning style, spiritual journeys, theological understanding, and much more. Learning one's personality type also makes us more aware and sensitive to the psychological needs, preferences, and differences of those around us.

If we are to care for, work with, or love other people, we need to know what makes them unique, and we will need to help them develop their own type potential and relate to them in ways that are meaningful to them. For example, people with developed sensate functions are usually characterized by simplicity in life style. They are interested in concrete facts and seldom in fantasy or make-believe. The basic interest of the intuitive type is in acquiring wisdom. Unlike sensors, they are fascinated by fantasy, hunches, and imaginative possibilities. However, routine tasks often bore them and they often do not follow through. They need new challenges, new problems, variety, and change. The thinking type wants things understandable and in logical order; consequently, thinkers do not like exceptions to rules. Often they make good executives, because the good of the whole takes precedence over individual desires. They can make decisions, but sometimes their apparent coldness alienates other types. The feeling type is most often characterized by an ability to experience joy. It is important to realize that the word "feeling" does not mean emotion, but rather signifies the capacity to evaluate data according to human values. Feelers are interested in other human beings and what influences them. They are excellent at getting along with others and are often found in the helping professions. Making unpleasant decisions affecting the lives of others is difficult for them.

Of the two middle letters in one's type (S or N, T or F), one will be the dominant function, the home base of operations, and the other will be the auxiliary, one's second most important function. It is impossible to love others unless we can recognize their type and place an adequate value upon their primary function. But here's a caveat: We should never try to have other persons change their type. They will do best if they develop what they are by nature.

When people are young, their energy is directed toward development of their most preferred, dominant function, and their behavior reflects this. For example, an introverted Feeling child will be a quiet observer, with an instinctive sense of others' feelings; an introverted Intuitive child will be actively exploring the variety of the surrounding world. An extraverted Thinking child will try to order his environment to fit with his logical principles; an introverted Thinking child will try to internally make sense of her world. Once children develop skills in their dominant function, the focus of energy and attention then shifts to the auxiliary function. The primary task of type development in the first part of life is to establish the leadership provided by the dominant function, balanced by the healthy development of the auxiliary function. Later in life, the focus of development shifts, this time to the less-preferred functions, aspects of the individual's personality and potential that have only minimally been explored. This redirection of energy is part of the midlife transition, which Jung saw as the gateway to later life development and satisfaction. The task of the second half of life, then, is to move toward full development of all of oneself, including those parts that were previously neglected and unrealized.

When people first learn Jung's theory, they often think the ideal is to develop all four functions with equal facility to achieve balance. That, however, is not how development works, for if a person tries to develop opposite ways of perceiving equally, for example, then neither Sensing nor Intuition will receive the focus or attention necessary to become fully reliable. The four functions tend to pull in opposite directions: Sensing, to the reality of the present; Intuition, to the possibility of the future; Thinking, to decisions based on objective logic; and Feeling, to decisions based on subjective values. People who do not establish dominance of each pair of functions are inconsistent in their behavior, pulled first in one direction and then another. The goal of type development, then, is not equal development and use of all the functions, but rather the ability to use each mental process with some facility when it is appropriate.

In conclusion, Jung's model of the human journey is based on the following assumptions:

- each person has an innate urge to grow
- the human psyche is self-regulating and capable of healing itself
- development means developing conscious control over and facility in the use of a function
- development is an interaction between a person's innate type preferences and the environment. If the environment is supportive, growth tends to follow innate type. If the environment is not supportive, the pattern may be affected by a person's adaptation to the requirements of the environment
- in the first half of life, growth takes the form of development of the preferred functions; in the second half of life, a person's focus of energy and attention naturally shifts to the less-preferred functions. This is a process of moving toward one's unexplored potential.

The following quote summarizes Jung's understanding of the psychological-spiritual task during the second half of life: "Among all my patients in the second half of life—that is to say, over thirty-five—there has not been one whose problem in the last resort was not that of finding a religious outlook on life."

Building on the insights of psychological type theory developed by Carl Jung and Isabel Briggs Myer, globetrotting minister and author Peter Tufts Richardson notes that four different approaches to human spirituality emerge from the MBTI.[5] How we perceive the world and how we respond to it (how we judge) seems to be directly connected to the spiritual path we find most personally satisfying. Utilizing the principle that one's spirituality flows out of one's individuality, Richardson locates the key to spirituality in the two middle letters of one's personality type. These cognitive pairs result in four possibilities: ST, SF, NT, and NF. One of these pairs defines each person's spirituality.

---

5. Richardson's approach is described in *Four Spiritualities*.

Richardson defines the four spirituality types, describes qualities and patterns unique to each path, and identifies mentors from different world religions for each journey:

ST – Journey of Works; STs are characterized by *a task-oriented spirituality.*

SF – Journey of Devotion; SFs are characterized by *an experience-based spirituality.*

NT – Journey of Unity; NTs are characterized by *a highly principled spirituality.*

NF – Journey of Harmony; NFs are characterized by *a questing spirituality.*

Temperament and Personality

People's involvement with the notion of "temperament" can be traced back to the traditions of ancient Egypt and Mesopotamia, where the health of the human body was considered to be connected with the four basic elements of nature—air, soil, water, and fire. The four elements, in turn, were related to body fluids (also called humors). In ancient Greek medicine, Hippocrates (c. 370 BCE) was the first to classify people according to their dominant body fluids: blood, black bile, phlegm, and yellow bile. The density of the fluids within individuals was believed to determine their personality. For Hippocrates, people could be classified as "cheerful," "somber," "calm," or "enthusiastic." The Roman physician Galen, who developed the ideas of Hippocrates (c. 190 CE), constructed a taxonomy of human behavior combining the four basic elements of nature with a matrix of hot/cold and dry/wet. Where all the elements were balanced, the individual was said to possess a balanced personality. Another possibility was that one element dominated the rest. This resulted in four less-balanced personality types, which Galen called Sanguine, Melancholic, Phlegmatic, and Choleric.

The sanguine individual, in which blood predominates, is claimed to be cheerful and optimistic, pleasant to be with, and comfortable with his or her work. The melancholic type, in which black bile or gall predominates, is said to be sad, depressed, and pessimistic. The phlegmatic type, in which phlegm predominates, is said to be slow, dull, and calm. The choleric type, said to have an excess of bile, is quick, passionate, hot-tempered, and often aggressive. While we might question the specifics of

Galen's bodily fluids, the personal element seems to have some merit, for we all know individuals that fit one of these four temperaments, particularly if we replace Galen's terms with more familiar ones: sanguine with cheerful, melancholic with broody, phlegmatic with calm, and choleric with excitable.

Nearly six hundred years before Galen, Plato had written in *The Republic* of four kinds of character that clearly corresponded with the four temperaments attributed to Hippocrates. Plato was more interested in the individual's contribution to the social than in underlying temperament, and so he named the Sanguine temperament the Artisan, endowed with artistic sense (driven by imagery and likely drawn to the arts, crafts, and creativity in general) and playing an aesthetic role in society. He named the Melancholic temperament the Guardian, endowed with common sense (driven by honor, duty, and trust in others and drawn to traditional leadership roles) and playing a caretaking role in society. He named the Phlegmatic temperament the Rationalist, endowed with reasoning ability (driven by cold and calm reason and likely drawn to logical, mathematical fields) and playing the role of logical investigator in society. And he named the Choleric temperament the Idealist, endowed with intuitive sensibility (driven by intuition and insight and likely drawn to activities involving ethics, relationships, and establishing harmony) and playing a moral role in society. A generation after Plato, Aristotle defined character in terms of happiness and not, as his mentor Plato had done, in terms of virtue. Aristotle identified four sources of happiness: sensual pleasure, acquiring assets, logical investigation, and moral virtue.

In his book *Please Understand Me* (co-authored with Marilyn Bates in 1978), clinical psychologist David Keirsey combined the personality theory of Isabel Myers and Katherine Briggs (MBTI) with the insights of the temperament hypothesis. While building on the MBTI behavioral descriptions, he subordinated Jung's idea of "function" or "type" to the concept of "temperament," noting that the latter has a much wider range as an explainer of behavior. While knowing a person's type has great value for anticipating behavior, the concept of temperament is said to be broader in scope, denoting a unification of otherwise disparate forces. Unlike Jungian typology, in which types are built through combination of "functions," temperament theory views types as emerging from temperaments by way of differentiation. A person becomes an ENFJ or INFP, for example, because of a given temperament rather than because extraversion or introversion somehow combined with intuition. Thus temperament theory replaces the principles of integration (viewed as reductionist) with the principle of differentiation. According to this theory, temperament determines behavior because behavior is the instrument for getting what one must have, satisfying the desire for that primary necessity that drives our personality, whether it be the hunger for power, status, freedom, or meaning.

Utilizing MBTI functions, Keirsey names his four temperaments after four Greek gods, all of whom Zeus commissioned to make humans more like the gods:, Dionysus, to teach humans joy, Epimetheus, to convey a sense of duty, Prometheus, to give humans science, and Apollo, to give humans a sense of spirit. The four temperaments are labeled as follows:

1. *Dionysian* or SPs (a combination of Sensing and Perceiving, namely ISTP, ESTP, ISFP, and ESFP), are characterized by Action and Freedom. SPs are essentially impulsive; *doing* is their thing, and they must be free to act in the present, using resources, utilizing tools, and enjoying people at once. When they feel constricted, SPs become restless and feel the need to move on. Socially, they tend to be charming and witty conversationalists. SPs bring to work and to play a sense of excitement, adventure, even risk. They thrive on uncertainty, where the outcome is not known and where there is freedom to test the limits. Of all the styles, the SP works best in crises.

2. *Epimethean* or SJs (a combination of Sensing and Judging, namely ISFJ, ESFJ, ISTJ, and ESTJ), are characterized by Duty and Hope. Driven by the Boy Scout motto "Be Prepared," SJs are industrious, maintaining a storehouse of commodities for the unknown future. *Belonging* is their thing, and this belonging must be earned. Moreover, they are the givers in a relationship, not the receivers; the caretakers, not the cared for. Theirs is not a desire for independence (as with the SP); rather, it is a desire to serve. While the SP is compelled to be free and independent, the SJ is, in effect, compelled to be bound and obligated. As SJs age, tradition becomes more important. If traditional ceremonies and celebrations are nonexistent, SJs manage to establish and maintain them. As conservators, they are the foundation, cornerstone, and stabilizers of society. If insufficiently appreciated, they can become exhausted, depressed, and even ill.

3. *Promethean* or NTs (a combination of Intuition and Thinking, namely INTP, ENTP, INTJ, and ENTJ), are fascinated by Power, not over people, but over nature. *Improving* is their thing. The ability to understand, control, predict, and explain realities, these are the four aims of

science; scratch an NT and you will find a scientist. These forms of power are but means to an end, for it is competency rather than power that is sought, the desire to improve. NTs love intelligence and related qualities such as capability, capacity, skill, and ingenuity. The most self-critical of all the styles, NTs can be perfectionists. Constantly alert to their own shortcomings, they question the credentials of others. This recalcitrance to established authorities can make them seem unusually individualist and even arrogant. Tending to be workaholics, NTs are forever learning; they enjoy developing models, exploring ideas, and building systems. They are regularly drawn to occupations that have to do with the formation and application of scientific principles. NTs tend to focus on the future, regarding the past as something dead and gone.

4. *Apollonian* or NFs (a combination of Intuition and Feeling, namely INFJ, ENFJ, INFP, and ENFP), are characterized by Spirit, elegantly expressed in the search for Self. While the purposes of SPs (freedom from responsibility), SJs (storing commodities), and NTs (storing capabilities) are understood by SPs, SJs, and NTs alike, although they may not embrace them, the NF cannot really grasp the others' commitment to what seems to the NF to be false goals. For NFs, *becoming* is their thing. While the SPs, SJs, and NTs can go after their goals directly and full bore, the NFs search for self is circular and perpetual. Hamlet, you might recall, wrestled with this dilemma: "To be or not to be, that is the question." Seeking to satisfy their longing for unity and uniqueness, NFs hunger for self-actualization. NFs can become disenchanted, moving from cause to cause in their search for meaning. They tend to choose the humanities and the social sciences as areas of interest. Passionate in pursuit of a creative effort, NFs can be dilettantes compared to NTs, flitting from idea to idea like intellectual butterflies. They are not content with abstractions but rather seek relationships. Their quest culminates not with action but with interaction.

The Enneagram

The Enneagram represents an approach to personality that concerns itself with normal and high-functioning behavior, and it condenses a great deal of psychological insight into a compact system that is relatively easy to understand. The term "Enneagram" was introduced by George Gurdjieff (1879–1949), an eccentric Russian who traveled widely, particularly to Mount Athos, a rugged and isolated peninsula in Greece that is home to twenty Orthodox monasteries. There he learned esoteric practices helpful in opening human consciousness. He taught these practices to his study groups in St. Petersburg and Moscow in 1916. Gurdjieff called his system of principles of inner growth The Fourth Way, claiming it transcended the three traditional spiritual paths of the monk, the yogi, and the fakir. He taught that it is possible to live The Fourth Way while active in the world, rather than detached from life in an isolated community of like-minded seekers.

The word Enneagram stems from the Greek *ennea*, meaning "nine," and *grammos*, meaning "points." The Enneagram refers to "a nine-pointed star diagram that can be used to map the process of any event from its inception through all the stages of that event's progress in the material world."[6] The Enneagram's value is in its ease of use, rooted in a time-tested tradition of understanding human nature—how it is formed, broken, and healed. The Enneagram types persons into one of nine boxes (the Perfectionist/Reformer, the Helper/Giver, the Achiever/Performer, the Idealist/Tragic Romantic, the Investigator/Observer, the Loyalist/Critic, the Enthusiast/Epicure, the Protector/Boss, and the Peacemaker/Mediator), providing information about the way that individuals are likely to behave and therefore to get along. While lessening the tension of having to live with the mystery of the unknown, the Enneagram is not a fixed system. It is a model of interconnecting lines that indicate a dynamic movement, in which each of us has the potentials of all nine types, or points, although we identify most strongly with the issues of our own type. Interconnecting lines indicate the versatility of movement available to the individual, as well as specific relationships between the different types of individuals.

Underlying the Enneagram is a distinction between one's essential nature and one's acquired personality. Essential nature is described as "hard wired" or what is "one's own," the potential with which we were born, rather than the personality we have acquired through education, the influence of authority figures, beliefs, and personal ideas. The Enneagram's nine-pointed star suggests that there are nine major aspects of essential being and that each may be approached in different ways. The search for a particular aspect of essence is motivated by the suffering caused by its absence. For example, if you are chronically afraid, then you

---

6. Palmer, *The Enneagram*, 10.

have suffered the loss of the child's essential trust, whether in the environment or in others. Therefore searching for courage becomes a motive in your life.

The realization that we are acting contrary to our essential nature indicates the presence of an inner observer. The Enneagram system encourages the practice of self-observation, whereby individuals focus their attention inwardly in order to recognize habitual patterns within their minds. The fact that one can observe and talk about one's own habits of thinking and feeling from the point of view of a detached observer helps to make these habits less compulsive and automatic.

In her book on the Enneagram, Helen Palmer identifies nine chief features (passions) of the emotional life (anger, pride, deceit, envy, greed, fear, gluttony, lust, and sloth). These emotional patterns are part of one's emotional shadow or the acquired personality, stemming from the need to cope with early family life. If a child develops in a healthy manner, then the passions are akin to mere tendencies, which can be identified with relative ease and dealt with accordingly. But if the psychological situation is severe, then one of the shadow issues becomes an obsessional preoccupation. In this case the capacity for self-observation weakens and the individual cannot move on to other things. The hope is that by identifying one's own Chief Feature, one can observe the many ways in which this habit has gained control over one's life. In this case, one's Chief Feature (one's passion), a neurotic habit that developed during childhood, can also become a personal mentor.

Having discovered how temperament and personality type influence our preferential, perceptual, learning, theological, and spirituality styles, chapters 9 through 11 below bring psychological and spirituality theory to life as various individuals illustrate practical discipleship through accounts taken from their individual faith and life stories. However, before examining these authentic and inspirational accounts, we explore discipleship in the Bible, focusing on the gospel of Luke and on the life of Jesus as paradigmatic for modern disciples, followed by two chapters discussing what Jesus would want modern disciples to know about theology and scripture and to do regarding political, social, economic, and ecological issues facing our world today.

Questions for Discussion and Reflection

1. Do you believe it is natural to want to have others agree with us or to have them conform to our values, beliefs, and behaviors? While this need or desire for conformity typifies first-half-of-life thinking and living, have you learned to let go of this need? If so, how did this transformation occur, and if not, why are you still clinging to a need that promotes conflict and that seems counterproductive to peace, goodwill, and sanity?

2. Explain and assess Carl Jung's view that personality is driven and distinguished by preferences rather than by singular instincts.

3. In your estimation, is human personality primarily determined by nature, nurture, or by some other factor? Explain your answer.

4. Do you agree that spirituality, like personality, is unique to each individual, or should we all seek to conform to a common spirituality? Explain your answer.

5. Of the four spiritual personality types identified by Hindu scholars, which type or spiritual path best describes your preference or experience? Explain your answer.

6. If you have taken the MBTI (available free online), what do the results say about your preferences and orientation to the external world?

7. Explain how awareness of one's personality influences not only self-understanding but also our understanding of those around us.

8. Can you say you have made peace with your personality, including its strengths as well as its weaknesses and dispositions? If there is one part of your personality, temperament, or character you could change, what would it be? Explain your answer.

9. According to Carl Jung, during a person's second half of life, his or her focus and attention naturally shift to the less-preferred functions. If this has happened in your life, can you provide examples?

10. The Enneagram (available free online) is a valuable tool for understanding the distinction between one's essential nature and one's acquired personality. If you have learned your Enneagram number or type, write a short statement that helps you understand your basic qualities, drives, virtues, and vices.

Chapter 4

The Centrality of Discipleship in the Bible, Part I

WHEN WE CONSIDER THE central message of the Bible, a good case can be made that discipleship is its core principle. The Hebrew scriptures (Old Testament) portray Israel as God's people, not simply a collection of persons but a divine company ("a priestly kingdom and a holy nation"; Exod 19:6; 1 Pet 2:9). Out of families, clans, and tribes God formed a nation, with a corporate personality: When one person suffered, everyone suffered; when one person was blessed, the people enjoyed the benefits; when one person sinned, the whole nation participated in the judgment; when one person received a promise, he or she did so on behalf of the nation.

In the Bible, God's covenant people, whether viewed as the people of Israel (Old Testament) or as the body or church of Jesus Christ (New Testament), are characterized by loyalty to God or Christ, by allegiance to fellow Israelites or to other Christians, and by commitment to Torah or gospel (the Israelite moral code or Christian message understood to constitute the will of God for society).

In the Old Testament, one way to view discipleship is what we may call "participation," in which an individual's behavior, beliefs, or attitudes are said to correspond to, reflect, or partake of the same character or quality as other Israelites. In the New Testament, discipleship centers on what we may call "imitation," viewed as "following after" Jesus, that is, learning his teachings and putting them into practice.

Underlying discipleship is the biblical idea that human beings somehow reflect the nature of God, or should seek to do so. However we understand the statement that humans are made "in the image of God"

(Gen 1:26–27), it presupposes some correspondence between God and humanity, not of equality, but one of intimacy and allegiance. The biblical teaching, "You shall be holy, for I the Lord your God am holy" (Lev 19:2), may initially have pointed more toward religious ritual than to moral sanctity; nevertheless, this text begins a tradition of "following God" that continues through the prophets and Judaism to Jesus and his disciples. What in the Old Testament is a universally presupposed fundamental concept becomes in the New Testament a new reality with the gift of the Holy Spirit.

Of the many passages in the New Testament that deal with the calling and mission of the disciples of Jesus, 1 Peter 2:4–10 is one of the most instructive. It establishes the biblical truth that followers of Jesus are not essentially a social organization or a human institution that can be analyzed sociologically, but are rather a creation of God built upon Jesus Christ, the "living stone" upon which foundation a "spiritual house" is built. As disciples, the members of this "spiritual house" are themselves, like Israel of old, "a chosen race, a royal priesthood, a holy nation, God's own people" (1 Pet 2:9; see Ex 19:6).

The place of disciples in the movement of God's purpose for the world is developed with majestic splendor in the epistle to the Ephesians. In addition to describing the followers of Jesus (the church) in terms of the image of the temple, of which Jesus Christ is the chief cornerstone (Eph 2:19–22), a second image is used, the distinctively Pauline image of the body, of which Christ is the head (Eph 2:16; see 1:22–23; 4:15–16).

The theme of peace is sounded in Ephesians 2:17, the words "to you who were far off" and "to those who were near" echoing God's great promise to Abraham in Genesis 12:4, "in you all the families of the earth shall be blessed." While we usually think of peace as the absence of war, in the Bible "peace" has a more positive meaning, pointing to a state of harmony, wholeness, and welfare in the community. And it is a basic biblical premise that there cannot be right relations within communities unless human beings are in right relation with God, for when separated from God, people are at odds with one another as well as with themselves.

As Old Testament prophets looked away from the fractured society of Israel, they anticipated the coming of the age of the Messiah, when the barriers of separation would be overcome and human beings would be brought into a new relation with God, with one another, and with the natural environment. In Ephesians love is not a commandment but a new reality in human relationships that has been initiated by God's prior love through Jesus Christ. The church is a fellowship of love, the highest endowment of God's Spirit (see 1 Cor. 13:13; 1 John 4:7–21).

In his guidance, Paul walks a careful line between legalism and antinomianism, recognizing the importance of Christian freedom while remaining subject to the needs of others. The reformer Martin Luther best entered the mind of Paul when he declared that a Christian is "subject to none" in respect to personal liberty, yet "subject to all" in respect to charity. This, for Paul, is the law of Christ because this was the way of Christ. And in this way, for Paul, the divine purpose underlying Moses's law is vindicated and accomplished.

This brings us to a concept that many scholars consider the unifying teaching of the Bible and the essence of discipleship, the moral principle known as The Great Commandment or the "law of love." It was this principle that Jesus both emphasized and exemplified in his ministry, namely, that the fulfillment of moral righteousness depends on the twin commandments of love to God and love to one's neighbor (Mark 12:30–31; Matt 22:37–40; Luke 10:27). This interpretation of the law is echoed by Paul when he says that the whole law is summed up in the single commandment, "You shall love your neighbor as yourself" (Gal 5:14)—or that "Love does no wrong to a neighbor; therefore agape [God's love in us] is the fulfilling of the law" (Rom 13:10). In the Bible, the command about loving God comes first, for it supplies the basis for loving the neighbor.

As radical disciples know, the Great Commandment is not a call to "be right" or to a lifestyle built on belief; rather, the Great Commandment is a call to "be in love," a call to a lifestyle built on trust.

Contrary to popular belief, in the New Testament the term "disciple" is not used specifically for the Twelve. While the gospels often speak of the Twelve, the lists given of this group do not always agree, for it is clear that Jesus' entourage also included a number of women who joined the apostolic band (see Luke 8:1–3), and that at least on one occasion Jesus commissioned at least seventy other followers to preach and heal (Luke 10:1–11).

The word "disciple" occurs about 260 times in the gospels and Acts, but nowhere else in the New Testament. While the term occasionally designates followers of Moses, of John the Baptist, of Paul, and even of the Pharisees, the term's most frequent designation is to followers of Jesus. Of over 230 instances of the term in the gospels, about 90 percent are not limited to the Twelve or else remain ambiguous as to whether these or some larger group is indicated.

While the singular form of the word is frequent in John's gospel, the singular form never occurs in Mark. In Matthew and Luke, the term appears only on Jesus' lips, and regularly in teaching about the nature of discipleship. In these teachings, discipleship regularly includes participation in the sufferings and deprivations of the Master. Disciples must be prepared to forego comfort, security, family, and possessions (Luke 14:26, 33), and like Christ, to carry their own cross (Luke 14:27). Strikingly, in Luke 6:40, Jesus equates full discipleship and full Christlikeness.

As the four canonical gospels are written by different authors to different audiences, each author painting unique and often contrasting pictures of Jesus and his ministry and message, so also each gospel presents different portrayals of the disciples and of discipleship. For example, Matthew is the only New Testament book to speak of "twelve disciples." While Mark never limits the term in this way, he often portrays core disciples in unflattering ways, depicting them as obstinate, fearful, and inconsistent, unlike later gospel writers, who reflect the increase in respect that the disciples received when they came to be regarded as apostolic pillars of the church.

Another difference, notably between Luke and John's gospels, is how their authors portray discipleship. Whereas John aligns discipleship with "believing in Jesus," that is, with allegiance or trust in Jesus and his message, Luke aligns discipleship more closely with imitation, that is, with patterning one's lifestyle and values after Jesus. The distinction is between discipleship as perpetuating a belief system or as a way of life modeled on Jesus' principles and priorities, encapsulated primarily in the "law of love."

In *Power Revealed*, my commentary on Luke–Acts, I note that the strategic placement of the book of Acts in the Bible—between the gospels and the letters—means that Acts functions as a lens or bridge that highlights the ultimate aim of the New Testament, namely, "to nurture Christian discipleship after the pattern of Jesus."[1] As the gospels disclose different understandings of Jesus and discipleship, so the two collections of letters in the New Testament disclose two distinct visions: the Pauline letters reflect the more progressive gospel of a Gentile mission, while the General Epistles reflect the more conservative gospel of a Jewish mission.

---

1. Vande Kappelle, *Power Revealed*, 48.

As a biblical scholar, I often describe myself as a progressive conservative, and while such a designation might sound like an oxymoron to some, I find it not only defines me but defines my rootedness in scripture.

In a recent podcast, progressive Christian journalist Diana Butler Bass discusses why, despite her disagreement with traditional Christianity, she remains Christian. The answer, she finds, is Jesus. In her 2021 book *Freeing Jesus*, Bass notes that her understanding of Jesus has changed throughout her life journey. Despite the text in Hebrews 13:8 that announces the view that "Jesus Christ is the same yesterday, today, and forever," Bass clarifies that she has changed over time, as has the church. In her estimation, Jesus too has changed, not only in our understanding of him but in a real way, for the sake of a changing world. If people are resistant of change and unwilling to allow new images of Jesus to emerge, chances are, she notes, that they are in a static place in terms of their spirituality.[2]

While I agree with Bass that our thinking and understanding changes over time, including our experience of Jesus, I don't believe it is Jesus who changes, but rather our way of reading scripture. The Bible, written over a long span of time and reflecting the views of many authors, does not contain one consistent set of teachings. Neither does it contain one understanding of Jesus. Thus, in this context, it is not Jesus who must change, nor we who must change, but our way of understanding scripture and tradition that must change. As the Bible contains different understanding of God, of human nature, and of doctrines such as salvation, atonement, creation, and eschatology, so it contains different images, views, and understanding of Jesus. Our task, then, is not simply to read the Bible, but to interpret what we read, for every reading is an interpretation. Reading scripture and understanding Jesus are largely subjective endeavors, and our task as individuals is to appreciate the wide variety of views and perspectives found in scripture, choosing which we wish to highlight and which no longer seem relevant or appropriate.

In my estimation, some passages, even some books of scripture, are altogether dated and irrelevant to modern thinking and practice. Their value is simply that of ancient history. Other biblical passages such as ancient laws and purity codes, are relevant only to traditional Jews. Likewise, some passages and teachings in the New Testament are relevant only to ardent Christian literalists, who accept those teachings without

---

2. Bass, *Freeing Jesus*, xxv; podcast, "Christianity is Many Things."

question. It is the role of religious education to help us sort out the timeless from the dated, the relevant from the irrelevant.

Some teachings and perspectives in scripture, however, including material across the spectrum of the two testaments, remain timeless, relevant, and inspiring because they transcend culture, history, trends, moods, and ideologies, which change over time. Many of those timeless teaching and perspectives on discipleship appear in Luke–Acts, to which we turn.

Discipleship in Luke–Acts

According to recent biblical scholarship, Luke's literary intention was to write a reliable account of Christian origins. He does so by writing two books, the first about the life and teachings of Jesus and the second about the origins of the church. He does not, however, write from a neutral or unbiased point of view. When speaking of Jesus, Luke uses many titles, including Son of Man, Son of God, Messiah, and Lord. In addition, other than a single reference in John's gospel, Luke is the only gospel writer to call Jesus "Savior."

When contemporary Christians hear the words "Savior" and "salvation" proclaimed on television or from the pulpit, they will likely associate the concept with the evangelical notion of obtaining eternal life, meaning gaining entrance to heaven in the afterlife and spending eternity with God. However, much of ancient religion, whether pagan or Jewish, had little or nothing to do with "being saved" in this sense. The salvation most ancients sought was decidedly this-worldly, whether from disease or disaster in this life, and the redemption many desired was freedom from slavery, debt, and other such forms of social bondage. Of course, Luke's view of salvation is considerably broader than the usual pagan sense of the term.

In ancient times, heads of state were frequently identified as "saviors" because of their expected or real benefactions. Luke's references to Jesus as a person with royal credentials (Luke 1:33; 19:38; 22:29, 30; 23:42; indirectly in 19:14, 27; 23:2, 3, 37, 38; Acts 17:7) form part of Luke's unified picture of Jesus as the Great Benefactor, whose purpose and mission is to effect salvation for all humanity (see Acts 10:38). In the Greek world, salvation was typically associated with the bestowal of various blessings and gifts, while in the Old Testament salvation was conceived more as deliverance from enemies.

In the Old Testament, salvation assures the individual renewed relationship with God, though it also conveys protection and liberation from foreign powers. For Luke, the concept of salvation also has social, physical, and spiritual dimensions. For example, in the paradigmatic speech of Jesus in Luke 4, salvation is equated with the preaching of good news to the poor, release to the captives, recovery of sight to the blind, and freeing of those oppressed. The social dimension is seen in the concern for the poor and the release of the captives, the latter of which includes release from demonic possession but is not confined to that realm. We see this dimension in the parable of the prodigal son (Luke 15), where family reconciliation is in view; in the story of Zacchaeus in Luke 19, who is being set free from social prejudice against tax collectors; and in the story of the sinner woman of Luke 7 who is freed from social stigma and being an outcast from society. Healing and exorcism are also seen as means or forms of salvation (in Luke 8:48 the text reads literally "your faith has saved [i.e. healed] you"). These same notions of salvation carry over into the book of Acts, though they do not exhaust Luke's concept of salvation.

For example, already in the gospel we hear of salvation in the form of forgiveness of sins (Luke 5:20), though even there the physical and spiritual concepts are interrelated. The latter, more "spiritual" view of salvation becomes more prominent in the book of Acts, as the paradigmatic speech in Acts 2 makes clear (2:21, 38). Yet the integral connection between healing and salvation continues to be clear in Acts, as chapters 3–4 show. In Acts 4:9–10 the healing of the crippled beggar happens in Jesus' name, which leads Peter to conclude, "There is salvation in no one else, for there is no other name under heaven, given among mortals by which we must be saved" (4:12).

Like the jailor in Acts 16:30–31, who asks Paul and Silas what he must do to be "saved," belief in Jesus is said to be sufficient not only for the jailor but for his household. It is hard to imagine that the jailor's faith would be sufficient to "save" in the spiritual sense his entire household. Surely what is meant here is that the jailor and his family would be spared from calamity if he believes (i.e., "trusts") in Jesus.

Viewing Jesus as Savior is important to Luke, for the title is illustrative of Luke's overriding theological conception, labeled "salvation history" by the German biblical scholar Hans Conzelmann, one of the first commentators to study Luke as theologian rather than as narrator or historian. According to Conzelmann, Luke's conception of human history, from creation to the end of the world, is arranged into three epochs: (1) the period of Israel, (2) the period of Jesus' earthly ministry, and (3) the period of the church. The period of Jesus' life on earth represented the "middle of time." As such, it was central to all history, but, just as it was preceded by a long "period of Israel," so it was to be followed by a lengthy "period of the church."

As simple as this arrangement seems, it has far-reaching theological implications. For one thing, it assumes a significant interim between the time of Jesus' earthly ministry and the end of the world. According to Conzelmann, that mindset led Luke to write not only a third gospel but also the first history of the Christian movement. After all, why write another account of Jesus and a book about history if you are expecting the end of the world to come any day? Recognizing that the *parousia* (the return or "coming" of Christ) was losing its significance as a key factor in Christian hope and therefore as a decisive motive for Christian living, Luke is said to have written for a new generation of believers, his purpose being to strengthen their faith and to offer them pastoral guidance to meet challenges that might cause them to doubt. If the church is to endure, it must make peace with the world and learn to coexist with society.

Impressive as it is, Conzelmann's proposal has not fared well. A better understanding of Luke's historical paradigm is that, like Paul and other New Testament authors, he divides history not into three parts, as Conzelmann claims, but rather into two epochs, namely, the "former age" (the time of prophetic promise), and the "new age" (the time of eschatological fulfillment in the church). Within the eschatological time of the church, there are also two great periods, the mission to the Jews (Acts 1–12), and the mission to the Gentiles (Acts 12–28).

Despite Conzelmann's arguments, Luke does not radically distinguish between the time of Jesus and the time of the church. In fact, he does not radically distinguish the time of Israel from the time of Jesus or the church because in his view the community of Jesus' disciples is the logical development of Israel according to God's plan. Jew and Gentile united in Christ are the beginning of Israel's restoration.

In addition to titles such as "Lord" and "Savior," Luke also uses the word "prophet" when referring to Jesus, for like Israel's prophets, Jesus discloses the character of God's rule and summons God's people to faithfulness. In addition, prophets meet resistance and rejection, as does Jesus.

When Jesus appeared, the masses immediately placed him in the prophetic category: "A great prophet has arisen among us!" (Luke 7:16; Mark 6:15; 8:28; John 4:19). For Luke, Jesus is "a prophet mighty in word and deed before God and all the people," as the two on the road to Emmaus call him (24:19). Their description is justified by Jesus' having raised a widow's son from death (7:11–17), as Elijah had done (1 Kgs. 17:17–24). Like Elijah, Jesus leaves the world by heavenly ascension, and, also like him, his return at the end of time is expected. Perhaps Jesus is nowhere more Elijah's antitype than in his attempt to bring the nation at large to repent and change its ways. The call to repentance occupies the greater part of Jesus' teaching on the way to Jerusalem in Luke 10–16. He curses unrepentant Jewish towns (10:13–15); he compares this unrepentant generation unfavorably with Jonah's Ninevites (11:29–32); he recalls ominously the murder of prophets (11:47–52); he holds up local disasters as warnings of worse to come if repentance fails (13:1–5); and a series of parables of repentance, beginning with the fig tree at 13:6–9, has its climax with the great parables in chapters 15 and 16, the parable of the Rich Man and Lazarus ending with prophetic indictment: "If they do not hear Moses and the prophets, neither will they be convinced if someone should rise from the dead" (16:31).

As Luke 13:31–35 indicates, not only his life but also his death show Jesus to be a prophet. Luke tells the passion story in such a way that Jesus is seen to be God's rejected prophet. Luke's version of the passion is also a final lesson in discipleship, for it culminates the teaching Jesus has been giving his disciples all along. In going to his death, Jesus shows what it means to be a servant, to face trials, and to take up one's cross.

Within the New Testament, the book of Acts sets out to tell the story of the infant church. Written around 85 CE, Luke describes the early church in ideal terms. Jesus had appointed apostles, and these became their leaders. Luke pictured the Jerusalem church as a charismatic fellowship so loving that believers shared what they possessed. United in practice and belief, the initial followers of Jesus, all good Jews, eventually expanded to include Gentile believers, and the notion of discipleship got complicated. A formal assembly of apostles and elders gathered at Jerusalem around 49 CE to discuss the matter, and at this council James, the brother of Jesus and a leader of the Jerusalem church, announced the consensus that all races, Jewish and Gentile, circumcised and uncircumcised, were to be welcomed.

However, despite the agreement of the Jerusalem Council, which accepted Gentiles into full church membership with limited restrictions (see Acts 15:28–29), the ecclesiastical controversy continued, for Paul's epistles are full of evidence that there were for a time Jewish Christians who insisted on greater adherence to Jewish laws and practices. What, then, does it mean to be a follower of the Way, a Christian disciple?

For Luke, the universalization of the gospel embraces not only all ethnic diversity but also people up and down the social scale, including both the oppressed and the oppressor. Furthermore, Luke and Acts also demonstrate a concern for the physical as well as the spiritual welfare of humankind, so that the gospel's liberation is not merely to come to all people but is to affect every aspect of their lives. Such a total salvation requires a total response of discipleship. In Luke's gospel, Jesus' disciples must be prepared to leave everything and follow (Luke 5:11), renounce all (14:33; 18:18–30), take up their cross daily (9:23), and put their hand to the plow and not look back (9:62)—agendas reiterated in Acts. The whole gospel must be proclaimed to the whole person in the whole world—that is Luke's pastoral agenda. Why? Because there is only one, all-sufficient Savior, and all must acquiesce to that Lordship.

For Luke, discipleship consists in being molded by God's Spirit, but more specifically, by the tradition about Jesus. Thus, remarkable correspondences can be discerned between what Jesus says and does in Luke's Gospel and what the disciples say and do in Acts. Indeed, as Jesus tells his followers, "A disciple is not above the teacher, but everyone who is fully qualified will be like the teacher" (Luke 6:40). Thus, in his writings, Luke intends to illustrate graphically how Christians living after Easter should take the earthly Jesus as their model.

There is more to being a Christian, however, than simply patterning one's life after that of Jesus. In Luke's view, disciples must follow Jesus by experiencing his call (5:11, 27–28; see Acts 9:1–31). Furthermore, disciples are not solitary individuals but participants in community. This dimension of the Christian life is emphasized throughout Acts, but it is also foreshadowed in Luke's gospel through the corporate life of Jesus' disciples, a community consisting of females as well as males (8:1–3).

Luke's concept of discipleship applies not only to the way Christians are to live but also to the mission they are to fulfill (Luke 5:1–11; 24:46–49). Luke records two stories in which Jesus sends the disciples out as missionaries (9:1–6; 10:1–24), emphasizing that the disciples are sent by Jesus but also that they are to undertake this mission in partnership with others. In both cases, discipleship consists of being molded by a tradition, being empowered by an experience, and participating in a community.

In addition to what has already been said about individual discipleship, Luke understands the basis of Christian community to be the tradition about Jesus. This affects all aspects of congregational life, including fellowship, worship and prayer, teaching, and mission. In Acts, Luke states that believers live communally, sharing possessions (Acts 2:44; 4:32). While such idealism might seem foreign or far-fetched to modern Americans living in relative prosperity, this image seems to build on patterns in Luke's gospel, taken from the corporate life of Jesus' disciples. There we find unusual attention given to meals, banquets, and table fellowship. Banquets and food feature prominently in Jesus' parables and teaching. In all, Luke mentions nineteen such meals, thirteen of which are peculiar to his gospel. As if to call attention to the prominence of this motif, Luke reports that Jesus' opponents call him a "glutton and a drunkard" (7:34) and criticize him for eating with tax collectors and sinners (5:30; 15:1–2).

Modern readers may have difficulty appreciating this theme, unless they realize that in the biblical world, food is life and the sharing of food is the sharing of life. Thus, examples of Jesus' participation in table fellowship become "acted parables" about life, and Jesus' instructions about eating together show how people should live together. Besides generosity, hospitality, and humility, another possible interpretation is to view meals in Luke's gospel as inclusive events, so when Jesus is depicted as eating with tax collectors and sinners, this also points metaphorically to eating and living inclusively, with people of other faiths, cultures, races, and social classes. Furthermore, meals also represent occasions for conversation, reconciliation, and role reversal, by which the lowly are raised up and the proud are put down (7:36–52). In other words, where Jesus gives instructions concerning matters of table etiquette, readers can look beyond the surface to deeper issues of fear, prejudice, bias, and inequity.

Luke–Acts not only contains the content of Christian proclamation, but also presents a theological basis for the church's mission in the world. That basis lies in the concept of servanthood, presented so clearly throughout Luke's gospel (see 22:27, where Jesus establishes the pattern of servanthood when he declares, "I am among you as one who serves"). Underlying the church's mission to evangelism, which leads to growth and expansion, the calling of every believer is to servanthood. This is the Bible's stress on election, that when God calls a people, they are called not to privilege but to service. The Bible makes it clear that just as ancient Israel's call was for the healing of the nations (Gen. 12:3)[3] that call also continues for the church. Christians are called to be servants and are expected to perform acts of love and mercy for others, in imitation of Christ. Luke's writings, of course, offer the church an exemplary portrait of Jesus as the Servant of God.

The depiction of Jesus as Servant of God in his ministry and passion is frequently associated with the gospel of Mark, the first gospel written and hence the most primitive. Finding numerous christological titles embedded in Mark, scholars note that beneath this collage lies a distinct and authentic portrayal of Jesus as a servant come to suffer in obedience to God. Mark presents Jesus as a person of action, using the term "immediately" over forty times in its brief format. He records mostly what Jesus did, and little of what he said. There is no Sermon on the Mount, for example, and relatively few parables. There is no genealogy and birth narrative, for these records would have little value for one whose worth is servitude. One of the most important passages regarding the servanthood of Jesus in the gospels is found in Mark 10:45, "For the Son of Man[4] came not to be served but to serve."

In the Old Testament and in the writings of ancient Judaism the expression "Servant of God," used religiously, was employed in a variety of ways, principally as (1) a self-designation of a pious worshipper or as an ascription in the plural of pious persons; (2) as a collective term for the nation of Israel; and (3) as a denotation of the Messiah. It is clear that at least certain sectors of Palestinian Judaism understood Isaiah's Servant Songs (Isa 42:1–9; 49:1–7; 50: 4–9; 52:13—53:12) messianically during the first centuries BCE and CE.

The New Testament explicitly calls Jesus God's "servant" in Acts 3:13, 26, and 4:27, 30, with both Isaian and Davidic nuances present. In five passages, quotations from the Servant Songs are applied to Jesus and to aspects of his ministry (Matt. 8:17; 12:18–21; Luke 22:37; John 12:38; Acts 8:32–33). Of these, only Jesus' quotation in Luke 22:37, Philip's text in Acts 8:32–33, and possibly Peter's statement in Acts 3:13 directly connect Jesus with a Suffering Servant concept as well as a Servant motif. In

---

3. The biblical word for healing, health, wholeness, and goodness is "salvation," similar in meaning to the Hebrew word *shalom*. In the Bible, the election of a people becomes the basis for good news, what the New Testament calls "gospel."

4. The term "Son of Man," a reference to the humanity of Jesus, is also Jesus' favorite self-designation.

addition, the traditional formulations in 1 Corinthians 15:3-5; 11:23-25; Philippians 2:6-11, and 1 Peter 2:21-25, together with confessional fragments found in Romans 4:25; 8:32, 34; 1 Timothy 2:6; and 1 Peter 3:18, evidence either verbal or conceptual affinities to Isaiah 53.

Surveying the passages where Jesus is explicitly identified as God's Servant, where the Isaian Songs are applied to him or to aspects of his ministry, and where the language of confession is based on Isaiah 53, there is little doubt that early Christians thought in terms of Servant Christology—even of Suffering Servant Christology. And judging by the fact that such a conception exists in Paul's letters, principally (if not exclusively) in confessional portions, and later in the writings of the early patristic theologians only in prayers and liturgical formulations, it is reasonable to conclude that such a Christology stems from the first Jewish Christians.

Setting aside Jesus' passion, clearly central to the gospel writers and the Christian movement, what does Luke's Servant Christology teach about discipleship? In chapter 5, Luke defines discipleship in the story of Peter. Discipleship is defined in terms of risk and trust. Peter is a veteran fisherman, so Jesus meets him by the sea, in his own environment, and helps him find in that familiar realm a sign of the transcendent. In effect, Peter says to Jesus, "This is my world; if you can turn my fishing world upside down, you are for real." And because Jesus was able to do that, Peter and his companions "left everything and followed him" (5:11).

In Luke's Sermon on the Plain, his abbreviation of Matthew's Sermon on the Mount, Jesus does not present a list of dos and don'ts necessary to enter God's kingdom. Rather, Jesus is describing for his disciples what it means to be a disciple. The sermon consists of five parts: (1) blessings and woes (6:20-26); (2) on love of enemies (6:27-36); (3) on judging (6:37-42); (4) on integrity (6:43-45); and (5) on hearing and doing (6:46-49). Whereas Matthew's setting is before a huge crowd, for Luke it is given primarily to the disciples, precisely because this is a description of discipleship (but see Luke 7:1, where the larger audience is included, perhaps as potential disciples).

In Luke 8, Jesus demonstrates power over evil. The second half of the chapter provides four miracle accounts, stories that show Jesus setting things free. First comes the calming of the storm (8:22-25). The Jesus who can set hearts free to live in the truth can free nature to live in peace, because he controls even the winds and the sea. Rather than viewing this event as a demonstration of Jesus' power over nature, the calming of the storm is, like the story that immediately follows, an exorcism of evil from nature. The language used in 8:24, "he . . . rebuked the wind and the raging waves" is the customary language of an exorcism. From ancient times, and even in some cultures today, large bodies of water are believed to be the abode of evil spirits, said to stir up storms against sailors. Jesus' word of rebuke here is a direct command to evil itself.[5] In the story of the Gerasene demoniac (8:26–39), Jesus also demonstrates power over evil. In the cure of the woman with the hemorrhage (8:43–48), Jesus cures what medicine cannot; in the raising of the daughter of Jairus (8:40–42, 49–56), Jesus displays power over death and sets the child free to live again.

In 9:1–6, Jesus gives these powers to the Twelve, sending them forth to overcome evil, heal, and preach the gospel of the kingdom. This is the first of four scenes in which the disciples are commissioned in Luke: (1) sending the Twelve to preach and heal (9:1–6); (2) sending the seventy in pairs (10:1–11); (3) Jesus' preparation of the apostles for their post-Easter mission (22:35–38); and (4) the commissioning of the eleven and the others at the end of the gospel (24:48–49). A further commissioning follows in Acts 1:6–8.

In Luke 9 the issues developed in the previous two chapters reach a climax. When reports of Jesus' work reach Herod, he asks, "Who is this about whom I hear such things?" (9:9). This section of Luke provides an answer to Herod's question. Jesus is "the Messiah of God" (9:20), but he is also the Son of Man who will be rejected and killed by the religious authorities. As we learn from Jesus' life, discipleship requires a total commitment of one's life. The five sayings on discipleship (9:23–27) that follow the first passion prediction also serve as an answer to Herod's question regarding Jesus' identity. Lordship and discipleship are always related. Surprisingly, the five discipleship sayings are addressed to "all"—both the disciples and the crowd (see Mark 8:34)—thereby extending the invitation to discipleship to all people.

The feeding of the five thousand in 9:10–17 (a variant of this miracle is told in each canonical gospel, making it the only miracle shared by all four evangelists) is reminiscent of the great Banquet, the coronation feast of God symbolic of the messianic age (see Isa 25:6–8). In his preaching Jesus made frequent use of this symbol, to denote either the presence of the kingdom with its rich invitation (5:34; 6:21; 14:16–24) or its ultimate, heavenly fulfillment (13:29–30; 22:15–18). The feeding highlights Jesus'

---

5. Craddock, *Luke*, 115.

compassion and especially his concern for the poor and hungry. In addition, the church finds in this event a model for ministry: Jesus working through his disciples.

Following the episode of the transfiguration of Jesus, it becomes obvious that the disciples do not understand that discipleship, like messiahship, entails suffering, because they debate among themselves as to which of them is the greatest. Jesus answers insightfully from the depth of self-understanding he received, beginning at his baptism: "the least among all of you is the greatest" (9:48).

Questions for Discussion and Reflection

1. Explain and assess the author's point that discipleship is a core biblical principle.
2. Explain the difference between discipleship as "participation" and as "imitation." Which of these best typifies your experience or understanding of discipleship? Explain your answer.
3. Explain and assess the meaning and significance of the biblical idea that all humans are made "in the image of God."
4. How, according to 1 Peter 2:4–10, are Christians connected with the hopes and mission of ancient Israelites?
5. In your reading of this chapter, what did you learn about the "law of love"?
6. In your estimation, what are some modern implications of Jesus' teaching that discipleship requires carrying one's cross? (See Luke 14:27.)
7. Explain and assess the contrast in the gospels between discipleship as "believing in Jesus" and as basing one's lifestyle on Jesus' values and lifestyle.
8. Explain and assess Diana Bass's idea that as our understanding of Jesus changes throughout our lifetime, so, for the sake of a changing world, Jesus also changes.
9. Assess the author's idea that some passages and even some books of the Bible may be dated and therefore irrelevant to modern thinking

and practice, while other passages and books might be more relevant today that when first written.

10. Explain and assess the difference between temporal and eternal meanings of the word "salvation," and how these differences influence our understanding of Jesus as Savior.
11. Explain and assess the meaning of Luke's use of the word "prophet" when referring to Jesus.
12. In your own words, describe what the book of Acts teaches about discipleship.
13. In your own words, describe what Luke–Acts teaches about servanthood.
14. In your own words, describe what Matthew's Sermon on the Mount teaches about discipleship.
15. In your reading of this chapter, which concept regarding discipleship in Luke–Acts do you consider most relevant to the view that Jesus inspired more compassion than any single person, movement, or force in history?

Chapter 5

The Centrality of Discipleship in the Bible, Part II

BECAUSE LUKE'S GOSPEL HAS much to teach twenty-first century followers of the historical Jesus, this chapter continues the focus on discipleship in the third gospel, concluding with a segment on the ethical implications of being twenty-first century kingdom people. In Luke 9:51—18:14 (often called Luke's travel narrative) we discover anew the close connection between Christology and discipleship. If the first part of Luke (chapters 1–2) introduces Jesus as a royal messiah from the house of David, and the second part (chapters 3–9) narrates Jesus' journey from baptism to transfiguration, focusing on his self-understanding as the Son of God, the third part (chapters 10–19) focuses on the identity and task of disciples as "kingdom people." The fourth and final unit of Luke provides Jesus' final teachings to his disciples, preparing them through word and deed for his death and the path beyond. The death, resurrection, and ascension of Jesus function as an interlude to the next episode in Luke's story, the birth and expansion of the church, when the disciples, led by God's Spirit, become leaders in their own right.

Two personal stories illustrate my perspective on disciples as kingdom people. Upon graduating from the Stony Brook School, a college preparatory school on Long Island, New York, I received a gift from one of my teachers. The gift was a book titled *A Leader Led*, a study guide on 1 Timothy. I have always treasured that book, not only because I received it from Thomas Little, the religion professor with whom five students and I traveled across the United States the summer after my junior year, but because the title suggests my identity as leader and my vocation as disciple of Jesus. That's what I see going on in Luke's travel narrative: the training of "kingdom people" as future leaders.

The second story is about Robert Cook, president of The King's College, my alma mater. Dr. Cook, a Christian author, radio broadcaster, and pastor, was associated with Youth for Christ before coming to King's. He often invited me to travel with him on speaking engagements, where I was encouraged to share my testimony. When we traveled, we often prayed, and I peeked on occasion to make sure Dr. Cook's eyes were open as he drove. Like Jesus with his disciples, he taught me through word and deed. Though he died in 1991, his broadcasts are still available on YouTube. The title of his books and programs, "Walk with the King Today," was striking and practical, its premise being that as children of God, you and I are nobility in training, raised at the feet of Jesus and walking daily with the King, the Lord of lords. As we read Luke's travel narrative, let us accompany Jesus as disciples, siblings, and friends—as leaders led.

When Jesus sets his face toward Jerusalem, he sends messengers ahead of him, to prepare the way in Samaria. The long-standing feud between Jews and Samaritans flares up again in this section, as does the Elijah theme. In 9:53–54 we find the disciples James and John trying to emulate Elijah, who felt the best way to deal with the enemies of Israel was to call down God's curse upon them. James and John had a lot to learn about discipleship. Intoxicated with limited authority and influence, they saw only one way to solve problems—by force. This is why Elijah's methodology gives way to that of Jesus, with his new way of loving enemies and dying for them.

As Jesus heads toward Jerusalem, he encounters three people with excuses that keep them from the spiritual path (9:57–62). Their reasons are all valid: (1) the necessity of home; (2) duties to aged parents; and (3) relationships with family. The three candidates for discipleship are warned to count the cost. Jesus makes some hard remarks here, but the fact that Luke brings up this issue shows that he is telling his community that the call of God's kingdom (God's rule) is absolute. It is the only thing that matters because it is the only thing that lasts. Jesus obviously isn't telling people to avoid family duties or family funerals, but instead is encouraging them to find ways to be responsible through a transformed consciousness. Family life is divinely appointed, but under certain conditions Jesus' followers must be prepared to sacrifice security, duty, and affection if they are to respond to the call of God's kingdom, a call that makes other loyalties pale by comparison (see Luke 14:26/Matt 10:37;

also Luke 11:23). The point is not to be stymied by life's problems and dilemmas but to keep moving forward, making a difference through one's presence. That's how one grows spiritually, by being attuned to God's Spirit, hearing and obeying God's marching orders. The most difficult choices in life are not between the good and the evil, but between the good and the best.

In addition to the mission of the Twelve (Luke 9:1-6), Luke also presents a mission of the seventy (or seventy-two). This number is believed to come from the list of nations in Genesis 10 (seventy in the Hebrew text, seventy-two in the Greek text). The sending of the seventy is recorded by Luke alone, and it raises some difficult questions, because the same material is placed by Matthew in his charge to the Twelve (Matt 9:37-38; 10:7-16, 40). Whether the mission is fact or fiction, the number is certainly symbolic. By invoking the number seventy, Luke may be alluding to Moses, who shared the burden of his work with his seventy assistants (see Exod 24:1, 9; also 18:21-23). Even though their commission, like that of the Twelve, was to the house of Israel, Luke is clearly anticipating the mission to the Gentiles begun at Pentecost (see Acts 2:5).

The missionaries are sent forth in pairs, and for good reason. Gospel work—kingdom work, church work—is not solo activity. The gospel of love cannot be communicated by one person because, in the end, love is something that happens between two. If only one disciple is sent, that ministry would likely be verbal. In the Bible, the gospel spreads between two or more people. That's why group Bible study is so important. God places us in corporate contexts because unless one is in right relationship with at least one other person on this earth, expansion is not possible. Eastern Orthodox know that intuitively, as do Mormon missionaries, who always travel in pairs. In Orthodoxy, no one is saved individually; rather Christians are saved together.

Other aspects of this mission deserve attention. For instance, when Jesus instructs the missionaries in Luke 10:4 not to greet people on the road, he is not saying they should be unfriendly; rather he is telling them to have a focused purpose, to be intentional about their activity. Their mission is an urgent one because they are harvesters: Israel is ripe for the harvest and must be gathered into the kingdom while the brief season lasts. The focus of their mission is the immanence and nearness of the kingdom (10:9, 11). This does not mean that the arrival of the kingdom is in the future, about which people must be warned during the interval that remains. For Luke the kingdom is present, and that presence is to be proclaimed by word of mouth but also actively demonstrated through deeds of love, compassion, and power. Whether we like it or not, whether we believe it or not, God's kingdom is inexorably present, a reign of peace to those who accept it and a sentence of doom to those who do not. The time is short because the opposition is gathering its forces, so that even now the disciples go out "like lambs into the midst of wolves" (10:3).

The parable about the Good Samaritan (10:25–37), occasioned by the lawyer's question in 10:29, "And who is my neighbor?" provides further clarification of the meaning of discipleship; the conversation between Jesus and the lawyer illustrates the difference between the ethics of law and the ethics of love. To the lawyer eternal life is a prize to be won by meticulous observance of religious rules, whereas for Jesus, love of God and love of neighbor is in itself the life of the heavenly kingdom, already begun on earth. Whereas the rabbis believed keeping the law of Moses in its entirety, with its 613 commandments, was the way of showing love to God, Jesus was convinced that loving God means devotion to God's purpose of compassion and grace. The story of the Good Samaritan tells us that the question, "Who is my neighbor?" is the wrong question. The proper question is, "To whom can I be a neighbor?"; and the answer is, "To anyone who needs my help." Importantly, Jesus chose an outsider, a Samaritan outside the Jewish system, to be the true neighbor. In this amazingly anticlerical story, Jesus focuses on the basics—pity, care, compassion—and does not get sidetracked by divisive peripheral issues such as religious membership or religious orthodoxy.

Scholars are now labelling the parable of the Good Samaritan an "example story" rather than a parable, since it appears only in Luke, and only Luke contains example stories (10:30–37; 12:16–21; 16:19–31; 18:10–14). Despite Luke's editorializing, this story likely goes back to Jesus, who intended it not as an example of "proper" behavior but as a portrayal of how the inbreaking of the kingdom transforms people and reorders their thinking. What we have here is an ethnic reversal, used to challenge current attitudes regarding ritual standards. The notion of a "good Samaritan" was a contradiction in terms for a traditional Jew, but such reversal is typical of Jesus the sage, "who seems to specialize in oxymorons like good leaven, light burdens, and here a good Samaritan."[1]

The Martha and Mary story (10:38–42), a uniquely Lukan passage, often leads to misunderstanding because we focus on the wrong person,

---

1. Witherington, *Jesus the Sage*, 194.

in this case on Mary. As the opening line makes clear, this is Martha's story, not Mary's. As hostess, Martha is the central figure, the stronger character. She is full of good works and entirely free from selfishness. But she earns a gentle reproof from Jesus because good works and even sacrifice can be spoiled by self-concern and self-pity. Jesus is not contrasting prayer and activism and putting primacy on a life of contemplation. Rather he is saying that the one prerequisite for being a follower of Jesus is listening to God's word. Listening is the better part. Martha is trying to get Jesus to reinforce her cultural understanding of women's roles, and Jesus refuses to do so while still affirming Martha warmly. Both virtues combined—good works and contemplation—represent the ideal. Good works alone can become misery to the doer and tyranny to others.

In chapter 11, Jesus illustrates his ministry by what appears to be a central metaphor of his teaching, the "sign" of Jonah (11:29–32). Without the sign of Jonah—the pattern of new life only through death—Christianity remains largely impotent, another way to "win" and avoid the pain of faith. Or it becomes a language of ascent instead of the treacherous journey of descent that characterizes Jonah, Jeremiah, Job, John the Baptist, and Jesus. Jesus' way, as he himself characterized the journey of discipleship, is "the way of the cross" (see 9:23–27). Those who miss the sign of Jonah miss the Christian message. Chapter 11 ends with a condemnation of legalism, which is what always recurs when people fail to follow the sign of Jonah. Opposition to Jesus increases in 11:47–54, for those preoccupied with "orthodoxy" find Jesus' view of discipleship hard to comprehend.

At the heart of Jesus' sermon in Luke 12 we find these words: "strive for [God's] kingdom" (12:31). According to this teaching, the kingdom[2] is to be the believer's first and main concern. It was certainly so for Jesus, who gave up everything for the sake of the kingdom. The theology of Jesus does not admit compromise; there must be a complete break with conventional morality or piety. For example, a rich young man is told by Jesus that he must sell all that he has and give to the poor (18:18–30). To understand the meaning of such severity, this story must be read contextually. Jesus is on his way to Jerusalem, and the final conflict in which he is to be engaged looms before him. At such a time there can be no hesitation; it must be all or nothing. This is a moment of crisis for those who would follow Jesus. In Luke's travel narrative, when Jesus says, "You

---

2. As mentioned earlier, one way to translate Jesus' term "kingdom" is "radical discipleship."

cannot serve God or wealth" (16:13), he is not giving a new commandment. He is simply stating a fact about the choices his followers must make. Before them lie two mutually exclusive worlds. Those who choose to live in one are automatically excluded from the other. When money has priority, God's lordship is compromised: "No one who puts a hand to the plow and looks back is fit for the kingdom of God" (9:62).

In 14:26–27, Jesus is quoted as saying: "Whoever comes to me and does not hate father and mother, wife and children, brothers and sisters, yes, and even life itself, cannot be my disciple." These powerful and troublesome lines, their rhetoric softened in the Matthean parallel (see Matt 10:37–38), were not intended to be taken literally (see Mark 7:9–13). They are an example of Middle Eastern hyperbole, so common in the gospels. Luke's audience was comfortable with extremes—light and darkness, truth and falsehood, love and hate—primary colors with no grey tones or hints of compromise. To say, "I like this and hate that" means "I prefer this to that." For the followers of Jesus, to hate their families meant to give them second place in their affection. However, as the reference to carrying one's cross in 14:27 indicates, there is a cost to discipleship, and that cost often implies relationships, as Paul notes in 2 Corinthians 6:14–16.

These are radical sayings. It is quite plain that if everyone gave away all their possessions to the poor, the only result would be that the rich of today would become the poor of tomorrow and vice versa; the social situation would be neither changed nor improved. Not every command is of equal application to every situation; there must be a measure of adaptation and flexibility. But before we become too easily dismissive of Jesus' radicalism, let us remember that Christian ethics are derived from Christian theology. The central point of that theology is the example of Jesus Christ and his demand that citizens of the kingdom recognize unconditionally the sovereignty of God.

In Luke 13:29 the kingdom of God is shown as a great gathering that includes all humanity. In Luke's version, the gathering takes place from the four points of the compass. This image, like the four-sided cross, is symbolic of the mystery of the kingdom, since its structure suggests the wholeness and harmony of God's kingdom. Its breadth and length, height and depth, embrace what is on the right and left and unite all in Christ, the center. In Ephesians 2:14–16, the reference is to the union, through Christ, of Jew and Gentile, but the image also applies to the union of our personality, the sensual and the intuitive, the spirit and the flesh, the inner and the outward, the knowable and the unknowable, logic and imagination, darkness and light.

We must always remember that the context of Jesus' sayings was the message that God's kingdom was near at hand. Jesus' claims placed persons on the very borderline between the old age and the new. Jesus' perspective made love, not duty, central. However, such love is no natural sentiment or calculated act but is patterned after the love of God. As God's love is bestowed unconditionally upon those least deserving to be loved, so likewise Christians must love even those who seem to be most loveless, including social outcasts or despised enemies. Jesus transforms religious laws by destroying legalism: Christ is the "end of the law" (Rom 10:4). Rather than setting a standard of perfection that drives us to despair, Christ teachings provide a compass that gives direction to our efforts to improve and transform society. Christian ethics, then, are essentially "resurrection ethics," since they derive their motive and patterns from the love of God manifested in Christ: "Beloved, since God loved us so much, we also ought to love one another" (1 John 4:11).

In chapter 14, Luke focused on eating and table-fellowship. As previously noted, in his gospel, Luke records numerous stories that have something to do with Jesus sitting at a table. For Luke, the table is the place of fellowship and communion. It is also the place where Jesus redefines the social order by doing things differently and challenging those who are in control of the social order—the rich, the elders, the scribes, and the "politically correct." For Luke, the theme of table fellowship seems to be Jesus' unique form of visual sermon, cultural critique, and social protest. When you have a party, Jesus says, "invite the poor, the crippled, the lame, and the blind" (14:13). As Jesus implies, the new order of the kingdom will not simply ignore the status symbols of the world, but reverse them. Human hierarchies mean nothing to God. What matters is our common humanity and the desire to be in fellowship. In his parables and stories, Jesus is empowering the outsider. The apostle Paul also implemented this message in his churches when he declared, in one of his most revolutionaries statements: "There is no longer Jew or Greek . . . slave or free . . . male and female; for you are one in Christ Jesus" (Gal 3:28).

In 14:33 Luke addresses the renunciation of possessions, an issue that resurfaces often in his writing, as it does in 18:18–30, in the idyllic summaries in Acts 2:44–45 and 4:32–37, and in the instructive story of Ananias and Sapphira in 5:1–11.

Among the Jewish people of Jesus' day, wealth was thought of as a sign of God's blessing. Jesus disagreed. Despite the wealth and prosperity gospel many preachers are proclaiming nowadays, power and success are not signs of God's blessing. "It is easier for a camel to go through the eye of a needle," Jesus noted, "than for someone who is rich to enter the kingdom of God" (18:25). Of course, we must not read this as an absolute law, or seek its enforcement, for that is not what Jesus was teaching. He was simply answering a question, discerning insincerity in the ruler's query. He seems to be saying, "If you want to enter into the freedom I am talking about, if you want to live authentically, here's my answer: Give it away. It will possess you more than you will ever possess it." When the man replies, "I am not ready to live like that," Jesus replies, "Okay, you asked, I answered."

If Americans were to select one book of the Bible and say, "This is going to be our guidebook, our philosophy of life," I doubt it would be Luke's gospel, because it hits us too deeply in areas where most are quite comfortable. Luke punctuates his discussion on wealth and discipleship with an impossible one-liner: "none of you can become my disciple if you do not give up all your possessions" (14:33).

Jesus and the Presence of the Kingdom

The dominant theme in the preaching of Jesus—indeed the center of his mission and message—is the coming of the kingdom of God (what we are calling "radical discipleship"). While the phrase "kingdom of God" is rare in contemporary Jewish writings, it is widely regarded as one of the most distinctive aspects of the preaching of Jesus. Because almost everywhere in the Old Testament the idea of the kingdom is related to the people of Israel and the rule of the house of David in Jerusalem, Jesus is at pains to divest his teaching of this former understanding of the nature of the kingdom. What Jesus proclaims is the immediate sovereignty of God, who will take control of the destinies of all humans, restore humanity to what God had intended it to be, and overthrow the evil powers that had led astray human beings from their proper destiny.

In Mark's gospel, Jesus' first act upon returning from his sojourn in the wilderness is to proclaim the coming of the kingdom (1:15). Here Jesus picks up where Second Isaiah (Isa 40–55) left off half a millennium earlier. Isaiah had envisioned a day when God would finally bring justice to the world, when the long-suffering faithful could rejoice at the end of oppression. Jesus shared Isaiah's anticipation but was more specific about when this time would come: "Truly I tell you, there are some standing here who will not taste death until they see that the kingdom of God has come with power" (Mark 9:1). His audience was to repent and "believe in the good news."

Whatever Jesus envisioned in his proclamation about the kingdom, it was going to be on earth. Despite Matthew's preference for the expression, "kingdom of heaven," it is clear that the concept, as Jesus used it, refers to the destiny of good people on a new, improved earth. It has nothing to do with the souls of dead people ascending to heaven.

In New Testament teaching, the coming of the kingdom is always dependent on divine initiative, never on human achievement. Humans may enter the kingdom; they may proclaim it and inherit it (Matt 25:34; 7:21), but they can neither earn it nor bring it forth. Because the word "kingdom" suggests a geographical region or realm, which is misleading in this context, scholars prefer the term "kingship" or "kingly rule of God."

While the term "kingdom" is complex and paradoxical at its core, Jesus didn't limit his thinking to belief in a glorious future, with its new world. Rather, he brought the doctrine into the present, living out of the resources of the future proleptically. This is why scholars label his teachings "realized eschatology" or "inaugurated eschatology." As later Christians went on to claim, God's kingdom is present here and now (Luke 17:21); eternal life is a present reality (John 3:36; 6:47); abundant life is available now (John 10:10).

Accepting the goodness of God's creation, as well as the damage caused by human pride and interference, Jesus came to offer new possibilities. Believing in the power of the Jesus story to transform society, Brian McLaren, together with Gareth Higgins, tells how Jesus came to subvert all stories of violence and harm.[3] Exposing and delegitimizing stories of domination, Jesus taught and embodied service, reconciliation, and self-giving. Instead of stories of violent revolution, revenge, or of compliant submission, he taught and modeled transformative nonviolent resistance. Instead of purification stories of scapegoating or ethnic cleansing, he engaged strangers and aliens with respect, welcome, neighborliness, and mutuality. Instead of competitive stories of accumulation,

---

3. McLaren and Higgins, *Seventh Story*.

he advocated stewardship, generosity, sharing, and a vision of abundance for all. Instead of apocalyptic stories of isolation and escapism, he sent his followers into the world to be agents of positive change. And instead of leaving the oppressed in stories of victimization, he empowered them with a vision of faith, hope, and love that could change the world.

Those six stories of violence and harm all claimed that the path to peace, security, and happiness was about "winning." However, in the Jesus Story, the story of reconciliation and love, humans still get to win, only not at anyone else's expense. In the Seventh Story, human beings are not the protagonists of the world. Love is.[4]

As an apocalyptic prophet, Jesus proclaimed that God's kingdom was coming to earth imminently (Mark 1:15). These words in Mark, the first words Jesus is recorded to have said in that gospel, provide a summary of Jesus' teaching. This would be a real kingdom with real rulers, a kingdom that would welcome some people but exclude others. Before the kingdom arrived, a scene of judgment would take place, in which the Son of Man, a cosmic figure from heaven, would appear to destroy God's enemies. This coming judgment would involve a massive reversal of fortunes; those who had prospered in this world through siding with evil would be displaced, but those who had suffered would be exalted. The judgment would come not only to individuals, but also to institutions and governments. In particular, the Jewish temple in Jerusalem, the heart of all institutional Jewish worship, would be destroyed.

Throughout his authentic teachings, when Jesus refers to the coming kingdom, he seems to mean an actual earthly kingdom, with actual rulers. Consider Jesus' teachings found in Q (a hypothetical source scholars call possibly the earliest gospel source): "Truly I tell you, at the renewal of all things, when the Son of Man is seated on the throne of his glory, you who have followed me will also sit on twelve thrones, judging the twelve tribes of Israel" (Matt 19:28; cf. Luke 22:30). While the arrival of the kingdom was "good news" for Jesus' followers, it was not good news for everyone. In a mighty act of judgment, evil rulers would be toppled and punished, and the oppressed would be raised up (Luke 13:23–29; cf. Matt 8:11–12). This coming judgment would involve a serious reversal of fortune, one that makes sense in an apocalyptic context (Mark 10:31; Luke 13:30).

---

4. McLaren and Higgins, *Seventh Story*, 38, 40–42.

Likewise, Jesus' ethical teachings make best sense in an apocalyptic context. These teachings, however, have come down to us today as perfect examples of how people ought to live normally. Nevertheless, it is important for us to understand that the meaning of Jesus' ethical teachings might have been quite different in their original context from their meaning in ours. In our context, Jesus' teachings assist us in knowing how to get along with one another, so that we can contribute to a healthier and more wholesome society, allowing us to experience peace and well-being for the long haul. But for Jesus there was not going to be a long haul. The Son of Man[5] would soon come in judgment, and people needed to prepare for entrance into his kingdom by showing that they sided with God rather than with the forces of evil that were opposed to him. Jesus' ethical teachings were ethics of the kingdom—they both reflected what life would be like in the kingdom and qualified one for entrance once it arrived.

In the kingdom, there would be no hatred; thus, people should love one another now. In the kingdom, there would be no oppression; thus, people should work for justice now. In the kingdom, there would be no war; thus, people should work for peace now. In the kingdom, there would be no sexism; thus, people should work for equality now. Only those who lived in ways that are appropriate to the kingdom would be allowed entrance when it arrived.

According to Jesus' teachings in the Sermon on the Mount, his followers should regard entrance into the kingdom as their most prized possession, and even be willing to give up all their possessions for the sake of the kingdom (Matt 6:25–33). Later on, Jesus indicates in his parable of the Pearl of Great Price (Matt 13:45–46) that the kingdom is like a merchant in search of fine pearls who finds a perfect pearl and then goes out and sells all that he has to buy it. The pearl is the kingdom, and it demands our ultimate allegiance; that's how valuable it is. For Jesus, nothing made sense apart from the kingdom of God that was on the verge of breaking into history. If its coming found one unprepared, all would be lost.

---

5. In the gospels, Jesus uses the term "son of man" in three different ways: (1) as a circumlocution for himself (speaking indirectly of himself as a man; see Matt 8:20); (2) to speak of his vocation, specifically of his earthly mission and coming passion (see Mark 8:31); and (3) with reference to an eschatological figure who will bring God's judgment at the end of time (Mark 8:38). The reference here is not to Jesus but to the future eschatological figure mentioned in Daniel 7:13–14, a figure many early Christians mistakenly associated with Jesus.

If Jesus' ethical teachings make best sense in an apocalyptic context, we need to rethink their meaning. Jesus, it appears, did not deliver timeless truths to guide individuals in leading long and productive lives. His teachings were meant to show people how to live in order to enter the kingdom that would soon appear. When we examine teachings such as "love your neighbor as yourself," and "love your enemies and pray for those who persecute you," he is teaching ethics of the coming kingdom. How else can we understand Jesus' teaching to the young ruler, that he should give up everything—all possessions and everything that binds one to this world (Mark 10:17-31)—except in this context? This emphasis on giving up everything for the kingdom means that Jesus was not a major proponent of what we now call "family values" (see Luke 14:26; 12:51-53). As with other hard sayings of Jesus, these should not be explained away so that they no longer mean what they say. Instead, they should be placed in an apocalyptic context.

Understood apocalyptically, Jesus' command to love one's neighbor and God above all else points to the coming kingdom, when God will provide such things as food and clothing (Matt 6:25-33). To those who trust God, all things are possible, for that is how God will care for us in his kingdom that is soon to come. Jesus, then, did not see himself as inventing a new system of ethics, so much as explaining the Law of Moses in view of his own apocalyptic context.

While later sources have Jesus proclaiming the kingdom as a present reality, this is not what Jesus actually taught. For him, the kingdom was imminent, but it had not yet arrived. Understanding Jesus' message of the coming judgment by the Son of Man, including the destruction of the temple in Jerusalem, helps explain Jesus' actions in the temple prior to his crucifixion. Viewed apocalyptically, they become a symbolic expression of his teaching, a prophetic gesture or enacted parable of the coming of God's imminent judgment on the earth, beginning with institutional Judaism. In cleansing the temple, Jesus was demonstrating on a small scale what would soon occur in a large way.

What Would Jesus Do?

Some years ago, it was fashionable for evangelical Christians and even for non-Christians to wear a bracelet with the letters WWJD, an abbreviation of "What Would Jesus Do?" The motto became popular in the United States in the late 1800s, after the publication of the widely read book by Charles Sheldon titled *In His Steps: What Would Jesus Do?* The phrase had a resurgence in the 1990s as a personal reminder for adherents of Christianity to live faithfully.

While adherence to Christian social and ethical values is commendable, it is based on a questionable premise, that we can know how a first-century Jewish mystic named Jesus might think and act in the twenty-first century. While the rationale behind this WWJD motto is based on the notion that Jesus' deeds and thought process are captured reliably in the four gospels of the New Testament, that motive is radically flawed, for the gospels reflect more the ethical and theological views and interpretations of second and third generation Christians than verbatim conversations, sermons, and factual eyewitness accounts.

For the authors of Matthew, Luke, and John, certainly, Jesus was primarily a divine being with certain human qualities, but not truly human at all. In these writings, the words and actions of Jesus are viewed through the authors' christological lens. For Mark, the first gospel writer, Jesus was born human but exalted to divine sonship at his baptism.

Before we moderns try to imitate Jesus' behavior, we must address two related questions, acknowledging that neither can be answered definitively:

1. Was the historical Jesus human or divine? If he was fully human, as I have been arguing, he was like us in every respect, and his ethical motivation and behavior would be relevant and imitable. If he was fully divine, then his motivation and behavior would ultimately be irrelevant and unattainable to fallible, mortal creatures.

2. If Jesus were alive in the twenty-first century, what would Jesus do? How would he behave, and what would his motivating values be?[6]

If Jesus taught and lived as an apocalyptic Jewish prophet in the twenty-first century, few if any Christians would follow him. Nevertheless, most Christians follow him as a first-century apocalyptic Jew. How ironic!

Was Jesus literally born of a virgin? Of course not. Did he literally walk on water, multiply food, or turn water into wine? I sincerely doubt it. Was he literally raised bodily from the dead? Not if he was fully human. Did he literally die for our sins? Only if we believe in animal sacrifices as vicarious atonement, something most of us neither believe nor practice. What, then, does it mean to follow Jesus?

6. This question will be addressed in chapters 7 and 8 below.

I believe there is no more important topic for inquiry today than the meaning and message of Jesus, no more important concern than one's answer to Jesus' perennial question, "Who do you say that I am?" (Mark 8:29), for in this quest, I believe, lies the solution to individual malaise and humanity's woes.

Questions for Discussion and Reflection

1. Explain and assess the author's suggestion that followers of Jesus are "kingdom people."
2. In reading the segment on Luke's "travel narrative," what did you learn about the meaning of radical discipleship?
3. Assess the meaning of the author's statement, "The most difficult choices in life are not between the good and the evil, but between the good and the best." Can you provide examples from your experience or from life in general that attest to this view?
4. Explain and assess the meaning of the statement that "gospel work—kingdom work, church work—is not solo activity."
5. Explain the difference between mission that focuses on the needs of people—and that by necessity is often diverted and interrupted—and mission that is focused and intentional. Which form do you prefer? Explain your answer.
6. In reading the segment about the Good Samaritan, what did you learn about discipleship?
7. In reading the segment on Mary and Martha, what did you learn about discipleship?
8. In reading the segment on loving and hating family and friends, what did you learn about discipleship?
9. In reading the segment on eating and food-fellowship, what did you learn about discipleship?
10. In reading the segment on wealth and possessions, what did you learn about discipleship?
11. In reading the segment on the kingdom of God, what did you learn about discipleship?

Chapter 6

Jesus as Archetype of the Self[1]

HAVING EXAMINED THE MISSION and ministry of the historical Jesus, this chapter focuses on the death and resurrection of Jesus as templates for growth in discipleship. In America today, as in most global economies, there is a mutual contract between personal egos and egoic cultures. This is the meaning of the phrase "the world" in the New Testament (see John 1:10; 8:23; 12:31; 1 John 2:15–17). In this sense, the word "world" is a way of speaking of the corporate False Self, what we might call "the system" or "the way the world works." Jesus said, "Take courage; I have conquered the world" (John 16:33).

Our False Self (our temporary egoic self) fears change, even creating moral disguises to achieve its selfish ends. Hence, the New Testament often personifies the ego—whether personal or corporate—as the devil or Satan. The devil's secrets are always disguised, as we see with the snake in Genesis 3:1. Satan's temptations are not always blatant and offensive, but often subtle and self-centered.

Like Jesus, the ego is tempted economically (to be successful), politically (to be powerful), and spiritually (to be right). The ego regularly acquiesces, finding such temptations seductive. When the corporate ego succumbs, the results can be disastrous. Temptations to dominate others or to remain isolated and self-sufficient seem obvious to us, unlike the third temptation, which fuels the ego with high octane. Our True Self (the permanent "image of God" in us), rooted in Ultimate Reality, has little need for limited answers and temporary certitudes. It has found its

---

1. This chapter is adapted from chapter 8, "Death and Resurrection as Metaphor," of Vande Kappelle, *Walking on Water*, 96–108. Ideas in this chapter were initially adapted from Rohr, *Diamond*, 43–102, 139–58.

certainty elsewhere and lives inside a "Yes" so eternal that it can absorb life's disappointments and fractures. The False Self, however, fears and denies all paradox and uncertainty, probably because it unconsciously knows it is itself a mass of contradiction and uncertainty. The True Self, symbolized by the Risen Christ, has already overcome the contradictions and paradoxes of life.

In speaking of the Christian life, pastoral theologian Andrew Purves distinguishes between imitating Christ (*imitatio Christi*) and participating *in* Christ (*participatio Christi*). While many believers today strive to "be like Jesus," early Christians thought differently, emphasizing the importance of participating in Jesus Christ through the power of the Holy Spirit. Trying harder was not the solution. Rather, they understood that God was the primary actor, and the Christian life a response to Christ's "vicarious humanity," experienced through the Holy Spirit.[2]

Jesus confronted the False Self's seductive lies by living within an entirely different frame of reference, the eternal "kingdom of God." The False Self is no longer a threat or an enduring attraction when viewed from the vantage of the True Self. This is what Christians mean at Easter when they proclaim that Jesus destroyed death. Perhaps it would be more accurate to say, "Jesus exposed the lie," because there is clearly plenty of "death" in our society that has not died.

Death and the False Self

Mature religion talks about the death of any notion of a separate, False Self, while recognizing that only a deep security in a larger love will give us the courage to do that. The True Self can let go because it is secure at its core. Our False Self, however, does not let go easily. Unwilling to die to the old, it resists all such change.

As Jesus and other great spiritual teachers made clear, there is a self that must be found and another that must be renounced. This teaching is found in each gospel (see Matt 10:39; 16:25; Mark 8:35; Luke 9:24), but is central to John's gospel, where it is coupled with "dying to the self": "unless a grain of wheat falls into the earth and dies, it remains just a single grain; but if it dies, it bears much fruit" (John 12:24). Hence, "those who love their life lose it [that is, their False Self], and those who hate their life

---

2. Purves, *Reconstructing Pastoral Theology*, 152.

[their False Self] in this world will keep it [their True Self] for eternal life" (John 12:25; see also 1 Cor 15:36–37, 42).

In one way or another, almost all religions say that you must die before you die—and then you will know what dying means, and what it does not mean. What it does mean, of course, is the relinquishment of selfish, possessive living, of egoic existence. This includes the death or renunciation of easy opinions, forced certitudes, intellectual or moral superiority, futile attempts at perfect control, and eventually any belief in our separatedness from God.[3] The ego self is the self before death; some form of death—psychological, spiritual, relational, or physical—is the way we will loosen our ties to our small and separate False Self. Only then does it return in a new shape, which we call the soul, the True Self, or the Risen Christ.

There are four major splits from reality that we have all made in varying degrees to create our False Self:

- We split from our shadow self[4] and pretend to be our idealized self.
- We split our mind from our body and soul, and live in our minds.
- We split life from death and try to live without any "death."
- We split ourselves from other selves and try to live apart, superior, and separate.[5]

Each of these illusions must be overcome, either in this world or at the moment of physical death. Spirituality, pure and simple, is overcoming these splits from Reality.

Anything less than the death of the False Self is inadequate religion. The False Self must die for the True Self to live, or, as Jesus put it, "if I do not go, the Advocate [the Holy Spirit] will not come to you" (John 16:7). Theologically speaking, what this verse is telling us is that Jesus (a good person) still had to die for the Christ (the universal presence) to arise. This is the pattern of transformation, where the letting go of the original

---

3. Rohr, *Eager to Love*, 26.

4. The shadow self, something everyone possesses, represents the least-developed part of one's personality. The shadow uses relatively childish and primitive forms of judgment and perception, often as an escape from the conscious personality and in defiance of conscious standards. One's shadow includes "good" qualities as well as "bad" or "shameful" qualities that one denies. As one makes room for one's polarities, one becomes healthier and more open to transforming grace.

5. Rohr, *Diamond*, 29.

indispensable self results in the arrival of a better reality. This pattern of death and rebirth—of cross and resurrection—is both spiritual and natural. As we know from science, the death and birth of every star and atom is this same pattern of loss and renewal.

Our True Self sees truthfully and will live forever. Our False Self is constantly changing and will eventually die. Our False Self is our necessary warm-up, our ego part that establishes our separate identity, especially in the first half of life. It is our incomplete self trying to pass for our whole self. The role of true spirituality, of radical discipleship and of mature religion, is to help speed up this process of dying to the False Self. Whatever one calls it, radical discipleship is the form of living embodied by Jesus. Such calm, egoless approach to life is invariably characteristic of people at the highest levels of doing and loving in all cultures and religions. These are the ones we call sages or holy ones.

Without what Jesus called "the sign of Jonah" (see Matt 12:39–40), Christianity remains a largely impotent ideology, another way to "win" instead of the "way of the cross" characterized by Jonah, Jeremiah, Job, John the Baptist, and Jesus. Viewed this way, Jesus become the teacher of the path rather than the cosmic problem-solver. The Jonah-Job-Jesus pattern has been hard for Westerners to recognize and accept, but it is taught by what we call Eastern religions. The sign of Jonah is at the heart of the matter.

Psychologically, the large fish (whale?) represents "the power of life locked in the unconscious. Metaphorically, water is the unconscious, and this creature in the water is the life or energy of the unconscious, which has overwhelmed the conscious personality and must be disempowered, overcome, and controlled. . . . In the story of Jonah, the hero is swallowed and taken into the abyss to be later resurrected—a variant of the death-and-resurrection theme."[6]

The egoic self is real, precious, unique, but temporary, for our False Self is what changes, passes, and ends when we die. There is no escape from death when the "me" is the egoic self. It is a manifestation of the True Self, but it tends to forget this and imagines itself to be apart from God rather than a part of God. However, such thinking is in error. There is no "me" separate from God, just as there is no wave separate from the ocean. When we die—psychologically and spiritually but also physically—we remain what we were and are: holy, sacred, and immortal.

---

6. Campbell, *Power of Myth*, 146.

To not let go of our False Self at the right time and in the right way is what it means to be trapped, addicted to ourself. This, I believe, is the meaning of Jesus' words to Mary Magdalene after his resurrection, "Do not hold on to me" (John 20:17). What Jesus is saying is, "Don't cling to the past, Mary, to your needy False Self. You and I are heading for something far better." Great love is both attachment and detachment. There is a spiritual art to attachment and detachment.

If all we have at the end of your life is our False Self, there will not be much to eternalize. However, there is no death when the "me" is the divine Self, for the True Self lives forever. When we are connected to the Whole, we no longer need to defend or protect the isolated part. We are now connected to something Real, eternal. When we are able to move beyond our False Self—at the right time and in the right way—it will feel like freedom and liberation, as if we had lost nothing.

It is no surprise that we humans would deny death's certain coming, fight it, and seek to avoid the demise of the only self we have known. This process of transformation is something we both deeply desire and desperately fear. It is the phenomenon Rudolph Otto termed the *mysterium tremendum*, an experience both alluring and frightful at the same time. Originally described in the language of symbol and myth, this experience has been acted out in ritual and other kinds of human activity long before it became a topic of philosophical and theological discussion. It is the union that will liberate us, yet we resist and flee.

The path of dying and rising is exactly what in-depth spiritual teaching must address. It is the letting go of all we think we are, moving into a world without any experienced context, and becoming the person we always were at depth and yet did not know on the surface. The surrender of our False Self in the final days and hours in any conscious dying has been called "enlightenment at gunpoint" by Kathleen Dowling Singh, a woman who spent her life in hospice work.

We put off enlightenment by decades if we are not present at deaths—and births. Remember, salvation is not so much a matter of *if* as *when* we get it, and maybe how much we can handle.[7] It makes us wonder why we have turned the spiritual journey into a forced march or into a game of *Survivor*, instead of a joyous proclamation of this necessary but good process of surrender into love. The reason seems obvious; it is because the False Self prefers win-lose over win-win, even, strangely enough, when it

---

7. Rohr, *Diamond*, 141.

ends up defining itself as a loser. The ego will always choose trumped-up competition over calm cooperation. Such a mindset—more "hell" than "heaven," seems almost the American way.

Once we know we are sharing in "the force field of resurrection," we can always live within it, drawing from its power.[8] Nevertheless, the price of such momentous realization is that we must first go into the tomb with Jesus, "so that, just as Christ was raised from the dead by the glory of the Father, so we too might walk in newness of life" (Rom 6:4).

Resurrection and the True Self

Religion (*re-ligio* meaning re-binding) is not doing its job if it only reminds us of our distance, our unworthiness, our sinfulness, and our inadequacy before God's greatness. Whenever religion increases the gap, it becomes antireligion instead. Such gap creating between God and creation is actually diabolical (*dia balein*, Greek for "to throw apart"). What we need, of course, are adequate symbols (*sym bolon*, "throwing together"), and that, precisely, is what the New Testament provides: an entirely symbolic way of understanding Reality.

Let us be clear; in his human mind, Jesus was limited. It seems likely, as modern biblical scholarship indicates, that Jesus did not fully know his True Self as the "Son of God" until after the Resurrection. Before his transformation, Jesus lived by faith and was like us in every respect except sin (Heb 4:15). This means he never accepted the "lie of separation," which is the core meaning of sin. He could affirm, without hesitation, "The Father and I are one" (John 10:30). That affirmation, and other equally remarkable affirmations attributed to Jesus, such as "before Abraham was, I am" (John 8:58), are not so much declarations of uniqueness as indications that in Jesus we have the ultimate model and trustworthy leader for all humanity.

When we examine other well-known biblical passages in this light, they come alive in new ways. For instance, when Jesus says, "I am the vine, you are the branches" (John 15:5), there really isn't a division between vine and branches, even though we can tell the difference between them. And when Jesus says, "I am in my Father, and you in me, and I in you" (John 14:20), there is no implied separation of the Self and God. The same holds true in Acts, when Paul defines God as that in which "we live

---

8. Rohr, *Diamond*, 144.

and move and have our being" (Acts 17:28). This realization that God is living in us and through us is how we plug into the much larger heart and mind beyond our own.

Thus, when I use the word Resurrection in this segment, it is for its symbolic value. Despite its uniqueness in Jesus, Resurrection is not about psychological optimism, religious miracle, theological proof that Christianity is the true religion, or even an affirmation that there is life after death. Rather, I am referring to something more constant and universal than any of these, something intrinsic to almost everything in life, even things we fear or dislike.

The False Self is energized by problems, challenges, and self-created goals. The True Self, however, is energized by a different fuel: union, contentment, and particularly, deep resonance (meaning) of any kind. Once we know that life and death are not separate but part of a whole, we will begin to view reality in a holistic way, and that will change everything. For one thing, it is the initial birth of nondual consciousness. No one can teach us this. It can only be modeled. Interestingly, the only person Jesus ever called "Satan" or "devil" is Peter, when he tried to oppose this central message of death and resurrection (Matt 16:23).

The eminent Swiss psychiatrist Carl Jung spoke of Jesus as "the Archetype of the Self," meaning that what happens in the life of Jesus happens always and everywhere.[9] Discovering in the Jesus story a map of the unconscious human journey, he feared that Western civilization could lose this pattern, and that the results would be disastrous. Jesus is our "Savior," then, because he is the one who charts and guides us on the necessary path. The contours of that path can be summed up in the twin concepts of death and resurrection, for they serve as the template for full and authentic human life, what Jesus called "abundant life" (John 10:10).

As resurrected Lord, the risen Christ is not being rewarded for a job well done as much as he is modeling the full, completed journey and goal of life. The New Testament depicts Jesus as the "pioneer and perfecter" of the entire human journey, as Hebrews 12:2 poetically states, the guarantee (Heb 7:22) and pledge (Eph 1:14) that life is stronger than death, that love is everlasting. Furthermore, this guarantee has been implanted in every heart by God's Holy Spirit.

When Jesus called his disciples, he was not asking others to join a new security system, a religious club, denomination, or order. He did

---

9. Jung, *AION*, 5.70, 115–16, 124; 12.283.

not invite them to a belief system, but rather to a lifestyle: "Follow me." Where faith was elicited, it was in the form of trust, not belief. When he called his first disciples, Jesus was talking about further journeys to people who were already settled, socially and religiously.

The gospels are essentially resurrection accounts, written after the fact. Their purpose is to unify Christian believers by evoking faith in Christ. The gospels can be misleading, particularly for those who view faith systematically, as a set of doctrines and beliefs. They were not intended to be read doctrinally or dogmatically. It took Christians several centuries to create a systematic understanding of Jesus and his mission, one that, in my estimation, they got wrong. When I think of Jesus, it is not about how he is dissimilar from other human beings but rather how he serves as the model and metaphor for all humanity that I seek to understand. In my estimation, the historical Jesus embodies the universal Christ, the True Self that gives all humans final meaning and definition. In that respect, Jesus' story is the universe story.

Longing for God and longing for our True Self are the same longing. Religion has only one job description: making one out of two. For Christians, that is the "Christ Mystery," the belief that God overcame the gap from God's side, doing "the heavy lifting," initiating the longing. What God is saying in the incarnation of Jesus is, "I am not totally Other. I have planted some of me in all things." Christians would say that it is God who is doing the longing in us and through us, by means of the divine indwelling we call the Holy Spirit. The core meaning of the Christian doctrine of the Holy Spirit is simply this, that God implanted a natural affinity and allurement between Godself and all God's creatures. Otherwise, the limited and the limitless would be incapable of union. Apart from God's Spirit, the finite and infinite could never be reconciled.

The Third Incarnation of God

What we call Resurrection is one of the greatest and most compelling symbols available to human beings, for it discloses the universal pattern of the undoing of death. The three Abrahamic religions saw God as the one "who gives life to the dead and calls into existence the things that do not exist" (Rom 4:17). For Christians, this pattern of incarnation, death, and resurrection revealed in "the Christ" was true long before Jesus of

Nazareth, from the very birth and death of the stars to the entire circle of life on this planet.

When we speak of Jesus, we also have in mind the eternal or Cosmic Christ. Christ is simply another word for "the body of God," another name for "God-as-materialized" (what scientists call the "Big Bang," which apparently happened about 13.8 billion years ago). This Cosmic Christ is God as revealed through every aspect of creation, as the New Testament makes clear (John 1:1–10; 1 Cor 8:6; Col 1:15–20; Eph 1:3–14; Heb 1:1–3; 1 John 1:1–3).

When ordinary people become Christians, that is, "little Christs," they embody or enact in their lives the "third incarnation" of God, or the "second coming" of Christ.[10] Let me explain what I mean. The first incarnation is the moment described in Genesis 1 as "the first day," when God became the Universal Christ, joining in unity with the physical universe and becoming the light inside of everything. This is described in Genesis 1:3–4 by the statement, "Then God said, 'Let there be light'; and there was light. . .and God separated the light from the darkness." This teaching is affirmed in the prologue of John's Gospel, by the relationship between God and Christ (the Word/Logos): "In the beginning was the Word, and the Word was with God, and the Word was God. . . in him was life, and the life was the light of all people. The light shines in the darkness, and the darkness did not overcome it" (John 1:1, 4–5). The first incarnation—what we are calling the Cosmic Christ—is the divine presence pervading creation since the beginning. From this perspective, wherever the material and the spiritual coincide, we have the Christ.

The second incarnation of God and the "first coming" of Christ represent what Christians believe about the historical incarnation we call Jesus. Let us be clear: Christ is not Jesus' last name. The word Christ is a title, meaning Anointed One. When Christians speak of Jesus Christ, they include the entire sweep of the meaning of the Christ, which includes all the divine activity since the beginning of time (see Rom 1:20). Of this activity, Jesus is the visible map, the one who brings this eternal message home personally.

The third incarnation of God (the "second coming of Christ") occurs whenever true discipleship occurs, when Jesus Christ is born in us. For Christians, evidence for the third incarnation appears in the Eucharist: "Eat it and know who you are," Augustine said. As any nutritionist

---

10. The concept of three incarnations, exemplified in what Richard Rohr calls an incarnational worldview, is articulated in his book *The Universal Christ*, 12–21.

knows, we are what we eat and drink. Christians are part of the Christ Mystery. No longer alienated from God, others, or the universe—at least in principle—Christians embody cosmic belonging, oneness with Christ, the name we give to everything purposeful and harmonious in the universe. Paul affirmed this truth when he declared, "It is no longer I who live, but it is Christ who lives in me" (Gal 2:20).

Exhorting believers to adopt the mind of Jesus (Phil 2:5), Paul also confirms that Christians incarnate Christ, since they possess "the mind of Christ" (1 Cor 2:16). When individuals become Jesus people—incarnations of Christ—they exchange one mindset for another, their "monkey mind" (the obsessive, noisy chattering we observe during silent meditation) for the mind of Christ. This is likely what Paul meant when he called believers God's "new creation" (2 Cor 5:17): "If anyone is in Christ, there is a new creation: everything old has passed away; see, everything has become new." For Paul, when the minds of believers are transformed into the mind of Christ, their bodies become temples, dwelling places of God's Spirit (1 Cor 3:16–17; see Rom 12:1–2).

As we travel inward, into the interior depth of soul, we discover that each believer is a chip off the old block, a miniature word of the Word of God, a mini-incarnation of divine love. This entails allowing God's grace to heal, hold, and empower us. It means entering the unknowns of our lives, and learning to trust the darkness, for the transformative power of divine love is already there.

The full Christ Mystery serves as a pattern for the entire journey of the True Self, from divine conception, to beloved status, through crucifixion, and unto resurrection. This whole process of living, dying, and then living again starts with God breathing life into the "dust of the ground" and calling this living being *adam* ("of the earth"). The point is that a drama was forever set in motion between breath and what appears to be humus (human, *adamah*, from the soil). Matter and spirit are forever bound together, divine and mortal endlessly intermingled. The changing of forms is called resurrection, and the return is called ascension, although it appears as death.

As scholars point out, taking the concept of the ascension of Christ literally is nonsensical and counterintuitive in a scientific age. The idea of an eternal heaven somewhere above us is the product of an antiquated cosmology often described as the "three-story universe." We know there is no known place in the universe where Jesus literally went. Even ascending at the speed of light, Jesus would still be traversing our galaxy today.

Astronomy and physics have eliminated ascension to heaven as a literal, physical possibility. However, if we understand ascension metaphorically, meaning Jesus has gone inward—not into outer space but into inward space, into the kingdom within, into the consciousness that is the source of all things—this we can imagine. The images are outward, but their reflection is inward. The point is that one can ascend with Jesus by going inward. This is a metaphor of returning to the body's dynamic source.[11]

This process of life, death, resurrection, and ascension is called incarnation. Because it is about Christ, it is also about creation, and that includes all humans, coming forth as individuals and then returning unto God, the Ground of all Being. As Jesus indicated, to God all people are alive (Luke 20:38); those who are deceased are simply in different stages of aliveness. This is the staggering change of perspective that the gospel was meant to achieve. This realization is the heart of all religious transformation (*transformare* is Latin for "to change form"). The Risen Christ represents the final perspective of every True Self: a human-divine perspective that looks out from God and sees all things as ultimately good and as united.

Resurrection is incarnation come to its logical and full conclusion. It fully demonstrates that this world, this physicality that includes our human flesh, is part of the eternal truth and forever matters to God. Resurrection is not a miracle to be proven, but a manifestation of the wholeness that we are all meant to experience, even in this world. The Risen Christ is the standing icon of humanity in its final and full destiny. Resurrection is about Jesus, but it also says something essential about us, namely, that we too are larger than life. Finally, we can live meaningfully, filled with hope. Our code word for this is heaven.

When we take the Resurrection metaphor absolutely seriously, it moves us far beyond the stripped-down literal meaning where so many flounder. It does not have to mean "an eternally enduring life" as much as "a present life of eternal significance." Science strongly confirms this principle, only with different metaphors and symbols, like condensation, evaporation, hibernation, sublimation, the recurring seasons, and even the constant death and birth of stars from the same stardust. God appears to be resurrecting everything all the time. It is not something we need to "believe" as much as something to observe and ponder.

---

11. Campbell, *Power of Myth*, 56–57.

We all want to know that life on earth has both temporal and eternal meaning. We can be assured it is going someplace good because it came from someplace good—a place of "original blessing" instead of a place of "original sin." For Christians, the model and exemplar is Jesus: "I know where I have come from, and where I am going, but you do not know," he states in John 8:14. If the original incarnation is true, then resurrection is inevitable and irreversible. The only difficulty is that transformation and "crucifixion" must intervene between life and Life. Loss always precedes renewal.

The great unfolding of God's Mystery involves all the events and stages of our life; nothing is wasted or discarded—not even evil, sin, or death (this is why the Bible includes those seemingly extraneous stories of murder, rape, deceit, and war). God is going somewhere with this whole thing called life. Why else would the Creator take the great risk in fashioning a universe where the parts evolve and develop but not the whole? Humans are preoccupied with stability, efficiency, and control; God, by contrast is clearly into freedom, imagination, and creativity.

The Risen Christ affirms everything with a big "Yes" (2 Cor 1:19), even its own earlier imperfect stages. The final astonishing gift is that our False Self has now become our True Self; the one and the many have become the One. That is precisely the metamorphosis we call resurrection. The raw material of every aspect of life is not ended but merely changed: "this perishable body must put on imperishability, and this mortal body must put on immortality" (1 Cor 15:53).

According to John's gospel, the Risen Christ appeared first to Mary Magdalene, not to one of the Twelve (John 20:1–18). At first, this seems surprising, until we realize that she is the symbolic stand-in for all longing humanity, all who have experienced sorrow, rejection, and pain. She is the gospel personage who most needs love to be stronger than death, and so she is the first to know it—and perhaps at the deepest level. She is the first one who symbolically comes to awareness, the first real knower, and thus is the clear "witness to the witnesses" (20:18). It is not surprising, then, that she is named as standing at the foot of the cross (19:25), with two other Marys—who walked through the mystery with Jesus. And they were also the first ones at the tomb on Sunday. Mary is the archetypal name for all those who live out of their True Selves and know its Source. This True Self cannot find or know God without wanting to bring everybody else to the same awareness.

The True Self has already overcome the contradictions and paradoxes of life, which is symbolized by the Risen Christ, who presents the full tension of death and life, earth and spirit, human and divine—precisely as overcome. Once we know that there is an implanted and positive direction to creation, we can go with the primary flow (faith); eventually we will learn to rest there (hope), and finally to actually live there in peace and joy (love). We are home at last in an inherently sacred universe.

We North Americans really don't know how to live in peace or without enemies. Our economy, our self-image, and our national psyche have thrived in a triumphalistic and paranoid stance for so long that it will be hard to change to a positive and creative mode. What we can and must do, however, is to live and to announce the alternative: a new way of living based on faith instead of fear, peacemaking instead of moneymaking, community instead of competition, for this is what radical discipleship (Resurrection life) looks like.

The Risen Christ knows that good is more powerful than evil, love stronger than hatred, life more durable than death. Until we know that in our bones, until we risk it in our actions, until we base our life's choices on such awesome trust, all our preaching is useless and our believing in vain (1 Cor 15:14). The mystery of the death and resurrection of Christ tells us that we live in a benevolent universe. God is on our side, we belong here, and there is no basis for existential fear. We no longer need to control or live in fear, because something far better is taking place. Resurrection says that the true apocalyptic message is not "The end is near!" but "The beginning is always happening!"

As the mystics and sages teach, the path of dying and rising is one continuous movement. It begins with learning to love one's life, and then with allowing oneself to die into it—and never to die away from it. Once death is joyfully incorporated into life, you are already in heaven, and there is no possibility or fear of hell. This is the Way, modeled by Jesus and enacted by his followers. "The Gospel is not a fire insurance policy for the next world, but a life assurance policy for this world."[12]

Questions for Discussion and Reflection

1. Explain and assess the merits of equating the imperial ego with Satan or the devil.

---

12. Rohr, *Eager to Love*, xxii.

2. In your own words, explain the difference between *imitatio Christi* and *participatio Christi*.
3. After reading this chapter, explain the meaning of Jesus' statement in John 12:25, "those who love this life will lose it and those who hate their life in this world will keep it."
4. Explain and assess the four shifts from reality that create one's False Self.
5. Assess the merits of the statement, "Anything less than the death of the False Self is useless religion."
6. Explain the meaning of "the sign of Jonah" in Matthew 12:39–40.
7. Assess the meaning of the statement, "If all you have at the end of your life is your False Self, there will not be much to eternalize."
8. Explain and assess the meaning of Kathleen Dowling Singh's phrase "enlightenment at gunpoint."
9. In your estimation, what did Jesus mean by "the Father and I are one"? (see John 10:30).
10. After reading this chapter, what did you learn about Resurrection?
11. Explain and assess the concept of the three incarnations of God.
12. Explain and assess the merits of the notion that "resurrection life" and radical discipleship are synonymous.
13. In your estimation, what is the primary insight gained from this chapter? Does this chapter raise any issues you might need to address in the future?

Chapter 7

What Jesus Would Want Modern Disciples to Know

IN THIS CHAPTER AND the next, we focus on Jesus as our contemporary. If he were physically present among us as a twenty-first-century individual, what would his priorities be, and what would he want his followers to know about religion, faith, God, and scripture? The answers given below are by necessity subjective and exploratory, limited at best and partial in coverage. Nevertheless, they are a start, one I hope you find perceptive, compelling, and sufficiently inspiring to categorize as radical.

Speaking of Jesus as our contemporary, the Jesus I have in mind would be a modern, educated individual living his love of God and others fully in Western society. But unlike most Western depictions, he would certainly not be white ("Caucasian"), and likely not even male. Might he not appear as a person of color, possibly even as female? I realize that this approach is arbitrary and likely not the position, place, or perspective the living Jesus would represent today. It is certainly possible that if he were alive in the twenty-first century, Jesus would likely be Jewish and not Christian. There is also a good chance he might not be mainstream Jewish but rather a Messianic or Hasidic Jew, possibly belonging to a form of Hasidic Judaism such as the Chabad-Lubavitch community, a charismatic messianic group that believes Rabbi Menachem Mendel Schneerson, who died in 1994, is the Jewish messiah. The belief among Hasidic Jews that the leader of their movement could be the Jewish messiah is traced to the Ukrainian Jewish mystic and healer Rabbi Israel ben Eliezer, known as the Baal Shem Tov (1698–1760), the founder of Hasidism.

During Schneerson's life, the Chabad movement hoped that he would be the messiah. Since 1994, most of Chabad persists in the belief in Schneerson as the Jewish messiah. Some Chabad messianists believe Schneerson will be resurrected from the dead to be revealed as the messiah, or go further and claim that he never died in 1994 and is waiting to be revealed as messiah.

These ideas are strikingly similar to views first-century Jewish followers of Jesus maintained. Jesus, you might recall, began his ministry as a follower of the apocalyptic prophet John the Baptist, a charismatic figure likely reared in the wilderness of Judea (Luke 1:80) by Essenes, a baptismal sect of apocalyptic Jews[1] who viewed themselves as the children of light and all others human beings, including the majority of Jews, as pagan or apostate children of darkness. Considering itself the true Israel and all others as enemies of God, the Essene branch of Judaism powerfully influenced John's beliefs and lifestyle, and through him, Jesus, who was baptized by John and who followed many of his beliefs and practices.[2] Key disciples of Jesus, as well as many other followers, had also been disciples or followers of John. During his lifetime and even long after his death, John's movement had a wide following and spread rapidly across the eastern Roman empire. By the middle of the first century, John's legacy was more widespread and better known than that of Jesus, as we learn from the book of Acts (see 18:25 and 19:3). While eventually John came to be seen as a forerunner of Jesus, that was certainly not the case initially. In fact, there is little doubt that the Essenes, particularly through

---

1. As biblical scholars remind us, biblical eschatology and its variant, apocalyptic eschatology, are metaphorical ways of thinking about historical reality. When ancient Jews and early Christians thought apocalyptically, they were not so much expecting the end of the world or the cosmos but the end of the current world order, in which pagans held power and the covenant people of God did not. There are good reasons for the scholarly practice that distinguishes between forms of eschatology such as realized, imminent, present, future, ethical, ascetical, and apocalyptic eschatology. While there are similarities between the terms "eschatology" and "apocalypse"—both imply divine revelation and include the vindication of goodness and the elimination of evil—apocalyptic forms of eschatology are often adopted by those who perceive themselves to be marginalized religiously, politically, and economically at a level so profound that only divine intervention can rectify. For a more detailed presentation of ancient Jewish and early Christian eschatological and apocalyptic hopes, see chapter 12 below.

2. In addition to practicing daily lavations, the Essenes required a baptismal ritual that led to initiation into the community. They also celebrated sacramental meals in anticipation of the day when they would share bread and wine with the ruling "Messiah of Israel" at the end-time banquet. Like the ascetic, prophetic John the Baptist, the Essenes were the only ancient Jewish sect that produced prophets, observed strict asceticism, practiced celibacy, preached repentance before an imminent judgment, and emphasized the role of the Holy Spirit in the anticipated messianic mission.

John the Baptist's apocalyptic movement, gave rise to earliest Christianity, when the followers of Jesus called themselves "The Way" (see Acts 9:2; 18:25; 19:9; see also Isa 40:3 and John 1:23 and 14:4–6), a designation the Essenes also used of themselves. While there are important differences between Christianity and the Essenes, their similarities give us a window into the thought and practice of first-century Judaism.

If Christianity is an offshoot of an offshoot of Judaism, a good case can be made that the same might hold true of a twenty-first-century Jesus. It is not this view of Jesus, however, that serves to inspire our thinking and living in this volume, but rather that of a truly modern Jesus living humbly yet authentically in our midst.

What Jesus Would Want His Followers to Know about Religion

As our contemporary, Jesus would remind us that despite the prevalence of religion historically and culturally, its role is secondary, not primary. While indispensable to society, religion should not be self-serving or an end in itself. Rather, religion serves as a pointer to a greater reality. As a system devised by humans to provide guidance and meaning to society, religion should never cause dissension, division, or conflict between humans. Neither should it promote arrogant supremacy, self-assuring smugness, or crusading spirituality. The task of religion is not to create polarities, institutions, hierarchies, or doctrines. Rather, its role is to promote harmonious spirituality.

In antiquity, practically everyone was religious, meaning people had a holistic view of reality. Rather than dividing reality into two domains, as most modern individuals do, one containing all that is sacred or divine and the other all that is secular or profane, people in antiquity viewed all reality on a continuum, and religion provided a nondualist way of seeing, acting, and experiencing reality. Hence, ancient people viewed religion as a way of respecting all powers, natural and supernatural, that govern human destiny.

As religion scholar Joseph Campbell reminds us, the word religion derives from the Latin word *religare*, which means "to tie or bind fast" or "to reconnect." To ancient polytheists, *religare* implied reconnecting to the higher powers around us. To ancient theists, *religare* meant to revere nature's ways, and to find one's place in the natural order. In each case, finding harmony with that which is considered to be ultimate in power and reverence, whether natural or supernatural, and with other human beings, was essential and mandatory. For the historical as well as the modern Jesus, *religare* would be best expressed in the Great Commandment, namely, to love God and neighbor as oneself.

At their inception, world religions were healthy, wholesome, and beneficial. Over time, particularly as religions became institutionalized, that changed, so much that we need to distinguish between "healthy" religion and "junk" religion. Healthy religion provides a foundational sense of awe. It re-enchants an otherwise empty universe. It encourages reverence toward all things, enabling people of faith to see the reflection of the divine image in the human, the animal, and the entire natural world, which now become enchanted, that is, inherently supernatural. When humans are fully alert in spirit, mind, and body, their identity transcends their imagination, and they can accomplish more than they suppose. Moments of awareness occur as a dawning of meaning, when the familiar suddenly becomes infused with new insight and possibilities, and when unfamiliar ideas challenge and pervade our consciousness. Such occasions feel like personal discoveries.

Instead of providing awe, reconnection, and awakening, junk religion—on both the left and the right of the religious spectrum—leads to sectarianism, ideological divisiveness, emotionalism, and even social and political hysteria. Similar to junk food because it only satisfies enough to gratify momentary desires, junk religion does not truly feed the intellect or the heart. Junk religion is usually characterized by dependence on the past, often leading to fear of the present as well as of the future. However, when religion leads us to encounter the divine, we are empowered to embrace not only the present but also the future without anxiety or fear. There is no fear of the present because it is viewed as full of potential. There is no fear of the future because a loving God is in charge. In addition, there is no fear of the past because the past has been healed and forgiven. In authentic religion, people do not use theology to avoid reality or to fabricate a private, self-serving reality. Authentic believers let God lead them into the fullness of Reality—not into delusions or distrust and not away from paradox and uncertainty but directly into the throes of their humanity.

Whatever reconstruction human beings need to undergo individually and as a society cannot be based on fear or on reaction. Such transformation must be based on a positive and fully human experience of God as a loving Presence. Healthy religion is ready to let God be God, and to embrace a future we do not yet understand—and no longer need to understand.

What Jesus Would Want His Followers to Know about Faith

If Jesus were with us today, he would not link faith with belief or dogma in our minds. Rather, he would equate faith with loyalty and trust in our hearts. Faith, of course, has always been central to Christianity, but an emphasis on faith as believing difficult things to be true is a relatively recent phenomenon in Christianity, the product of the last few hundred years.

Because religion by nature is primarily experiential, constructing religion on the foundation of belief leads to endless conflict, frustration, and unanswered questions. Faith, however, makes a better foundation and prepares one more adequately for life. Some readers may wonder about my distinction, because all through life they have equated faith with belief. But faith should not be equated with beliefs. Faith may reach conclusions about beliefs, but its foundation is experiential and relational rather than doctrinal. Based on experience, faith makes conscious choices that square with that experience.

In the history of Christianity, faith has four primary meanings.[3] The first of these sees faith primarily as a "matter of the head," whereas the remaining three understand faith as a "matter of the heart." For each term the opposite is given, for antonyms are often as illuminating as synonyms.

1. *Faith as belief*, that is, as "believing" certain doctrines or dogmas to be true. According to this understanding, the opposite of faith is doubt or disbelief. This understanding is dominant today, both within the church and outside it. Its dominance in modern Western Christianity is due to the Protestant Reformation, which not only emphasized faith, but also produced numerous denominations, each defining itself by what it "believed," that is, by its distinctive doctrines or confessions. Following the Reformation, orthodoxy began to mean "right belief," and faith began to mean "believing the right things." While this view is widespread, it puts the emphasis in

---

3. This typology is adapted from Borg, *Heart of Christianity*, 28–37.

the wrong place, for it suggests that what God really cares about is the beliefs in our heads, as if having "correct beliefs" is what will save us. In this respect, perhaps a better antonym of faith is "certainty." The birth of modern science and scientific ways of knowing in the Enlightenment also affected the meaning of "faith" and "believe." When Enlightenment thinkers began identifying truth with factuality, that is, as something verifiable, they began calling into question the reliability of the Bible and of many traditional Christian teachings. As a result, "faith" and "belief" came to be contrasted with knowledge and certainty. For skeptics, faith came to mean "opinion or conviction," something one turned to when knowledge ran out. For believers, faith is what one turned to when beliefs and knowledge conflict.

2. *Faith as trust* in something or someone. In the Bible, it means radical trust in God. Significantly, it does not mean trusting in the truth of a set of statements about God, for that would simply be "belief" under a different name. While our behavior is important, God seems to be less concerned with our actions than with our character, for our actions flow from our will.

3. *Faith as faithfulness.* In the Bible, faith is the trustful acceptance of God's promises, particularly of God's desire to bless all peoples and nations of the world. But faith is also trust in God's faithfulness to the promise to deliver Good News to everyone, something that God accomplishes through Jesus Christ and his followers. Because God is steadfast and faithful, we too are called to faithfulness, not to beliefs about God, whether biblical, creedal, or doctrinal, but rather to radical centering in the God to whom the Bible and creeds and doctrines point. Faith as faithfulness means loyalty, allegiance, the commitment of the self at its deepest level. Its opposite is not doubt or disbelief. Rather, as in human relationships, its opposite is infidelity, being unfaithful to our relationship with God. To use a striking biblical metaphor, the opposite of faithfulness is idolatry, meaning not so much the worship of idols as false gods, but centering in something finite rather than the sacred, which is infinite and beyond all images. As the opposite of idolatry, faith means being loyal to God and not to would-be lords such as one's nation, affluence, achievement, family, or desire.

4. *Faith as vision*, that is, as a way of seeing reality, for how we view the whole affects how we respond to life. If we see life as hostile or threatening, we tend to respond defensively. If we see reality as indifferent to human purposes and ends, we likely will be concerned primarily with ourselves and with those most like us. However, seeing reality as life-giving and full of promise, as filled with wonder and beauty leads to radical trust and a desire to nourish and spread its goodness. To understanding faith as vision is to see reality as gracious; its opposite, un-faith, views reality as hostile and indifferent. This meaning of faith is closely related to faith as trust. Trust and vision go together; trust in God—the God of promise and faithfulness—and how we view God go together. In this way of life, radical centering in God leads to a deepening trust that transforms the way we live our lives. Seeing, living, trusting, and centering are all related in complex and salutary ways.

Faith starts with the willingness to recognize and question the core mysteries at the heart of existence: why we exist at all and how to make meaning out of our existence. Religious answers are like wisdom; often they are paradoxical. Sometimes they require us to examine things backward: to increase by diminishing, to multiply by dividing, to hold on by letting go. With the habit of faith, we are willing to ponder such questions in our hearts and minds. As Augustine indicated, belief is "giving assent to something one is still thinking about."

As we have noted, faith is relational, but this does not mean that beliefs don't matter. There are affirmations that are central to the Christian faith, affirmations such as the reality of God, the centrality of Jesus, and the significance of the Bible. These beliefs are essential, not only for Christians, but for people of all faiths, when properly understood. Faith as a way of seeing at the deepest level requires avoiding the human tendency toward excessive precision and certitude. Christian theology has often been plagued by both—the desire to know too much and to know it too precisely. Our minds tell us that such knowledge is not possible—perhaps not even desirable—and people cannot easily give their heart to something that their mind rejects. Properly understood, a deep but humble understanding of Christian faith as belief is close to faith as vision. As we have seen, biblical and theological faith need not be viewed as assent to narrow propositions or as fulfilling specific requirements, but as a persuasive and compelling way of seeing reality.

If Jesus were our contemporary, he would likely agree with Søren Kierkegaard, the Danish existentialist philosopher, who affirmed that one becomes a Christian by means of a leap of faith, a leap representing the commitment of one's entire being. Though doubt can never be completely overcome, the leap is not irrational, if it is impelled by one's heart, nurtured by one's will, and fueled by one's faith. Faith involves the will, but not a will uninformed by reasoning nor a will devoid of the concerns of the heart. We leap, not because there is a shortage of evidence, but because we recognize the reality of the domain of the heart.

The role of reason in Christian faith is informed by the French philosopher Blaise Pascal's famous distinction of three orders within human nature: body, mind, and heart. Since, according to this conception, faith and reason belong to different orders, they need not be opposed to one another. In this view, Christian faith is not a leap *within* the order of the intellect—a leap which violates the essence of that order—but a leap *from* the order of the intellect to the order of the heart.[4]

The key point for this understanding of religious faith is to acknowledge that belief in doctrines is not central, since they are themselves unprovable. While Christians honor physical, emotional, and intellectual knowledge, they place particular value on faith, both as source and end of knowledge, for faith involves heart-knowledge in addition to head-knowledge, the giving and committing of one's life to whatever we consider ultimate.

Whereas liberals and conservatives of his day focused on the content of religious faith, Kierkegaard opposed both by seeking not intellectual certainty but existential authenticity, focusing not on the content of Christianity but rather on what it means to be a Christian. For Kierkegaard, one does not become Christian by coming to know something one did not previously know. Rather, one becomes a Christian as one becomes a human, by embarking on a path. It would be quite normal to start on the path without ever reaching the goal, since one never actually becomes a Christian; one simply strives to become one.

While faith involves the mind, faith is primarily the way of the heart. Given the premodern meaning of "believe," to believe in God is to love God and to love that which God loves. The Christian life is as simple and challenging as that.

---

4. Allen, *Christian Belief*, 145.

What Jesus Would Want His Followers to Know about God

Throughout human history, there has been no more important question than that of God's existence. This concern, we might argue, is also the central religion question in modern Western culture. While polling in the United States reveals that throughout the twentieth century some 95 percent of North Americans reported they believed in God, that figure has dropped to about 85 percent in recent years, and to a low of 64 percent of respondents who now report they are "convinced" God exists. The results are far lower in most European countries, such as in England, where the figure for those reporting belief in God is about 35 percent.

Interestingly, for Americans reporting belief in God, many accept the modern worldview called secularist, naturalist, or materialist, to which they simply add God, despite the incongruities. The implications of such a view are that God is primarily transcendent, meaning God is all-powerful and all-knowing, but only minimally involved in world affairs. As Creator, God was directly involved with humanity in the beginning, but since then only occasionally, such as with the nation of Israel, in the incarnation of Jesus Christ, and currently in the lives of Christian believers through the Holy Spirit. For many modern believers, God will be actively central in human affairs again only at the end of history, an event highly anticipated by evangelical Christians and widely believed to be near at hand.

The majority of people who use the term "God," particularly in the Western world, have in mind a theistic concept of God, meaning an all-powerful and supreme ruler of the universe. Supernatural theism, by implication, includes the view that all finite things are dependent in some way on this ultimate reality, a reality generally described in personal terms. After all, imaging God as a personal being is very common in the Bible. It is also the natural language of worship and prayer, and there is nothing wrong with it in such contexts. A transcendent reality that does not possess at the very least those qualities that constitute the dignity of human beings, qualities such as intelligence, feeling, freedom, power, initiative, and creativity, could not adequately inspire trust or reverence in human beings. In this sense, God would have to be "personal" to be God. It is doubtful whether believers could worship something that does not have at least the stature of personality.

While the idea of a "personal God" is beneficial in that it makes God relational and accessible to humanity, the extremes of this position, such as presented in the Hebrew scriptures, raise insuperable problems for people in the modern era. This God fights wars and defeats enemies, chooses people and works through them, sends storms, heals the sick, spares the dying, rewards goodness, and punishes evil. Many people have trouble intellectually with these anthropomorphic renderings of God and with the seeming irrationality of belief in a personal God. While only the most traditional believers and the most literal readers of scripture believe such things anymore, this deity remains the primary object and substance of the Christian church's faith. It is this understanding of God that is becoming meaningless to increasing numbers in the modern world.

While it is attractive to speak of intimacy with God and accessibility to God, religious philosophers have long warned against ascribing human qualities and attributing human feelings to God. Still, the joy of familiarity with God and the need to recognize and be recognized by God override the philosopher's critique. There is, however, a critical flaw in this perspective: Once we conceive of God as a person like ourselves, God becomes open to criticism.

To protect God, apologists and theologians urge us to discard this way of thinking. God is not like us, says twentieth-century theologian Karl Barth; God is "Totally Other." This understanding views God as different not only in degree but also in kind. Humans can only speak of God indirectly, says thirteenth-century theologian Thomas Aquinas, for they cannot "know" God directly. Humans can only speak of God or "know" God indirectly, by saying what God is not (the *via negativa*), or by saying what God is like, thereby resorting to analogies or metaphors (the *via analogia*). Augustine, the great fifth-century theologian, articulated that very idea when he declared, "*Si comprehenderis, non est Deus*" (If you understand, then what you understand is not God). God, it seems, cannot really be known, but only related to.

In the history of Christianity, there have been two primary ways of thinking about God and the God-world relationship. Many religious scholars today are labeling these "supernatural theism" and "panentheism." Supernatural theism imagines God as personlike, though clearly as an exceedingly supreme personlike being. While involved in human affairs, this being dwells "in heaven" and not on earth. As a result, God's relationship with the world is interventionist and primarily spiritual in nature, mostly in worship and particularly in response to prayer.

Many people today find panentheism, the second way of thinking about God, increasingly attractive. One can find historical traces of panentheism in both Western and Eastern orthodox theology, though the word itself was popularized by English philosopher Alfred North Whitehead (1861–1947). Panentheism is not the same as pantheism, the concept that "all things are God." Rather, pan*en*theism is the concept that "all things are *in* God." Panentheism views God not as a supernatural being separate from the universe, beyond nature and history, but as the encompassing Spirit around us and within us. According to this conception, God is more than the universe, yet the universe is in God. Viewed spatially, God is not "out there" but "right here." Whereas supernatural theism emphasizes God's transcendence—God's otherness, God as more than the universe—panentheism affirms both the transcendence and immanence of God. It does not deny or subordinate one in order to affirm the other. For panentheism, God is both more than the universe and yet everywhere present in the universe.

Fortunately there are alternatives to the concept of theism, for "theism" and "God" need not be the same. Supernatural theism is but one human definition of God. Panentheists affirm that "God" does not refer to a supernatural being "in heaven," apart from nature, but rather to the sacred at the center of existence, the holy mystery that is around us and within us. Panentheism affirms the centrality of mystery in the universe and the possibility of relating intellectually and experientially to that mystery. It is possible, then, to be an agnostic or even an atheist regarding the God of supernatural theism and yet be a believer in God in the way offered by panentheism.

Alfred North Whitehead characterized God's relationship to the world as that of a "Persuasive Lover;" and others have offered variations on Whitehead's theme. The love relationship is an apt metaphor, for love is the fundamental and most intimate of relationships. Two qualities make this analogy particularly attractive: (1) that the essence of love is persuasive rather than coercive, and (2) that the experience of the beloved is to flourish and grow and emerge into fullness of life as a result of being loved. If this is so in human experience, then in a much more profound way God's unconditional love for the creation must be such as to invite the creation into ever more complex levels of being. To accomplish this, the God of infinite love freely accepts the integrity of nature, its processes and its laws, thereby inviting the world through the complex interplay of all of its elements to emerge into more novel forms and greater beauty through the evolutionary process.

Significantly, panentheism is a form of theism. This view does not mark the end of theism, as some are suggesting, but rather the end of supernatural theism. A panentheistic way of thinking about God is just as biblical as supernatural theism, and is, in significant ways, more biblical and more orthodox, for it emphasizes both the transcendence and the immanence of God on earth and in the universe.

In his accessible book titled *The God We Never Knew*, biblical scholar Marcus Borg examined the variety of images of God in the biblical and Christian traditions and discerned therein two primary "models":

1. The "*monarchical model*," which clusters images of God as king, lord, and father. This approach leads to what Borg calls a "performance model" of the Christian life.

2. The "*Spirit model*," which clusters images of God that point to intimate relationship and belonging. This model leads to a "relational model" of the Christian life.

Both models, Borg discovered, are found throughout all periods of Christian history, though the first is more common. From roughly the fourth century—when Christianity became the dominant religion of Western culture—through the present, the monarchical model has dominated. But alongside it, as an alternative voice, the Spirit model has also persisted. These models reflect two different voices within the Christian tradition.

The monarchical model portrays God as male, as all-powerful, as lawgiver, and as judge. Images of God in this model suggest that God is distant. Within this model, humans have offended divine majesty and deserve judgment. But because God loves his subjects, God creates a way for his people to escape the punishment they deserve: through appropriate sacrifice and true repentance. In the royal theology of ancient Israel, atonement was institutionalized in temple rituals. In the Christian version of the monarchical model, the king's (Lord's) love is seen especially in Jesus. Because God loves us, he sends his son into the world to die on a cross as the sacrifice that makes our forgiveness possible.[5]

The Spirit model, as used in the Bible, is broader than the specific Christian doctrine of "the Holy Spirit," which sees the Spirit as one aspect of God. In the Bible, Spirit is used comprehensively to refer to God's presence in creation, in the history of Israel, and in the life of Jesus and the early church. While the monarchical model also affirms that God is

---

5. Borg, *God We Never Knew*, 63–64.

Spirit, of course, and that affirmation can be a source of confusion that limits our understanding of God, there is a difference. When Spirit is assimilated to the monarchical model, God is not Spirit but a spirit—that is, a spiritual being out there, not here. But when Spirit is set free from the monarchical understanding, Spirit retains the suggestive meanings associated with breath and wind: God is the encompassing Spirit both within and outside us.[6]

The Spirit model of God affects the meaning of a number of central Christian teachings. It does so by changing the framework in which things are seen. Borg provides four examples:

1. *Creation looks different.* According to the monarchical model, God's creation of the world is understood as an event in the distant past involving the creation of a universe separate from God. The Spirit model depicts God's creation as an ongoing activity: in every moment God as Spirit (as the nonmaterial "ground" of all that is) is bringing the universe into existence.

2. *The human condition looks different.* Our central problem is not sin and guilt, as it is within the monarchical model, but "estrangement," meaning that humans are separated from that to which they belong. Our problem is blindness to the presence of God, separation from the Spirit that is all around us and within us and to which we belong.

3. *Sin looks different.* For the monarchical model, sin is primarily disloyalty to the king, seen especially as disobedience to his laws. The Spirit model addresses "sin" is more profound ways: for the metaphor of God as lover, sin is unfaithfulness; for the metaphor of God as the compassionate one who cares for all her children, sin is failure in compassion. Thus sin remains, but as betrayal of relationship and absence of compassion. Repentance also remains, only now it does not require sacrifice and contrition but a turning and returning to that to which we belong. Judgment also remains, only now not as the threat of eternal judgment but rather as living with the consequences of our choices. To remain estranged from God is to remain unsatisfied and unfulfilled.

4. *God as king and lord looks different.* God as Spirit is glorious, radiant, and splendid, like the splendor of a king. In the Spirit model,

---

6. Borg, *God We Never Knew*, 72.

God as king and lord is the subverter of systems of domination, not the legitimator of domination systems.[7]

The images of God associated with the Spirit model dramatically affect how we think of the Christian life. Rather than God as a distant being with whom we might spend eternity, Spirit—the sacred—is right here. Rather than sin and guilt being the central dynamic of the Christian life, the central dynamic becomes relationship—with God, the world, and each other.

In the 1930s and 1940s, Paul Tillich, a refugee from Nazi Germany, proposed that when Christians think of the word "God," if they had in mind a reality or entity that might or might not exist, they were not thinking of God. Tillich's point was that the word "God does not refer to a particular existing being (such as the God of supernatural theism). Rather, the word "God" is the most common Western name for "ultimate reality," for Being itself, or what Tillich called "the ground of being." This God was not a person but rather was the mystical presence in which all personhood could flourish. This God was not a being but rather the power that called being forth in all creatures. This God was not an external, personal force that could be invoked but rather an internal reality that, when confronted, opened us to the meaning of life itself.[8] Tillich, who believed that the word "God" had been distorted by the inadequate images of the past, was convinced that those images must die before the word "God" could ever be used again with meaning. He urged a moratorium on the use of the word "God" for at least a hundred years.

Following Tillich, Anglican Bishop Spong provided a model that integrates the Christian doctrine of the Trinity with this understanding of God. The meaning of God, according to his conception, is understood as (1) the source of life, (2) the source of love, and (3) the ground of being. Spong found in this triune understanding a portrait of God embodied in Jesus of Nazareth, a whole human being who lived fully, loved lavishly, and had the courage to be himself under every circumstance.

Thus, the call of this internal God found in our depths becomes primarily a call into being, a call that is not unique to religion. It is a call that refocuses what has been known as the religious dimension. In this scenario, the task of the church becomes less that of indoctrinating or relating people to an external divine power and more that of providing

---

7. Borg, *God We Never Knew*, 77–78.
8. Spong, *Christianity Must Change*, 64.

opportunities for people to touch the infinite center of all things and to fulfill all their potential. This understanding of God places a premium on the church's vocation to oppose anything that prevents us from the fullest expression of our humanity.

If Jesus were physically present today, I believe he would speak of God as personal, for he would want us to relate to God intimately and fully, viewing God as loving yet sovereign. When Jesus was with his original disciples, he taught them to call God "Father" (see Matt 11:27; 16:27; Luke 22:29), a term of both intimacy and respect. In addressing God, however, he went deeper, calling God "Abba" (Mark 14:36; see also Rom 8:15–17), meaning something close to "Daddy."[9] For Jesus, the term "God" had about it an almost inexpressible sacredness, yet it also possessed unsurpassable intimacy. In speaking of God, Jesus was certainly bringing the world "good news," for he had in mind everything humans could possibly say or imply about a personal, loving God.

Personifying God with personal characteristics is the natural language of intimacy and devotion. Problems arise only when we literalize or semiliteralize these personifications. Whatever God is ultimately like, our relationship with God must be personal, for this relationship engages us as persons at our deepest and most passionate level. To use language of the Jewish theologian Martin Buber, God has more the quality of a "you" or a "thou" than of an "it" or a "source." That is why Jesus, like the Jewish tradition, grounds experience with God in the notion of "covenant," for covenant is a relational model of reality. To say that radical disciples are in a covenant relationship with God implies dialogue or communication. This does not happen verbally or orally. Rather, God speaks through scripture, devotional practices, and through other people, as well as through visions and dreams and particularly through internal "longings," "leanings," and "prodding." As contemporary author Frederich Buechner advises, "Listen to your life. Listen to what happens to you because it is through what happens to you that God speaks." Paula D'Arcy states this truth more bluntly: "God comes to you disguised as your life."

Because the idea of a personal God raises incomparable problems for many people in the modern world, some theologians speak of God as transpersonal. Such language is useful, for it provides another alternative

---

9. Abba is a word we too can use with regard to God, for it is this relationship of unique filial consciousness that is at the core of reality. While the Jewish scriptures often speak of God as Father, the term Abba has no parallel in Jewish literature. Abba is a word no one before Jesus had ventured to use in addressing God.

to "personal" and "impersonal." Furthermore, the term "transpersonal" is attractive because it still maintains some element of the term "personal" without succumbing to normal literalizations of the word. However, personal language for God seems more appropriate than impersonal language, for as Jesus would remind us, God is not less than personal.

To speak of God as personal is important because it powerfully impacts our image of discipleship. Radical discipleship is not concerned with monarchical views of God, which imagine God as concerned with requirements and rewards. As Jesus might remind us, while God is a God of justice, God is also a God of love. Discipleship is about a relationship with God that transforms disciples into more compassionate beings, for the God of justice and love is the God of relationship and transformation. This God is also the God of grace, who loves us faithfully and unconditionally and has done so from the very beginning.

The "good news" of Jesus is the invitation into a new life here and now, one that transforms us personally and seeks to restore all reality to its original holiness.

What Jesus Would Want His Followers to Know about Scripture

The Bible represents the heart of the Christian tradition, providing Christians their identity, their sacred story. Of course, Christianity is ultimately centered in God, but it is the God of whom the Bible speaks and to whom it points. Despite its formational nature, the Bible has become a stumbling block for many Christians today. In particular, many are leaving the church because the Precritical Paradigm's way of reading the Bible—with its emphasis on biblical infallibility, historical factuality, and moral and doctrinal absolutes—ceased to make sense to them.

The Postcritical Paradigm provides an alternative to biblical literalism. Utilizing three adjectives—*historical, metaphorical,* and *sacramental*—it describes how scripture should be understood. These three approaches apply as well to the creeds and other normative Christian teachings.[10]

1. To speak of *the Bible as a historical product* is to see that it is a human product, not a divine product. Not "absolute truth" but relatively and culturally conditioned, the Bible uses the language and concepts of

---

10. The following points are adapted from Borg, *Meeting Jesus Again*, 43–60.

the cultures in which it took shape. It tells us how our spiritual ancestors saw things, not how God sees things. The Bible is not verbally inspired, since the emphasis is not upon words inspired by God but on people moved by their experience of God.

For the Postcritical Paradigm, describing the Bible as sacred scripture and therefore as "holy" is to value the historical process known as canonization. The documents that make up the Bible were not "sacred" when they were written, but over time were declared sacred, meaning that they became the most important documents for that community, providing its foundation and shaping its identity.

2. Much of the language of the Bible is metaphorical: one-third of the Old Testament is poetry or semi-poetical literature. To speak of *the Bible as metaphor* is to emphasize that this language should not be interpreted literally. Metaphor does not mean that the Bible is not true, but rather that it is not primarily concerned with facticity. The Bible does contain history, but even when a text contains historical memory, its meaning is more than (not less than) literal. For example, although the exile in Babylon in the sixth century BCE really happened, the way the story is told gives it a more than historical meaning. As we noted earlier, it became a metaphorical narrative of exile and return, providing images of the human condition and its remedy. In other cases, as the Genesis stories of creation, there may be little or no historical factuality. Though these stories are not literally factual, they are profoundly true.

3. To speak of *the Bible as sacrament* is to say that it mediates the sacred. If a sacrament is a physical vehicle or vessel for the Spirit, the Bible is sacrament in the sense that it is a visible human product whereby God becomes present to us.

For the Postcritical Paradigm, "the Bible—human in origin, sacred in status and function—is both metaphor and sacrament. As metaphor, it is a way of seeing—a way of seeing God and our life with God. As sacrament, it is a way that God speaks to us and comes to us."[11] The Bible is a two-way bridge, a path to the divine and a way to connect to our deepest self. Like a backboard in the game of basketball, scripture is a means to an end, not an end in itself.

Characterized by modern biblical scholars as a Spirit person, that is, as a "mediator of the sacred," Jesus was one of those persons in human history to whom the sacred was, to use William James's terms, firsthand

---

11. Borg, *Meeting Jesus Again*, 59.

religious experience rather than a secondhand belief. For Jesus, religious practice was central, by which I mean all the things devout people do together and individually as a way of paying attention to God. These include being part of a worshipping community, including its fellowship, spiritual formation, and its collective deeds of hospitality and compassion. In addition, this would include devotional discipline, especially prayer, contemplation, and Bible study.

Committed to monotheism, likely in its panentheistic version, and affirming that all human beings possess the divine Spirit, he would be anxious to share his intimacy with God and his activated divine Spirit with all his followers. Instructing us, he would probably indicate that our task, as his, is to arouse or awaken the dormant Spirit or True Self in ourselves and in others that has been immobilized or deactivated by the dominance of the egoic self, driven socially and biologically by the need to thrive and survive autonomously rather than through connection, dependence, and subservience to the divine.

Acknowledging the obvious human element in the Bible, and viewing it as the product of two faith communities—ancient Israel and the early Christian community—the modern Jesus would likely take a both/and stance regarding biblical authorship. Accepting: the biblical writers, including their words and experiences, to be human, he would also view them as witnesses to divine revelation, serving as vehicles to a higher voice and a deeper reality. In his understanding of revelation, this Jesus would agree with twentieth-century neo-orthodox scholar Emil Brunner (1889–1966) that God's self-revelation to humanity takes two forms—general revelation, available to all people, and special revelation, given to humans in scripture, which interprets and clarifies revelatory events in history and in nature, given them meaning.

As its name implies, general revelation is available to all humans regardless of time, place, culture, or other historical factors. General revelation is non-verbal. It is God's self-disclosure in nature, the human mind (or conscience), and through the events of history. The purpose of general revelation is clear: all humans live in nature (viewed as God's created order) and in history, and through such experience humans can know God and gain insight into the qualities that give meaning and purpose to life. According to the Bible, if humans were not sinful, general revelation would be sufficient for them to know God accurately and relate to God authentically. However, as Paul indicates in Romans 1, sinfulness leads humans to "suppress the truth," distorting the truth about God's sovereignty, providence, and standards, resulting not only in ignorance but also in idolatry and autonomy.

In claiming that the Bible is God's Word, orthodox Christians affirm that God inspires the authors of the Bible in such a way that what they write is what God intends for humans to know about salvation and spirituality in general. Most neo-orthodox theologians, however, distinguish between verbal revelation (that God speaks to humans by means of propositions or statements) and revelation through encounter (through existential, spiritual encounter that cannot be fully or even accurately conveyed in words), arguing that religious truth is neither objective nor subjective but something that occurs through encounter. Dialectic theology maintains that God does not reveal information or doctrine but rather reveals Godself, thereby overcoming the subject-object dilemma. God's revelation is not objective, that is, not an idea or object of thought, but rather self-revelation, as a person encounters another, establishing relationship with the other.

This view maintains that divine inspiration applies only to the *activity* of receiving revelation from God, and not to the *content* of the words themselves. Hence, believers should not directly equate God's Word and the Bible. According to Swiss theologian Karl Barth (1886–1969), considered the greatest Christian theologian of the twentieth century, the Bible can become a means of revelation, attesting to divine revelation, but the Bible is fallible—it contains errors, historical and scientific inaccuracies, and theological contradictions. However, despite its fallibility, the Bible *can become* the Word of God, but only in those parts and at those times when God chooses to reveal Godself. Consequently, the Word of God is not something humans can possess, not something that resides permanently in the Bible, for the Word of God resides only with God.

The historical Jesus, likely minimally literate, had no Bible to study or read individually. In his time it was the synagogue, and more specifically the religious leaders of his community, that interpreted the scripture. Today, most everyone is literate, and most people own Bibles that they hear read in worship or read and study individually and with others. Like the historical Jesus, a modern Jesus would advocate a rich devotional life. In addition, he would encourage his followers to use scripture devotionally and liturgically, that is, studying the Bible individually and with others in order to become adept at interpreting its message for themselves.

In this regard, a good place to begin is to look for a "canon within the canon," that is, to look for a biblical concept central to scripture and essential for all time. That concept or principle could then function as a lens or foundation for all individual reading of scripture. Fortunately, others have preceded us in that quest. For example, when Jesus was asked to summarize biblical teaching, he pointed to the Golden Rule ("Do unto others as you would have them do unto you") and to the Great Commandment ("Love the Lord your God with all your ability and your neighbor as yourself"). Likewise, the early Christian teacher Paul of Tarsus summarized biblical teaching with the "principle of charity" ("the greatest of all values and ideals is love"), as did the great Christian theologian Augustine of Hippo, who claimed that scripture teaches nothing but love. Rabbi Hillel, a contemporary of Jesus, once summarized the entire Torah (the revealed will of God) with the words: "What is hateful to yourself, do not do to your fellow man. That is the whole of the Torah. The rest is commentary."

Given his love of parabolic teaching, another aspect of scripture Jesus would emphasize is its story nature. Such approach, called "story theology," forces readers to rethink much of their theology, which has been given by extracting meaning from a story, and then expressed conceptually, theoretically, and systematically as dogma. At the heart of scripture lie three macro-stories that have shaped the Bible as a whole and have imaged our understanding of Jesus and the religious life in a particular way. Two of the stories are grounded in the history of ancient Israel: the story of the exodus from Egypt and the story of the exile and return from Babylon. The third, the priestly story, is grounded in an institution, namely, the temple, priesthood, and sacrifice. As the three formational stories of the Hebrew Bible, they shaped the religious imagination and understanding of both ancient Israel and the early Christian movement.[12]

The macro-stories, when taken together, are holistic. They share four powerful elements:

- all understand something profound about the human condition, that life involves suffering and alienation;
- all make powerful affirmations about God, portraying God as intimately involved with human life;
- all are stories of hope, new beginnings, and new possibilities; and

---

12. These stories are discussed more fully in Borg, *Meeting Jesus Again*, 119–37, and also in Vande Kappelle, *Beyond Belief*, 111–12.

- all are stories of a journey. This includes the priestly story, for taken in context with the others, the priestly story means that God accepts us just as we are, whatever our place on the journey.

These stories, all taken from the Hebrew scriptures, have powerful application in Christianity as well. In addition, the New Testament has a journey story of its own, that of discipleship. The initial clue is the meaning of the word "disciple," which does not mean to be "a pupil of a teacher," but rather a "follower after somebody." Discipleship in the New Testament, of course, is a journeying with Jesus. To follow Jesus means being on the road with him; it means undertaking the journey from the life of conventional wisdom to the alternative wisdom of life in the Spirit. Journeying with Jesus can involve denying him, even betraying him. Journeying with Jesus also means to be in a community, to become part of the alternative community of Jesus. And discipleship involves becoming compassionate, compassion being the defining mark of the follower of Jesus. Compassion is the fruit of life in the Spirit and the ethos of the community of Jesus. This understanding, unlike the conventional moralistic images of the Christian life, presents a transformist, dynamic understanding of the Christian life, where everything old passes away and where everything new becomes better (2 Corinthians 5:17).

Questions for Discussion and Reflection

1. If Jesus were a contemporary of ours, would he be a member of a specific Christian denomination or practice a nondenominational form of his faith? Would he even be a Christian? Explain your answer.
2. Define "dualistic thinking," and in a few sentences assess its attractiveness to religious individuals as well as its disadvantage as a way of viewing reality.
3. Based on the etymology of the term "religion," what are the implications of *religare* for discipleship?
4. In your own words, distinguish between "healthy" religion and "junk" religion. What does this distinction teach about radical discipleship?

5. In your own words, briefly summarize the four meaning of the term "faith." Which of these meanings do you favor? Why?

6. In your own words, explain the role of faith in radical discipleship.

7. Explain what Søren Kierkegaard meant by a "leap of faith," and what Blaise Pascal meant when he emphasized that Christian faith is not a leap *within* the order of the intellect but a leap *from* the order of the intellect to the order of the heart.

8. What are the advantages and disadvantages of the idea of a "personal God"?

9. Explain the meaning of Augustine's dictum, "If you understand God, then it is not God."

10. Explain the meaning of the term "panentheism," and assess its usefulness in conceptualizing God.

11. Which of Borg's two biblical models for God do you find most attractive, the "monarchical" or the "Spirit" model"? Must we choose between them? Is there a better model?

12. Assess the advantages and disadvantages of Tillich's reference to God as Ground of Being.

13. What are the advantages and disadvantages of the idea of a "transpersonal" God?

14. What do Christians generally mean when they say that the Bible is "holy"? Does the word "sacred" necessarily imply anything supernatural about the origin or nature of scripture? Explain your answer.

15. Of the three adjectives used to provide an alternative to biblical literalism, which of the three—historical, metaphorical, or sacramental—best describes your customary reading of scripture? Explain your answer.

16. Explain and assess the meaning of Karl Barth's dictum that because of its fallibility, the Bible cannot be equated with the Word of God, for the Word of God resides only with God.

17. Explain and assess the author's reference to a "canon within the canon." In your estimation, what does such a canon teach about radical discipleship?

Chapter 8

What Jesus Would Want Modern Disciples to Know and Do

CENTRAL TO SPIRITUALITY IS what some people call "mindfulness" and mystics call "being present." For Christians, the model and exemplar of such transformative awareness is Jesus, who came to tell us—and show us—that what is human shares in the divine nature, a divinely implanted reality that can be experienced here and now, in our present mortal state. As all mystics know and teach, spirituality is about seeing rightly, for "how one sees is what one sees." As Jesus says in Matthew 6:22, "The eye is the lamp of the body. So, if your eye is healthy, your whole body will be full of light." Moses could never have seen burning bushes as divine, could never have persevered with so much unknowing, unless he had moved to a higher level of seeing. William Blake, the seminal mystic poet who worked to bring about change both in the social order and in common ways of thinking, taught that "All we need to do is cleanse the doors of perception, and we shall see things as they are—infinite."

In Jesus' day, most of his contemporaries, particularly social, religious, and political leaders, simply could not see what he saw (Matt 13:13–17). This was not due to Jesus' unique identity or access to truth, for he keeps saying, in effect, "You should all know better. You do not know your own wonderful Jewish tradition." The same could be said of conventional Muslims, Buddhists, Hindus, or Christians today, "You do not know your own wonderful religious heritage."

Like any true reformer or prophet, Jesus evaluates his tradition from within, by its own criteria and its own documents. This is what I hope to do here for Christianity or any religion. Too often, religion offers doctrinal conclusions, additional competing truth claims in the increasingly growing marketplace of religious claims, but seldom does it give people a vision or process whereby they can legitimate those truth claims for themselves by inner experience and actual practice.

During the medieval period, two influential Christian philosophers at the monastery of St Victor in Paris—Hugh of St. Victor and Richard of St. Victor—wrote that humanity was given three different sets of eyes. The first was the eye of sensation, the second the eye of reason, and the third the eye of understanding. The third eye builds on the first two, yet goes further. It represents the full goal of all seeing and knowing.

The first two ways of seeing, when separated from the third, result in dualistic thinking, an "us versus them" way of seeing, the foundation of much violence and discontent in the world. The third way of seeing—typifying the seer, the poet, the saint, and the authentic mystic—grasps the whole picture. Today's world has many eccentrics, fanatics, rebels, and self-promotors. What the world needs is more individuals who see with all three sets of eyes. Such people are both humble and compassionate, for knowing that they do not know, they experience the unknowable.

Some call such knowing conversion, some call it enlightenment, some transformation, and some holiness. This way of knowing is Paul's "third heaven," where he "heard things that are not to be told, that no mortal is permitted to repeat" (2 Cor 12:2-4). Far too often, organized religion has a stake in keeping members in the first or second heaven, for this keeps them coming back, and keeps clergy in business. This is not always intentional, but rather an extension of the principle that you can lead others only as far as you yourself have gone. Lacking the contemplative gaze, such leaders remain functionaries and technicians, their parishioners without the resources to guide them into experiencing Mystery.

What I call the contemplative gaze is not a technique for acquiring benefit, for getting ahead, or even a requirement for entry into heaven; nor is it a pious exercise that somehow pleases God. It is much more like practicing heaven now. Paradoxically, if we misuse spiritual awareness, or keep it to ourselves, it "hides," and we cannot go deeper. This is why many remain at the level of mere "religion," and it is surely what Jesus means when he says, "For to those who have, more will be given, and they will have an abundance; but for those who have nothing, even what they have will be taken away" (Matt 13:12). How does the "secret" of God's kingdom, of God's reality and nature, become "unhidden"? It is disclosed when people stop hiding—from God, themselves, and others, and becomes transparent to those who see reality through Jesus' eyes.

All who witness this mystery, who experience its reality, "become children of God" (John 1:12), and, as Paul puts it, if children, then also "heirs of God and joint heirs with Christ" (Rom 8:15–17; see also Gal 4:7). While the Judeo-Christian tradition tells us we are already children of God, made in "God's image and likeness" (Gen 1:26–27), most of us have no clue what this means, and far fewer live out of its resources.

Continuing our discussion on Jesus as our contemporary, what would he want his followers, whether within the boundaries of the institutional church or beyond its boundaries and jurisdiction, to know and do as responsible global citizens? While global citizenship entails many concerns and responsibilities, in this chapter we focus on three areas: politics, social justice, and ecology.

A starting premise for our discussion, certainly central to the biblical Jesus, is that all human beings, shaped in the image of God, are inherently members of the family of God. As equal members of this sacred family, all human beings deserve to be treated fairly, kindly, and compassionately, with dignity and respect. How might this starting point influence such concerns as racial discrimination, women's rights, gender identification, poverty, and healthcare?

In addition, Jesus would think about Reality in nondualistic ways, viewing all life as an interconnected whole, a whole primarily spiritual in nature. He would, in essence, continue to tell us that the task of humans is to work with nature and not rule over it, reminding us that "this is my Father's world." While as a modern person Jesus would embrace many of the advances of science and education and be aware of the complexities of culture, society, and history, his perspective would counter modern Western assumptions such as hierarchy, individualism, triumphalism, greed, and anthropocentrism.

Three broad areas of concern face disciples in the twenty-first century. The first has to do with politics, particularly with advocating for peaceful resolutions of national and international problems and working to avoid violence and war. The second is poverty and social justice, with its corollary racism and prejudicial treatment of people of color and minorities in general. The third is caring for the environment. These three have many overlapping dimensions. For example, the eradication of poverty fosters international peace, and a sane, sustainable, and just use of natural resources also promotes social justice and international harmony.

Racism and prejudice may not be the reason governments declare war on others, but they certainly contribute to violence and the proliferation of weapons.

What Jesus Would Want Modern Followers to Know and Do about Politics[1]

It is easy for many religious people to brush off this topic as irrelevant to Jesus, even to Jesus as our contemporary. In their minds, religion and politics should be kept separate, as his statement "Give to the emperor the things that are the emperor's, and to God the things that are God's" (Matt 22:21) seems to indicate. That passage, given by Jesus in response to those who would entrap him, has many interpretations, including that people should obey civil as well as divine laws. However, the core teaching, found in the second part of Jesus' response, seems to be that as "divine image bearers," all human beings should give to God what is God's, namely, their ultimate allegiance and their entire self.

During his lifetime, the historical Jesus lived under two forms of government, both theocratic Israelite and imperial Roman, the first monotheistic and the latter pagan and polytheistic. Neither form of government was democratic. If Jesus lived in the twenty-first century, whether in the modern state of Israel or in a Western nation such as the United States, it is likely he would favor some form of democracy, whereby each citizen has guaranteed rights such as the right to vote, of representation, and other political rights found in Western constitutional forms of government.

Given that literacy and secondary education are no longer privileges but rights guaranteed to all citizens of Western nations, Jesus would insist that his followers stay informed politically and vote for candidates who are competent, trained, and qualified to lead by enacting and enforcing nonpartisan policies and legislation guaranteeing the safety, security, and well-being of citizens, visitors, and aliens alike.

Much as Jesus would oppose dictatorial or totalitarian rule, he would also oppose two-party political systems that reduced electoral choice to

---

1. While writing the segments on politics and social justice, I came across a book titled *Progressive Conversations*, a collection of newspaper essays written for a weekly column on religion and ethics by Roger Ray, the pastor of a nondenominational Christian church in Missouri. While I am indebted to his ideas in this segment and the next, I cite specific references where they are most appropriately needed.

either-or options. Supporting pluralism and nondualistic policies, he would likely encourage his followers to commit themselves to causes that are holistic and inclusive, guided by comprehensive compassion rather than by inflexible partisanship.

The United States has often used its military to conquer, control, and enforce its policies and perspectives. Jesus would challenge these priorities, insisting that national governments prioritize efforts at peacemaking and peacekeeping, working to elevate international cooperation over national sovereignty. For example, in American politics, Jesus would question the recent military role the United States has played in Iraq, Afghanistan, and other struggling nations in the Middle East.[2] It seems clear that the United States invaded Iraq in 2003 under false pretenses, for weapons inspectors had clearly reported the absence of weapons of mass destruction in Iraq, and while a cruel dictator was removed from power, the U.S. invasion left the country less stable and more violent. While the military action was also intended to lessen Iran's role in the region, such action may have backfired.

Like former president Donald Trump's false claim that Mexico would pay for the building of a border wall, Americans were first told that they would not have to pay anything for the invasion of Iraq. The Bush administration assured its critics that oil proceeds from the vast resources of Iraq would pay for the invasion, and American troops would be welcomed as liberators. Of course, anyone with knowledge of Muslim thought and religion would have known that Americans would not be greeted as liberators. Furthermore, the economic impact estimate was grossly misrepresented. Within a few months, the Bush administration offered a recalculated figure of $80 billion, and many citizens called for a halt to American plans, indicating what this sum of money could accomplish for poverty, education, and health issues alone. As it turned out, the $80 billion figure was way off; the real cost was not $80 billion, and not even $800 billion, but $2.4 trillion, thirty times the 2003 calculation.[3] At that time, congressman John Boehner suggested that the Social Security retirement age be raised to seventy in order to pay for the wars in Iraq and Afghanistan. If that happened, how many of us would be sufficiently pleased with the outcomes of recent wars that we would gladly willingly work five years longer to pay for them? Of course, that would only affect

2. Portions of the segment on the American role in Iraq and Afghanistan, including statistical information, are adapted from Ray, *Progressive Conversations*, 40–54.

3. Ray, *Progressive Conversations*, 38.

Americans who are dependent on Social Security, not the billionaires squeezing life from middle- and lower-class Americans.

After eight years of war, more than a trillion dollars of unfunded military spending, and more importantly, the loss of 4500 American soldiers' lives, the war ended with no real sense of accomplishment. The same was true of the withdrawal of Afghanistan. As bad as the Taliban are in that country, the expenditure of twenty years of American life and wealth has made little if any permanent change in the character of that nation.

Consider what impact this loss of life and wealth has had on our economy, on our shrinking middle class, and on our growing income gap in America. What if instead of invading Afghanistan and Iraq, the federal government had allocated these funds toward maintaining infrastructure, providing healthcare to the sick, and educational and economic opportunity for all?

Given a choice between better national infrastructure or invading another Middle Eastern nation, would people want temporary regime changes if it meant that one of their children had to die on the battlefield, the others couldn't afford to go to college, and they would become unemployed or homeless? As we saw in Iraq, after all the bodies had been buried, stockholders in the corporate complex became wealthier, but the people of Iraq continued to languish, their condition hardly better than before. Before Americans sign off on future military ventures, they should make clear their willingness to sacrifice personally to achieve the stated goal. While the use of military forces should have broad popular support, in all cases the intention should be honorable and moral.

A twenty-first-century Jesus would certainly combine a mystical nature with an activist spirituality. As an activist, there are many military and political issues he would challenge, not the least of which would be the possession and stockpiling of nuclear weapons. As an advocate of a clean environment and of the rights of all peoples and nations to coexist peacefully on this planet, he would certainly work to make the earth a nuclear free zone. It would only take about fifty pounds of weapons-grade uranium to produce a bomb that could wipe out any city in the world. Given that there are now more than a thousand tons of weapons-grade uranium in the world, much of it managed by unstable governments, it is reasonable to assume that the greatest challenge to world security still comes from the threat of nuclear bombs.

Any discussion of military-style weapons, designed to stop aggression by foreign powers or rogue units, prompts the issue of the threat of such individually owned weapons. If Americans demand progress in automobile safety in the engineering of roads and cars, why can't engineering skill be applied to gun safety? If the 30,000 gun deaths in America every years have not prompted sensible gun violence legislation, how many casualties would it take to change our thinking?

After the Sandy Hook tragedy in December 2012 that killed twenty-six people, of whom twenty were schoolchildren between six and seven years of age, it seemed like American legislators were ready finally to do something about our country's dangerous gun laws. However, when all was said and done, much more was said than done. Despite lengthy debate in Congress, the legislation that was passed in the Senate was so full of loopholes that it failed to deter any terrorist, criminal, or mentally unstable individual who wanted to purchase a gun.

Ironically, public outrage was not sufficient to outlaw assault rifles and large-volume ammunition magazines. In fact, sales of such weapons continued unabated. Since it is abundantly clear that the gun industry's political donations keep gun legislation from being seriously discussed, could American voters exert their moral will to make it illegal for the gun industry to lobby Congress? Significantly, in 2022 Congress passed the Bipartisan Safer Communities Act that takes steps to restrict gun access for young buyers, domestic violence offenders, and others who could pose a risk. This legislation also funds school safety and mental health programs.

While we are on the subject of legislators and lobbyists, is it ethical for an elected official, once out of office, to leverage his or her working relationship with other elected officials as a paid lobbyist? Despite whatever positive role lobbyists might play in informing legislators and helping to shape legislation, wouldn't our government be far better off if lobbying were outlawed?

Most everyone in America is aware our country has a political culture that is not only ponderous and unwieldy, but that also favors corporations and the wealthy over its general citizenry. To change the current stalemate, can we start with curbing reliance on violence? While some might think that war can improve the economy, didn't the 2022 Russian invasion of Ukraine demonstrate how bad war is for business, not only locally, but globally?

In most years, the United States has about 15,000 homicides, whereas Germany has about 150, and Japan has fewer than 10. This amazing transformation has taken place in the course of a single lifetime. While these nations are territorially smaller than the United States, they have significantly sizeable populations. If countries like Germany and Japan, where homicide rates have plummeted in recent years, have made a break with their violent past, can't we?

Twenty-five years ago Americans smoked cigarettes in college classrooms, restaurants, airplanes, and even in hospital rooms, but that has dramatically changed. If Americans can change in their attitudes toward cigarettes, can't the same happen with guns? Must we continue to accept the massacre of Americans through gun violence?

What Jesus Would Want Modern Followers to Know and Do about Social Justice[4]

When Jesus was alive in the first century, he was ridiculed and belittled by the social, intellectual, and religious elite of his day. Later, when he was arrested, falsely accused, beaten, and crucified, it was not only because he was viewed as a troublemaker and potential insurrectionist, but for his resolute desire "to speak truth to power." If he were with us today, would he sit quietly on the sidelines, issuing an occasional tweet or a statement on the editorial page of his local newspaper, or simply philosophize about the sad state of affairs in the world today? To the contrary, I am confident he would be a strong activist, enacting a morally responsible social and economic prophetic agenda and leading by example. Let's start our discussion in this segment with civil rights.

The year 2020 marked the sixtieth anniversary of a momentous event in the Civil Rights movement, when on February 1, 1960, four young Black men sat down at the Woolworth's lunch counter in Greensboro, North Carolina, to be served in the "whites only" eatery. By remaining in their seats after their request was refused, they ignited a movement to challenge injustice and racial inequality throughout the southern United States. Not to be dissuaded in their challenge of the Jim Crow laws, the four college freshmen returned to the lunch counter every day for six

---

4. Portions of the segment on healthcare and social justice are adapted from Ray, *Progressive Conversations*, 63–65, 68–73, and 82–93.

months, and sat there ridiculed and physically assaulted until at last the lunch counter became integrated.

It wasn't only Jesus and his apostles who were arrested, beaten, and sometimes executed for their civil disobedience. We cannot forget that the very people we now teach our children to admire, such as Gandhi, Martin Luther King, Jr., Dorothy Day, Dietrich Bonhoeffer, Nelson Mandela, and Archbishop Oscar Romero, all suffered arrests and beatings, and in some cases, martyrdom, for defying unjust social, political, and economic circumstances.

Some years ago, while I was chaplain and professor of religious studies at Washington & Jefferson College, Sister Helen Prejean came to the college to deliver the baccalaureate address to the graduating class. During her talk, she mentioned how most of us live in a "bubble," unaware of the world around us. As the author of *Dead Man Walking*, she spoke about racism in America, particularly in our penal system. "Did you know," she asked, "that most of the criminals who are executed are Black, or that executions are almost always only sought when the victim is white?" We assume that the death penalty deters crime, when it clearly does not.

While Sister Prejean frequently addresses students at the colleges and universities where she speaks, she also addresses church members in her talks, begging them to make themselves aware of what's going on in the world, and imploring them to be courageous enough to act to end injustice and poverty. A contemporary Jesus would agree with Sister Prejean in describing the moral and spiritual path all disciples must take, going from passive acceptance of the status quo toward becoming ethically aware actors on the local and global stage.

What has happened to our civil resolve today? The general populace has seemingly sat back and watched as our government has used tax dollars of every citizen to fund a healthcare system that only serves about 80 percent of the population, and many of these leave hospitals to find themselves being forced into bankruptcy. In addition, we have sat back and watched as our national resources have been used to bail out our country's banks and then, when the people who caused the banking crisis rewarded themselves with billions of tax dollars in personal bonuses, the media and the pubic have stood by idly.

In his book, *Progressive Conversations*, Roger Ray speaks of attending a healthcare debate at a local Chamber of Commerce around the Affordable Care Act. While the pro-business speakers acknowledged the need to cover the uninsured and to lower healthcare costs, they frequently referred to the 83 percent of Americans who have healthcare coverage, as if to suggest that one in five Americans not being covered is not really all that bad. As heartless as this attitude is, it also fails to take into consideration that many of those who are insured have to accept high deductibles in order to keep their insurance premium low enough to still afford to buy groceries. If one has a deductible of $5000 or higher, is one really insured? Such coverage is actually catastrophic insurance, and any visits to the doctor come straight out of wallets already depleted by paying hundreds of dollars each month that is useless except on catastrophic occasions.[5]

Nearly one-fifth of America's economy is consumed by healthcare, and there seems to be no permanent solutions to this crisis as long as insurance companies remain in control. The wealthy will always have access to the best healthcare in the world. But given that society has a vested economic and moral interest in the health and productivity of its entire population, shouldn't there be a basic healthcare program that includes everyone?

In spite of misleading anecdotal accounts, Canadians have created a national healthcare program that manages costs far better than the United States government, covering everyone instead of just the majority, as the United States does. I know there are Americans who prefer to have better care than what they might have in a national healthcare system, even if that means millions must go without adequate healthcare, but as Jesus would surely remind us, such an argument is morally and spiritually bankrupt and hardly deserving of consideration.

Having spoken of lobbyists in the previous segment, I must add that most people are not aware that there are three times as many pharmaceutical lobbyists on Capitol Hill than there are elected officials. The primary concern of these lobbyists is to make their companies more profitable. Their efforts, however, are a barrier to healthcare reform. Why is it that American-made medicines are cheaper in Canada than in the United States, sometimes by as much as 60 percent? The reason is that Canadian provinces cap prices at a level that is still profitable for the pharmaceutical companies but not as wildly profitable as in our unregulated economy.

Our country is in serious social and economic trouble. There is no question that the growing income gap between the rich and the

---

5. Ray, *Progressive Conversations*, 82–83.

working class is destroying our democracy. However, like a pickpocket who distracts our attention while stealing our wallet, both Republicans and Democrats keep trying to get us to believe that the solution lies in voting for their candidates rather than the opposing candidates, while both continue to accept political donations from institutions that fuel the class disparity. A cursory look at our election system reveals two inevitable facts: the candidate with the largest campaign fund wins 94 percent of the time, and the largest donors to both parties tend to be the same corporations.

Another reason we are in serious social and economic trouble has to do with our military spending, which is greater than the combined total of military spending in the rest of the world. And we do this while insisting that we cannot afford to rebuild the infrastructure of our nation, provide healthcare to the sick, and education to the next generation of Americans. Without infrastructure, education, and healthcare, our defense department will shortly have no country left to defend. In addition, if our only option to correct this downward spiral is to vote for a different set of corporate sponsored politicians, there is little reason to believe that anything will change.

Along with most Americans, I am concerned about the viability of our two-party system. We need at least two honorable parties to keep our democracy strong, and in my opinion, such honorability is woefully absent in our politicians and in their legislation. When it comes to healthcare and to the availability of adequate standards of living for all, what I don't hear is our two parties debating how best to deliver healthcare benefits in the most effective and economically efficient manner possible to those who need it. A primary issue that isn't being discussed is why an estimated 45,000 Americans die every year as a direct result of not having adequate health insurance.[6] That number is greater than all who die from automobile accidents, gunshot wounds, terrorism, or wars. These are 45,000 entirely preventable deaths if America would find a way to do what almost every other industrialized nation in the world has already done.

Why is it that the United States spends more on healthcare than any other nation in the world and yet is ranked thirty-eight in overall healthcare, far below the nations that have national healthcare programs? What is happening, in effect, is that American politicians are turning

---

6. Tailor and Stillman, "Dead Man Walking," 1881.

public resources over to insurance companies, which cannot diagnose illnesses, perform surgeries, or prescribe mediations, but that take billions of dollars out of healthcare to pay enormous salaries to their executives and dividends to their stockholders. There is no question that the United States will end up with a universal healthcare program. Anything else will bankrupt its economy.

One of the current hot topics in politics and economics is the issue of raising the minimum wage. Any proposed change in the economy will have winners and losers, but it is clear that adjustments to the wealth gap are necessary. However, the people at the top of the economic chain, the current winners, never want to see a change in the rules. The increasingly impoverished middle class naturally wants to see changes that would increase buying and selling and producing and consuming, but ironically, fear and anxiety often cause members of the middle class to vote against their own interests in support of the status quo.

However, the economy is not stimulated when we take from the poor what little they have and give it to the wealthy. Our economic policy of cutting estate taxes, cutting capital gains taxes, and creating tax loopholes for off-shore investments is, in fact, taking from the poor to give to the rich. We cannot raise everyone to executive-level salaries and expect that to work, but neither can we realistically defend the existence of a minimum wage that is below a reasonable living wage and pretend that this protects the jobs of the poor. The coronavirus epidemic changed the economic situation significantly, causing many employers to raise wages in order to fill previously low-wage positions. Furthermore, predictions that raises in the minimum wage will result in job losses have been shown to be false, so why is it that so many still offer that objection? For example, the city of Seattle raised its minimum wage to $15 per hour and in one year reduced its unemployment by 25 percent. Those who defend a minimum wage that is below a living wage seem to be lacking in compassion, patriotism, or both.

In our day, coercive, deceptive, and abusive political and economic practices demand an alternative. Jesus, as a teacher of radical compassion and self-sacrificing devotion to the core biblical principle that humans love neighbors as themselves, continues to be a mentor of the kind of spiritual depth his followers must claim as their own in order to transform the world in ways that bring good news to everyone, providing a bulwark against the abuses of the powerful.

If the United States were in a class warfare, it would be clear that the wealthy are winning. Congressional Budget Office figures demonstrate that over the past thirty years, the share of the wealth produced in America paid to the middle and lower classes has dropped between 10 to 30 percent (with an even steeper decline for those at the bottom of our economic ladder) while the share of wealth going to the top 20 percent has risen by nearly 30 percent, and for the super-elite of Americans it has risen by nearly 130 percent.[7] The results are now clear: the poor are becoming poorer and the rich are becoming wealthier. While the very wealthy will continue to exploit the talent and labor of the middle class, they cannot be allowed to win the class war outright, for there is no American democracy without a strong middle class.

The bottom line economically is that there should be no working poor in twenty-first-century America. A spiritual sense of connection to the poor, war refugees, the uninsured, the uneducated, and the hopeless is the best response we can give to a system that continues to transfer resources that should be fairly spread among the people of the world into the hands of a smaller and smaller super-elite.

What Jesus Would Want Modern Followers to Know and Do about Caring for Our Planet

Due to human activity and negligence, we humans are responsible for such destructive environmental acts as deforestation, overfishing, and species loss. According to Bill McKibben, there are currently half as many wild animals on the planet as there were in 1970. Furthermore, many plant species, including the planet's oldest and largest trees, are dying rapidly, as climate change attracts new pests and diseases. The baobab tree can live as long as 2,500 years, but five of the six oldest species on the planet have died in the last decade. Yet nothing seems to slow human destructiveness—just the opposite. "By most accounts," McKibben notes, humans have "used more energy and resources during the last thirty-five years than in all of human history that came before."[8] Around the world, human pollution is the biggest public health crisis, killing nine million people a year, far more than AIDS, malaria, TB, and warfare combined. The list of severe environmental problems grows longer each day,

---

7. Ray, *Progressive Conversations*, 71.
8. McKibben, *Falter*, 12.

including dead zones in the oceans and lakes where fertilizer pours off farms along with irreplaceable topsoil; vast quantities of plastic waste gathering in the sea; suburbs spilling across agricultural lands and agriculture overrunning tropical forests; and water tables quickly sinking as aquifers drain.

When the modern environmental movement came of age in 1972 with the publication of *The Limits of Growth*, the authors warned that the most probable result of unleashed human growth would be "a sudden and uncontrollable decline in both population and industrial capacity." Though modern societies have taken the environmental challenge semi-seriously, passing laws to clear air and water, they remain committed to further growth. Now, McKibben warns, it may be too late for change. The American way of life is unsustainable, and the human game on earth may be starting to play itself out. In 1989, when McKibben wrote *The End of Nature*, he painted a bleak picture. The situation since has not improved; instead it has become bleaker, possibly dire.

When we speak of climate change, we need to recall its cause and its magnitude, for it is by far humanity's greatest calamity. Over the past two centuries, humans have consumed immense quantities of fossil fuels, burning them in car motors, basement furnaces, power plants, and steel mills. When we burn fossil fuels, the carbon atoms combine with oxygen atoms in the air to produce carbon dioxide. The molecular structure of carbon dioxide traps heat that would otherwise radiate back out to space. This means that human usage of fossil fuels has changed the energy balance of our planet, trapping excess amounts of solar heat that would otherwise have returned to space.

If we consumed small amounts of fossil fuels, it wouldn't matter. But we have burned enough to raise the concentration of carbon dioxide in the atmosphere from 275 parts per million to 400 parts per million in the course of 200 years. We are currently on our way to 700 parts per million or worse.[9] To clarify what this means, the extra heat we trap near the planet because of the carbon dioxide we have created is equivalent to the heat from 400,000 Hiroshima-sized bombs every day, or four each second. At present, we are pushing about forty billion tons of carbon dioxide into the atmosphere annually, an amount unprecedented in the earth's 4.5-billion-year history. Even during the end of the Permian Age, when

---

9. According to experts, 350 parts per million is considered the limit for healthy atmosphere. The limit has now been crossed, and we surpassed 400 several years ago, climbing steadily beyond that figure annually.

most life went extinct, the carbon dioxide content of the atmosphere grew at perhaps one-tenth the current pace.

The results of our current pollution have been extraordinary. The past thirty years have seen the twenty hottest years ever recorded. "Faster than expected," is the watchword of climate scientists, that is, regarding the damage to ice caps and oceans. In January 2019, scientists concluded that the earth's oceans were warming 40 percent faster than previously believed. Droughts are intensifying globally, and in unexpected places such as Cape Town, South Africa; Säo Paulo, Brazil; and the Po River Valley, Italy's agricultural heartland.

As land dries out, it often burns, which explains the rash of forest fires in Northern California in 1987, when a thousand blazes broke out simultaneously. And every year seems to be worse. Since 2000, more than a dozen U.S. states have reported the largest wildfires in their recorded histories. Furthermore, each degree Fahrenheit we warm the planet increases the number of lightning strikes by 7 percent, and once the fires get going in our hot, dry new world, they are all but impossible to fight, as we saw in the devastating Camp Fire burning of Paradise, California in 2018.

According to experts, global warming is affecting the earth negatively in polar opposite ways, namely by making dry areas drier and wet areas wetter. As ocean temperatures rise, there is an increase of water in the atmosphere, increasing the level and intensity of storms. It wasn't the winds that made 2017's Hurricane Harvey the most damaging storm in American history; it was the amount of rain that hit Houston, Texas—127 billion tons worth, enough to fill 26,000 New Orleans Superdomes—its weight alone causing the city to sink by several centimeters. In places, the rainfall topped 54 inches, by far the largest rainstorm in American history. When Hurricane Florence hit the Carolinas in 2018, it set a new record for East Coast rainfall—the storm dumped the equivalent of all the water in the Chesapeake Bay.

The effects of global warming is now irreversible, at least for the near future. A 2018 study concluded that even if human beings stopped emitting *all* greenhouse gases today, more than a third of the planet's glacial ice would melt anyway in the coming decades. Beside the damage, the cost associated with global warming is staggering. Climate change is currently costing the U.S. economy about $240 billion a year, and the world, $1.2 trillion annually.

Climate related disasters are also resulting in increased poverty and hunger globally. In 2017, a United Nations agency announced that after a decade of decline, the number of chronically malnourished human beings had started growing again, by 38 million, to 815 million. The planet is becoming crowded as climate change is pushing people closer together, resulting in civil conflict and unrest and producing more migrants and refugees. In addition, if carbon dioxide levels continue rising, human cognitive ability will fall. If carbon levels increase to a thousand parts per million (a possibility by the year 2100), human cognitive ability will fall by as much as 21 percent.

As ice sheets melt, they take weight off land, increasing the risk of earthquakes—seismic activity is already increasing in Greenland and Alaska due to this effect. As faults are activated, landslides and tsunamis will increase in number and intensity. Climate change will also affect food supply. Since World War II, human ingenuity has kept crop yields growing ahead of fast-rising populations. That climb, however, now seems to be thwarted by rising heat and drought.

Assuming increased temperatures and rainfall, in June 2018, researchers found that a two-degree Celsius rise in temperature could cut U.S. corn yield by 18 percent. A four-degree increase would cut the crop almost in half. The effects of such a loss are incalculable, since the United States is the world's largest producer of corn, which is the planet's most widely grown crop. Global warming is also making food less nutritious, resulting in a loss of minerals such as calcium, iron, and zinc. Global warming studies also reveal an increase in crop pests, which thrive in the heat. Even if we hit the UN target of limiting temperature rise to two degrees Celsius, pests will cut wheat yields by 46 percent, corn by 31 percent, and rice by 19 percent.

Just as people have gotten used to eating certain amounts of food every day, they have gotten used to living in particular places, such as by oceans or in river valleys. From the earliest cities to the largest metropolises, proximity to saltwater meant wealth and power. Now, however, such proximity means increased vulnerability and potential fatality. As polar ice thaws, sea levels are rising. In 2018, researchers concluded that Antarctica had lost three trillion tons of ice in the last three decades, with the rate of melt tripling since 2012. As a result, scientists are now predicting not a half-meter or even a meter in sea level rise, but "several meters in the next 50 to 150 years," according to James Hansen, the world's premier climatologist. As Jeff Goodell notes, such a rise would "create generations of climate refugees that will make today's Syrian war refugee crisis look like a high school drama production." The UN estimates that climate change will produce from 200 million to 1 billion refugees this century alone. Where will they go?

Seeing with the eyes of Jesus, the spiritual mandate to protect our planet is threefold. The first is a reverence and awe for creation in all of its wonder and beauty. Henry David Thoreau was not the first to find more of the divine in nature than in the church, and he will not be the last. Of course, one need not preclude the other, but people of faith should certainly partner with naturalist and humanists in inspiring and educating ecological care and concern.

The second reason to protect our planet is that environmental issues have a huge social justice concern. Many of the major sources of pollution are by industries that choose short-term gain over long-term environmental health. The poor of the earth generally wind up living in areas where these industries dispose of their harmful byproducts. The resources of the earth should not be the sole possession of those who succeed in manipulating governments and banking interests into given them exploitative rights of natural resources.

Finally, there is the matter of concern for future generations. No single generation has a right to misuse the resources of the earth in ways that leave future generations at risk. In the twenty-first century, as in every age and place, Jesus calls mortals to be stewards of land and resources that are divinely ordained to last throughout time. Stewards are not driven by short-term gains, but rather by more vital interests that trump the desire for personal profit. In this respect, we have much to be grateful for, including the efforts of environmentalists who have gone before us, committed to reversing the trends of planetary degradation. Together, the peoples of the world can persuade governments to restore forests and clean up rivers and lakes. We have, through individual and governmental agencies, been able to reverse the erosion of the ozone layer of our atmosphere.

In light of what is currently at stake, namely, the future of humanity and other living creatures on earth, there is much we can do for the health of our planet. The largest consumption of fossil fuels is expended in two categories, the heating and cooling of our homes and in transportation, so this is where we can concentrate our efforts. In addition, learning to recycle, to insulate our homes, and to be more cautious about the use of energy can save us money immediately and in the long term.

But wouldn't it be wonderful if human beings were all motivated to do the right thing because it is the right thing to do? However, doing the right thing is always a bit easier if it saves us money at the same time. Strengthening our conscience and protecting our financial resources are not always mutually exclusive.

Some nations have made great strides in private transportation and mass transit systems. The technology exists. All that stands between us and making huge progress in protecting our environment is the collective will to change.

Perhaps a good place to begin is with the following parable. Imagine a lifeboat quickly sinking in rough seas with ten passengers trying to make it safely to shore. Six people are rowing the boat, two are bailing out the ever-rising water from the boat, and the other two are busy drilling holes in the bottom of the boat. What should be done to get the boat and its passengers to safety? Should the six who are rowing work harder? Should the two who are bailing work faster? Sadly, as these questions are asked to members of the United States Congress, legislators have tried everything but ask the two who are drilling holes in the hull to stop. Perhaps this is because big oil and big coal companies think they own the boat. While they may believe that nature has gone through such changes before and somehow stayed on course, what is happening to our planet these days is so catastrophic that it may well result in the sinking of our lifeboat, at which point everyone will inevitably drown.[10] Our dependence upon carbon-based fuels (gasoline and electricity generated by burning coal) is sinking our only boat. No excuses about being "bad for business" or "hurting jobs" can justify making the planet uninhabitable!

Questions for Discussion and Reflection

1. In your estimation, what does seeing rightly—or what some call "mindfulness" or "being present"—teach about radical discipleship?
2. In your own words, distinguish between dualistic seeing and thinking and seeing with the contemplative gaze, that is, with the eye of spiritual understanding or discernment.

---

10. This analogy, used by environmentalists, is taken from Ray, *Progressive Conversations*, 78.

3. In your own words, what would Jesus have modern followers know and do about the priority of a nation's military in its overall budget? Explain your answer.

4. In your estimation, what should modern American followers of Jesus learn from the U.S. invasions of Afghanistan and Iraq? Explain your answer.

5. In your estimation, what would Jesus have modern followers know and do about the possession and stockpiling of nuclear weapons? Explain your answer.

6. In your estimation, what would Jesus have modern followers know and do about gun safety in the United States? Explain your answer.

7. In your estimation, what would Jesus have modern followers know and do about the presence and influence of lobbying efforts on elected officials? Explain your answer.

8. In your estimation, what would Jesus have modern followers know and do about civil rights in America? Explain your answer.

9. In your estimation, what would Jesus have modern followers know and do about affordable healthcare coverage for all Americans? Explain your answer.

10. In your estimation, what would Jesus have modern followers know and do about a livable wage and America's current minimum wage policies? Explain your answer.

11. Do you agree with ecological activist Bill McKibben that the American way of life is unsustainable? If so, what should responsible modern disciples of Jesus do about it?

12. In your estimation, what would Jesus have modern followers know and do about global warming? Explain your answer.

13. In your estimation, what does it mean for modern followers of Jesus to be stewards of land and resources? Explain your answer.

Chapter 9

Radical Discipleship Illustrated, Part I

THIS CHAPTER AND THE next two chapters contain responses by the author and several of his friends and family members to the following questions: (1) What is your understanding of (radical) discipleship in the twenty-first century? (2) Illustrate your understanding of discipleship from your life and faith journey. Before we proceed with the result of this assignment, however, we need to define the terms "disciple" and "radical," lest they be misunderstood.

To be a disciple is to be an apprentice of another, a follower or imitator of an accomplished or worthy mentor. In our case, what we have in mind is following or imitating the historical Jesus. Of course, the times have changed, and imitating or following a first-century individual implies modernizing and updating that person's pattern and influence. By using the term "radical," what I have in mind has both a lexical meaning and a social application. The term "radical" goes back to the Latin word *radix*, meaning "root." As we saw earlier in John 15:5, Jesus called himself the vine and his disciples the branches. Despite differences between vines and branches, the similarities are far greater, and it is our similarity with Jesus, our continuity rather than discontinuity of ministry, I emphasize in this study. The term "radical" has social implications, for it implies that what is radical departs markedly from the usual or customary understanding of Jesus and his mission. In this study, both definitions are significant, for to be a radical disciple of Jesus means to imitate him in ministry and intent, but also to do so in ways that differ markedly from the perfunctory practices of many first half of life Christians.

Second half of life Christians accept the history of Christianity, which they know cannot be changed. However, being properly Christian is not important to them, for like Jesus, they know that it is the task of every generation of disciples to rethink its theology and practices, for only thus can they provide society with transformative vision. In this respect, theology must be simultaneously conservative and progressive. If belief and practice are only conservative, discipleship can become conformist, repetitive, judgmental, and unimaginative. However, if theology is only progressive, belief and practice can become merely novel, trendy, arbitrary, and uninspiring. A theology that is stagnant reflects a religion that is limited in both usefulness and effectiveness. Modern Christians spend a great deal of time trying to connect the dots, attempting intellectually to penetrate the core of reality to see what is good, beautiful, true, lasting, and transcendent. While most early Christians sought the same things, they did not approach life and faith analytically, as we do today. Rather, they applied what they believed mystically, spiritually, and intuitively. As a result, they lived kindly, in harmony with nature and others.

Since the Enlightenment, modern believers have approached reality in a more detached and scientific way, looking to facts, evidence, and objective truth for hope and truth, favoring doctrine over direct experience. In trying to defend its ground in the face of rationalism and scientism, modern religion tried to become "rational" and lost its alternative consciousness. Losing access to higher levels of consciousness—the transrational, transpersonal, and transcendent—many Christians settle for finality and conformity, content to rest in shallow waters rather than plumbing the depths. Tragically, many lose the inner experience that underlies the outer belief system. That is the heart of religion's problem today, taking the symbols too literally, and now the emerging generation is throwing them out as useless. Without searching, nothing can be found, but how one searches determines what one finds or even expects to find.

Despite the complexity of the figure of Jesus, for our purpose, when we think of him, our focus is on how he serves as the model and metaphor for all humanity. The historic creeds and dogmas of Christianity reflect less an incorrect view of Christian teaching than a limited and incomplete view, the church's attempt to define its foundational or organizational (first half of life) identity. Later, during the fifteenth and sixteenth centuries, reformers began questioning doctrines and practices established during the medieval period, including ecclesiastical hierarchicalism, sacramentalism, the centrality of belief for salvation, and the role and interpretation of scripture. Unfortunately, the Protestant Reformation, charting a new organizational identity for Christianity, also focused on first half of life issues, including statements of belief (creeds and confessions) and a closed canon, further fragmenting the church.

According to the New Testament, Christians are kind of hybrid creatures who live in two dimensions. They are citizens of the present age while at the same time living under the dominion of Christ's kingdom. As Paul put it somewhat paradoxically, Christians live "in the flesh" (human nature) as well as "in the Spirit" (the new dimension introduced by Christ). Awareness of this dual citizenship led early Christians to say that they were "strangers" in the historical era on earth (Heb 11:13). Ever since the New Testament period, Christianity has had to steer between two dangers: the temptation (1) to withdraw from society, on the assumption that Christ's kingdom is not of this world (John 18:36), and (2) to make a too easy identification of the kingdom with something in this world, such as the institutional church or the ideal human society. However, the essential message of the New Testament is this: The kingdom is not of this world, yet it has been manifest in this world through the life, death, and resurrection of Jesus.

Every verse of the New Testament presupposes the new people of God, a new community called the church. From the beginning, Christians were characterized as "the body of Christ," followers of Jesus who showed by their lifestyle that they were a part of the new order that Jesus had announced and that they believed had now arrived. Theologically, the church was a microcosm of the transformation that God's new order would bring for the whole world. To be in the church was to have a foretaste of life as God's new people. Socially, the church in the Roman empire was an alternative society, based not on selfishness, greed, and exploitation, but on the new freedom and fellowship that Jesus had announced: freedom to love God and to love and serve others (Mark 12:29–31). As the church expanded across the Mediterranean world, it was indeed a new society—a context in which people of diverse social, racial, and religious backgrounds were united in a new and radical friendship. Because they had been reconciled to God, they found themselves reconciled to each other.

The mission of radical disciples is to serve as midwives in the birthing process of twenty-first-century believers as they help the church transition from first to second half of life values and principles. Most of us are never told that we can set out from the known and the familiar to take on a further journey. This "further journey" is not chronological, nor does one magically stumble upon it at midlife or in times of crisis, thought these often serve as catalysts. While the second journey represents the culmination of one's faith journey, it is largely unknown today, even by people we consider deeply religious, since most individuals and institutions remain stymied in the preoccupations of the first half of life, establishing identity, creating boundary markers, and seeking security. The first half of life task, while essential, is not the full journey. Furthermore, one cannot walk the second journey with first-journey tools. One needs a new toolkit.

In our study of the meaning and message of the historical Jesus, it is important that we acknowledge the variety of individuals represented by modern disciples. In addition, discipleship is a deeply personal experience. Each disciple engages discipleship within a unique set of life circumstances and realities that even he or she cannot understand completely.

Called to Discipleship

Having asked family members and friends to reflect personally on their understanding of radical discipleship (see chapters 10 and 11 for these responses), at some point in the process it became evident that I was not exempt from their assigned task, so the following represents my response.

Responding to the first question of the assignment, I would define my understanding of discipleship in the twenty-first century by stating that discipleship involves viewing my vocation or career as a "calling" from God. According to this perspective, one's vocation can serve as one's primary form of service and ministry to God and others. The "radical" part of discipleship requires turning theory into practice, that is, converting talk into action. Radical discipleship, then, requires eliminating the gap between "talking the talk" and "walking the walk," a modern version of sayings such as "actions speak louder than words" and "practicing what you preach." If I were to summarize my understanding of discipleship in my vocational "calling" in one sentence or phrase, it would be "combining head and heart in my teaching and writing ministry."

To illustrate how this works from my life and faith journey, I start at the beginning. I grew up the only child of missionary parents in Costa Rica, a rugged and peaceful country in Central America. I spent my first eight years in a mountainous area of that country, on an orphanage/farm we called La Finca (The Farm) or El Hogar Bíblico (The Bible

Home), where on a clear day one could see both the Atlantic and the Pacific oceans. Working for the Latin America Mission (LAM), my parents served as houseparents, teachers, and worship leaders, and my father oversaw the local workers who tended the 180-acre farm, including the vegetable gardens and the dairy cows and livestock, enough to provide for the needs of sixty to eighty orphans. The farm also served as a coffee plantation, the coffee bushes used to produce income for the orphanage.

I never regretted growing up in that land of haunting beauty, often called "The Switzerland of the Americas." Bilingualism and biculturalism, inherited gifts, exposed me to diverse perspectives and lifestyles. A byproduct of that upbringing was a healthy curiosity about the world, its people, cultures, and terrain.

From the start, I loved to roam, and my earliest memory is about the time I got lost. As a toddler, I was often under the watchful eye of older children whose maternal and paternal instincts were already in bloom. My parents, with their busy schedules, appreciated those helping eyes and hands. However, youngsters are easily distracted, and it was during a careless moment that I wandered off. By the time my absence was discovered, I had vanished.

¿Donde está Roberto?" The cry of alarm quickly spread among the children, "Where did Robert go?" They looked everywhere, inside the house, in the school, and on the playground. Concern mounted as a search through the familiar haunts proved futile. They finally found me, lying next to a cow, fast asleep.

Given my upbringing, it seemed natural that I make a profession of faith at an early age, and I did so, sincerely, at the age of four. My first dramatic encounter with God, however, occurred two years later. It was siesta time, and my parents were inside, resting. Though I was free to play outdoors, I was warned not to climb trees, and especially not to eat the fruit of the *níspero* trees. However, like that young alchemist in the fables who was warned not to think of pink elephants whenever he attempted to make gold from base metals, lest the magical transformation be foiled, I couldn't resist the thought of juicy *nísperos* melting in my mouth.

Behind our dwelling, isolated from view, were several *níspero* trees, and on that day no one was around. I climbed one of the trees and began eating the forbidden fruit. However, in that moment, I was overcome by an eerie feeling. Everything was quiet, too quiet. The birds had stopped their singing, the insects their chirping, and I was existentially alone. Then I heard a rumbling sound. The trees began to shake and the earth convulsed. My heart pounded while I grasped the limb as tightly as possible. Our home, its flooring resting on three-foot-high columns, was shaking from the tremors. By then my entire body trembled with fear. My arms and legs shook like JELL-O, and I was unable to hang on to the limb any longer.

As soon as I hit the ground, the tremors subsided. The earthquake, quite common in that seismic region, was not particularly severe, but that day I understood the wrath of God, and I was sure that the earth had moved as punishment for my disobedience. God had been watching, and my guilt was exposed. Two years earlier I had experienced the embracing love of God, but this time it was God's wrath. I am thankful that my first experience with God, one of faith and not of fear, became the lasting one, for my relationship with God has remained one of affirmation and love.

Was I a disobedient or irresponsible child? Did this incident point to some fatal flaw in my character or disability in my developing spirituality? Not at all! On the contrary, it disclosed an adventurous self, a personality ready to push the boundaries, impelled by curiosity and in search of newness. Now, after having taught courses in world religions and as a professionally credentialed interpreter of the Myers-Briggs Type Indicator, I identify with the Hindu personality type called raja yoga, meaning that I self-identify spiritually with those who are scientifically or experimentally inclined. This identity is confirmed by my results as an NF in the MBTI and a three on the Enneagram (a Performer or Achiever, an ambitious personality driven to inspire others), and as an Apollonian on the Kiersey typology (a questing spirituality expressed in the search for Self, in hunger for self-actualization, and in longing for both unity and uniqueness).

When I was twelve, my parents were asked by the LAM Board to leave their idyllic Costa Rica and relocate to turbulent Colombia, a country that had recently emerged from a decade of violent social and political upheaval. It was a place of deep sectarian conflict, where the Protestant community had undergone violent persecution and where Fidel Castro had been inspired to become a militant Marxist. Since Colombia was not safe and did not provide sufficient academic opportunity, I enrolled at The Stony Brook School, a private Christian preparatory school in Long Island, not far from New York City, and that school became my home for the next three and a half years. While at Stony Brook, my faith deepened, as did my social and intellectual life, for it was there that I began integrating head and heart, fully embracing the school motto, "character before career."

From 1961 to 1965, The King's College (TKC) was my home. Located in a former resort on the outskirts of exclusive Briarcliff Manor, New York, I thrived in this Christian setting, excelling academically and spiritually. My years at TKC were some of the best of my life. I made great friends, had wonderful experiences, and befriended individuals at all levels of college life, including the resident custodian in the men's dorm, members of the maintenance crew, with whom I worked part-time, and members of the faculty and administration. In addition to serving in student government, I also played varsity soccer. My faith was nurtured at daily chapel services, Sunday evening services, and accompanying the college president, Dr. Bob Cook, on his speaking and preaching engagements. I also spent two summers traveling the country representing the college as pianist for musical gospel teams. One summer, in addition to musical accompaniment, I preached over sixty times at church services and other church related events. Following graduation, I remained at the college for a year, working in the language lab and supervising an off-campus dormitory.

In 1966 I enrolled in a graduate program in Latin American Studies at Indiana University, in preparation for possible missionary work or a career in teaching or diplomacy. Though I found Latin American Studies fascinating, I remained undecided about a career and applied to Princeton Theological Seminary, one of America's leading theological institutions, intending to study ethics and ecumenism. During my first year in the divinity program my attention gravitated to biblical studies, partly because of my strong background in the subject but also through the influence of one of the leading scholars at the institution, Dr. Bruce Metzger, a gracious scholar with a stellar international reputation and a conservative approach to the Bible.

Upon completing a divinity degree, I transferred my church membership to the Presbyterian Church and remained at Princeton Seminary, enrolling in the PhD program in biblical studies. Discerning a call to ministry, I sought ordination in my adoptive denomination and accepted the pastorate of a small congregation while I completed the dissertation phase of my program. Though my work at the church was meaningful, I found the administrative side tedious. Aware that my gift definitely lay in academics, I accepted a teaching position at Grove City College, a Presbyterian-related liberal arts college, and later at Washington &

Jefferson College, where I taught religion courses in addition to serving as department chair and as college chaplain. For the next forty years, I taught a college course in either Old or New Testament every semester, in addition to courses in theology, world religions, and spirituality.

The Journey of Faith: A Transformative Process

In retrospect, I find that my spiritual journey followed a religious paradigm that views one's faith story as a journey through three stages: precritical understanding (also called primary naiveté), critical understanding (a skeptical stage reflection the collision between one's childhood beliefs and those of modernity), and postcritical understanding (also called secondary naiveté). While many individuals experience all three stages fully and chronologically, as I did, some remain in the precritical phase—a state in which they accept without question those values and beliefs they received from parents and other significant authority figures in their lives. For others, this state is short-lived, abandoned in their adolescent years or during college or early adulthood, a time in life when they began questioning the existence of God and other inherited religious beliefs.

While many seekers today choose to remain in this critical phase, perplexed by the competing views promoted by multicultural traditions, world religions, and by secular worldviews, those who persevere in their faith journey discover that agnosticism and atheism are not final destinations but rather temporary stops. That has been my experience. Though my engagement with the critical perspective began seriously during my graduate and postgraduate studies at Princeton Theological Seminary, I did not fully commit to that phase until the final years of my midlife, well into the second half of my teaching career at Washington & Jefferson College. Then, for a two-week period, I became an atheist. During that brief period I became convinced that God, however conceived, did not exist. Strangely, despite a sense of deep loss, I found the awareness exhilarating, for I had based this conclusion on my own experience.

For a year I had immersed myself in scientific and philosophical literature, searching for an understanding of God in these academic disciplines. I took seriously the conclusions of Richard Dawkins and other "new atheists" and found convincing the methodology of former evangelical John W. Loftus outlined in The Outsider Test for Faith. This device encourages people from various faith traditions to assess their truth claims from the perspective of an outsider and with the same level of skepticism they use to evaluate other faith traditions. Applying this methodology to my own religious perspective, I spent a year subjecting my religious beliefs to logical scrutiny, temporarily replacing faith presuppositions with rational and scientifically verifiable premises. This undertaking infected me with rational thinking, labeled "the philosopher's disease" by a Zen Buddhist sage. While the critical phase brings euphoria, closure, and a sense of freedom to some, my experience left me scarred, emotionally and intellectually, a condition exacerbated by my religious upbringing, my vocation, and my ordination vows.

Eventually those who persevere in their faith journey find their religious perception transformed by what might be called "an experience of sacred mystery." Something happens to them—a mystical experience, something traumatic, a relationship, a sudden realization, a wilderness experience, an experience of "something more"—and the word "God" becomes meaningful once again, only this time not as a reference to a supernatural being "out there" but to the sacred at the center of existence, the holy mystery that is all around us and within us. God is no longer a mere idea or an article of belief external to oneself but rather an element of experience. Such persons have reached postcritical understanding, a state where one participates in religious rituals because they are meaningful and not because they are required, where one hears ancient biblical stories as "true" while knowing them as not literally true.

During my first year at Princeton Theological Seminary I read Bishop John A. T. Robinson's best-seller, *Honest to God*. The book, published in 1963, sent shock waves around the Christian world. Robinson, the English Bishop of Woolwich, had taken the writings of three seminal Christian thinkers—Rudolph Bultmann, the leading New Testament scholar in his generation; Dietrich Bonhoeffer, the German Lutheran pastor who had participated in the underground anti-Nazi resistance movement and who had been hanged at a German prison camp in 1945; and Paul Tillich, the most widely read theologian in the twentieth century—and made their thought accessible to the population at large. Bultmann referred to the biblical scripture as "mythology" that needed to be "demythologized," since its message had been framed in the presuppositions of an ancient world that no longer existed. Tillich, who suggested that God could no longer be conceptualized through the analogy of a person, developed a transpersonal theology in which God was perceived as "the Ground of All Being." Bonhoeffer called for the development of "religionless Christianity," arguing that just as Christianity in the first century could not be contained within Judaism, so in our day Christianity could no longer be contained within religion.

Like other seminarians, I studied Bultmann, Bonhoeffer, and Tillich and found their ideas intriguing and perceptive. Although Robinson's book and others like it were conceptually exciting, they did not square with my Christian upbringing or current "belief system." I eventually set them aside as contextual to my divinity training and continued preparing for ministry within the church. Such thinking was "modern" and I remained guarded.

Later, at Chautauqua Institution, I heard lectures by cutting-edge scholar Karen Armstrong and "Jesus scholars" Marcus Borg and John Dominic Crossan. I purchased their books and read them thoroughly, incorporating some of their ideas into my lectures. I read books on comparative religions and grappled with John Hick's notion of "religious pluralism" and Brian McLaren's concepts of "a new kind of Christian" and "a generous orthodoxy." Although these writers tilled the soil of my spirit and sowed transformative seeds, none prompted the wake-up call that I experienced during the first week of the 2010 Chautauqua season, when I attended a weeklong series of lectures delivered by Anglican Bishop Spong, who was promoting *Eternal Life: A New Vision*, another intriguing volume in his controversial writing career.

For that series of talks, which included a panel discussion and five public lectures, a crowd of over one thousand people gathered to listen, to question, and to interact with key concepts from Spong's writings. In keeping with my customary response to such presentations, I took copious notes, purchasing and then reading several of the speaker's books. During the ensuing academic year, while transcribing notes from that experience, I recognized the effect cosmic and human evolution had upon Spong's theology, and my outlook changed dramatically. Shortly thereafter, while watching a videotaped lecture series by evolutionary biologist Richard Dawkins titled *Growing Up in the Universe*,[1] the defensive walls of my worldview were breached as I accepted biological evolution

---

1. *Growing Up in the Universe* is a series of lectures given by Richard Dawkins as part of the Royal Institution Christmas Lectures, in which he discusses the evolution of life in the universe. The lectures were first broadcast in 1991, in the form of five one-hour episodes, on the BBC in the UK. The Richard Dawkins Foundation for Reason and Science was granted the rights to the televised lectures, and a DVD version was released by the foundation in 2007.

as foundational for my worldview. That decision forced me to re-examine my belief system and its assumptions. No concept, however sacred, was exempt from scrutiny.

As a result, I arrived at nine realizations that inform my belief and behavior:

1. the certainty of human evolution
2. the compatibility of science with religion (Christianity)
3. the harmony of faith and reason
4. the inherent limitations of dogmatism
5. the need to read scripture metaphorically
6. the multivalency of scriptural texts
7. the Jewishness of original Christianity
8. the fallibility of supernatural theism; and
9. the experience of love in the universe.

In 2011, while doing research for *Beyond Belief*, my book on faith, reason, and science, I came across the term "panentheism." For some time I had struggled with the idea of a personal God, knowing that while such a view makes God accessible to human beings, supernatural theism, which attributes personal qualities to God, is unambiguously anthropomorphic. While it is natural to personify God in worship, insuperable problems arise when we literalize these personifications. The extremes of this position, such as presented in the Hebrew scriptures, raise serious problems for people in the modern era. This God fights wars and defeats enemies, chooses people and works through them, sends storms, heals the sick, spares the dying, rewards goodness, and punishes evil. Many people have trouble intellectually with these anthropomorphic renderings of God and with the seeming irrationality of belief in a personal God.

In panentheism I found a theological model that provides a satisfactory conception of God and of the incarnation. This perspective finds the Being of God including and penetrating the entire universe, but (as against pantheism) God's Being is more than the universe. According to this view, God is in everything and everything is in God. Yet God is greater still. Unlike pantheism, which depersonalizes and dehistoricizes, panentheism personalizes reality, seeking God as the inner truth, depth, and center of all being.

Openness to Adventure

Earlier in this chapter, I described temperamental qualities and personal experiences from my childhood that disposed me to newness and opened me to adventure, both in my faith and life journey. Here I add further examples from later stages in my journey. During my studies at Princeton Theological Seminary, I read about John Goddard, an adventurer who spent his life pursuing 127 goals that he had devised at the age of fifteen. These goals, amazingly varied, included exploring the Nile River; writing a book; composing music; learning to play "Clair de Lune" on the piano; teaching a college course; studying primitive cultures in New Guinea; learning French, Spanish, and Arabic; running a five-minute mile; climbing the Matterhorn; circumnavigating the globe; and flying an airplane. I found such an approach to life quite compelling, although I knew I would never be that adventurous. At that time I purchased a Schwinn Varsity bicycle from a high school student who had discovered that a bicycle pedal could not compete with a car's accelerator. I paid $50 for the ten-speed bike, knowing very little about frame sizes or components.

During the next sixteen years, as I began a career in the pastorate and then as a college professor, the Schwinn saw limited use, primarily on short rides around town with my family or on summer vacations at the shore. By the summer of 1984, in my second teaching position, I was ready once again for adventure. I had recently acquired cross-country skiing and flatwater kayaking skills, but I needed a more expansive outlet. I dusted off the old Schwinn, oiled its moving parts, pumped up the tires, and began to set goals. Initially, short trips provided adequate exercise, but as my conditioning improved, I looked for greater challenges. Soon I was climbing some of the hills for which western Pennsylvania is famous, and my trips turned into outings.

One day, while looking through a bicycle catalogue, I decided to buy a better bicycle. The Schwinn Varsity was great for kids. It was sturdy and durable, but at forty-two pounds it was too heavy for touring and its twenty-three-inch frame was too small for my lanky six-foot-one-inch body. At a bicycle outlet in Ohio I selected my first new bicycle, a metallic-blue fifteen-speed touring bike. This time I knew something about frame sizes and components, and I gladly paid $350 for a custom chrome-moly twenty-five-inch Japanese touring bicycle that weighed fifteen pounds less than the old Schwinn. I purchased a roof rack, a good helmet, a pair of gloves, and some cycling apparel. The thrill of bicycle riding was rekindled and I was ready for some serious riding. Ten- and fifteen-mile-rides turned into twenty- and thirty-mile trips. Cycling was becoming addictive.

In the fall of 1987 I began cycling year-round, a strategy that led to planning my own bike trek across the United States. In 1989, after receiving approval for a sabbatical that fall, I initiated plans for a late-summer trip across the North American continent, following a course close to the Canadian border. *The Invisible Mountain*, my second book, focuses on that period of forty-two days in the summer of 1989 when I translated my dream of a cross-country cycling trip into a trek on behalf of Habitat for Humanity, utilizing adventure as a means to help disadvantaged citizens. As I cycled across the "northern tier" of the North American continent, I matured as an individual and grew spiritually by going "Homeless for Habitat."

The lessons I learned through that trip prepared me for the two-month pilgrimage related in *Into Thin Places*, a journey that began a mere three weeks after the cycling trip. That journey—a quest for ancestral, cultural, and spiritual identity—was intentional. I mapped out an overland route, noting must-see cultural, archaeological, and religious sites along the way. As a professor of religious studies and an ordained college chaplain, I designed an itinerary through Europe, the Middle East, and Africa that would enable me to appreciate and better understand my roots. My objectives included (a) visiting religious and cultural centers in the region, (b) exploring archaeological sites and museums, (c) conversing with Israelis and Palestinians on matters of mutual concern, (d) gaining a perspective not ordinarily achieved in guided tours, and (e) exploring my identity to better understand its spiritual core or center. The experiences of 1989 led me to embrace as motto the memorable spiritual principle, "Life is an adventure to be lived, not a problem to be solved."

My training, experience, and writing ministry eventually led me to a model of the spiritual journey known as the "second half of life." As I noted earlier, this "further journey," largely unknown today, represents the culmination of one's faith journey. The first task of the journey is to build a strong "container" or identity; the second is to find the contents that the container is meant to hold.² The first task—surviving successfully—is obvious, one we take for granted as the purpose of life. We all want to complete successfully the task that life first hands us: establishing an identity, a home, a career, relationships, friends, community, and security, all foundational for getting started in life. Many cultures throughout history, most empires in antiquity, and the majority of individuals in the modern period have focused on first half of life tasks, primarily because it is all they have time for, but also for lack of vision.

Most of us are never told that we can set out from the known and the familiar to take on a further journey. Our institutions, including our churches, are almost entirely configured to encourage, support, reward, and validate the tasks of the first half of life. Shocking and disappointing as it may be, we struggle more to survive than to thrive, focusing on "getting through" or on getting ahead rather than on finding out what is at the top or was already at the bottom. As wilderness guide Bill Plotkin puts it, many of us learn to do our "survival dance," but we never get to our actual "sacred dance."

How can we know we are entering the second half of life? The following road markers are quite reliable: when we

- experience new urges
- sense a new vision
- are ready to let go of old securities
- are ready to risk giving up the patterns of the past for the promise of the future
- are ready to embrace nonduality³
- are as focused on the "inner" life as on the outer dimension of life.

While individuals can describe their experience of the second journey and even serve as mentors, they cannot define or outline the journey

---

2. Rohr, *Falling Upward*, xiii.

3. Duality thinking, also called polarity thinking or all-or-nothing thinking, is the bane of spirituality. More than with any other personality trait in our lives, all-or-nothing thinking causes huge mistakes and bad judgments. It results in withholding love, misinterpreting situations, and hurting both others and ourselves. Dualistic thinking is not wrong or bad in itself—in fact, it is necessary in most situations. However, it is completely inadequate for the major questions and dilemmas of life. Second half of life people are "yes/and" thinkers who avoid getting trapped in the small world of "either/or," except in the ways of love and courage, where they are "all in."

for others. This is due both to the uniqueness of the journey and to a subtle factor, known by generations of mystics and spiritual masters but elusive to many of our contemporaries: We do not choose this second journey; rather it chooses us. It finds us by means of our soul, our personal center and true home, the source of our true belonging. The soul comes to our aid through dreams, deep emotion, love, the quiet voice of guidance, synchronicities, revelations, hunches, and visions, and at times through illness, nightmares, and terrors. This is the identity that defines us, aligning us with our powers of nurturing, transforming, and creating, with our powers of presence and wonder. It is the soul that guides us, preparing the way and declaring us ready for this further journey.

Recently, former U.S. Vice President Mike Pence was greeted by a pro-Trump rally with hissing and booing. Trying to speak over a disgruntled minority, who apparently defined him by partisan standards, Pence responded by baring his soul, informing the audience that he was a Christian, a conservative, and a Republican, in that order. While labeling others or oneself is not generally helpful, since self-awareness changes over time, sometimes situations require taking a stand. Mike Pence took a stand, and if I were forced to name my top three descriptors, they would be human (a global citizen), panentheist, and nondualist, in that order. What such terms mean, of course, changes frequently. If asked to define your current identity in three words, how would you respond?

In the Bible, spirituality is truth telling. However, the Bible communicates its truth not superficially, such as through facts or formulas, but profoundly, through story and myth. Think of "creation" in the Old Testament and "incarnation" in the New. Such teaching is not meant to be rational nor informative. In other words, these accounts do not use fact or science to convey truth, but rather metaphor and poetry to convey meaning.

When I am concerned with meaning and spirituality, I seek to unify head and heart, for discipleship, like spiritual truth, is understood holistically. The following lines clarify my understanding of discipleship:

Those who are unaware, theorize;
Those who are aware, actualize.
Those who are unaware, criticize;
Those who are aware, harmonize.

Questions for Discussion and Reflection

1. This chapter provides a tentative definition to the phrase "radical discipleship." In a sentence or two, offer your own definition or understanding of the phrase.
2. Do you agree with the author's statement that in order to provide society with transformative vision, each generation of Jesus' disciples needs to rethink its theology and practice? Explain your answer.
3. If Jesus were a contemporary of ours, would he be theologically progressive or conservative? Explain your answer.
4. If Jesus were a contemporary of ours, would his reading of scripture be primarily literal or metaphorical? Explain your answer.
5. Assess the merits of considering one's vocation or career as a "calling" from God and therefore as a primary part of one's discipleship.
6. In your estimation, explain what role (whether positive or negative) your upbringing had in affirming or supporting your current understanding of radical discipleship.
7. If possible, identify specific experiences or aspects of your childhood and adolescence that helped shape or nourish your personality and spirituality types.
8. If possible, identify specific experiences or aspects of your educational training that influenced your personality and spirituality types.
9. In speaking of his journey of faith, the author outlines a three-stage process of precritical, critical, and postcritical understanding. Does your faith journey follow a similar pattern? Explain your answer.
10. Assess the merits of John Loftus's Outsider Test for Faith.
11. Explain and assess the merits of the spiritual journey as two halves of life. Using this model, are you currently in the first, the second, or in some other phase of your spiritual journey? Explain your answer.
12. If you were to define your current spiritual identity in three words, what would they be? Explain your answer.

Chapter 10

Radical Discipleship Illustrated, Part II

THIS CHAPTER CONTAINS FOUR strikingly different accounts, each a journey into Christian discipleship. Despite their differences, all four participants illustrate their understanding of discipleship from their life and faith journey. The first and third accounts are by two of my family members. The first, by my wife Susan, focuses on discipleship as a mentoring process, and the third, by my daughter Sara, a busy mother who set aside an important career to focus on her family, speaks of discipleship as the journey of a lifetime. The second and fourth accounts are by two friends of mine, Tony and Marybeth, one a licensed psychotherapist, peace activist, and renowned baritone, and the other a skilled nurse serving in an administrative capacity in a large urban hospital. Both are members of a local discussion group whose members read and study my published books.

When I first asked my wife Susan to complete the assignment on discipleship, her initial response was direct and succinct: "Discipleship is about putting others' needs above your own." In my estimation, that definition of discipleship is classic, about as attractive and alluring as D. T. Niles's famous definition of evangelism: "Evangelism is one beggar telling another beggar where to find bread." Thankfully, I received a lengthier typed response from Susan a few weeks later.

As Susan's husband, I am amazed at her vision, strength, and tenacity. An eight on the Enneagram, she is a strong advocate of others, especially those in need or otherwise marginalized by society. Pastoring a Presbyterian congregation throughout much of my teaching career, she also devoted time to rear two strong, caring, and resilient children, now devoted parents and committed Christians whose faith stories appear in this and the next chapter. In addition Susan was elected to serve as the first clergywoman moderator of the Synod of the Trinity, a higher judicatory in the Presbyterian Church (USA) that includes oversight of all member churches in Pennsylvania, West Virginia, and parts of eastern Ohio.

During her career, she mentored seminary students and led various men and women into church ministry while serving on numerous governing and oversight committees and boards, including at Washington Hospital, the C.A.R.E Center (a substance abuse counseling and rehab facility), Resurrection Power (a ministry with housing for men and women in recovery), Pittsburgh Theological Seminary, and as president of the board of The Presbyterian House at Chautauqua Institution, in addition to her work with Gestalt Pastoral Care Associates, Inc.

Susan's Discipleship Story: Consenting to Grace

Growth in the Christian faith is a journey under the guidance of others toward becoming the person one is created and called to be. This discipleship process happens under the guidance of the Holy Spirit and takes many forms. It can be a result of crisis and the ensuing opportunity that comes along with trauma or it can be a slow and intentional training.

For me, discipleship began at a young age. My father was a strict and loving disciplinarian. He set high standards for the whole family in loving neighbor and making the world a better place. He personally mentored young men through the Boy Scout program. However, my mother was my primary mentor as she showed me how to navigate a troubled world in her personal contact with individuals whether she was volunteering in her children's schools or directing volunteers at a large medical hospital. I followed in their footsteps as I led young women as a Girl Scout leader and offered personal care to others through my profession as a local church pastor.

In the Christian Education department of a large downtown church in Buffalo where Sunday school classes were provided from pre-school through adult, the female leaders asked me to assist in pre-school classes when I was still in elementary school. Later in middle and high school, I assisted elementary school teachers in their classrooms. The youth pastor and his wife took me and other high school students under their wing in small groups and retreats to lead us into personal relationship with Jesus

Christ and a life commitment to God. In summers before college, I was a camp counselor at a church camp on Lake Erie.

After college and a personal encounter with the living Christ in a small congregation in Connecticut, I volunteered to lead the high school youth in activities and Christian development. From there I left for seminary to prepare for a career in pastoral ministry. Women have mostly been my guides and mentors in discipleship. While women were not commonly found in pastoral roles during the 1970s, I met two strong women from the Black church who led retreats, preached in a few churches, and crafted me in the most important aspects of discipleship—taking on the mind of Christ and following in the footsteps of Jesus to reach out to others in love, healing, and discipleship.

Mostly women and some men discipled me along this soul enhancing journey continuing through seminary and later as a pastor and finally in a doctoral program of pastoral care and spiritual formation. At that point I began the process of mentoring younger disciples. While I served as pastor, several seminary students asked me to provide oversight of their required practical church training.

Not only with individuals, but also when I sat on nonprofit boards, the Holy Spirit led me to creative change and making a difference in the structure and sometimes in the progression of the organization. I was privileged to serve Pittsburgh Theological Seminary on the Board of Directors for almost twenty years. Relationships with faculty and administrators enhanced mutual personal guiding and spiritual formation along the journey that does not end in one's early adulthood, but continues along the whole spectrum of life experience.

For me this full circle process was enhanced in retirement as I took in-depth training for a ministry of healing and spiritual growth under the founder of Gestalt Pastoral Care (GPC), Tilda Norberg. In her book, *Consenting to Grace* (2006), Norberg introduces techniques associated with Gestalt Pastoral Care, an approach to caregiving that pays particular attention to another person's way of perceiving the world. Gestalt Pastoral Care ministers, as taught by Norberg and other trainers, are on their own journey to healing. Practicing contemplation and allowing God's love to flow through them, GPC ministers seek to enter the world of the persons they are guiding, knowing that people have their own perceptual style, life experience, and pain.

Gestalt Pastoral Care is an amalgam of Gestalt theory, spiritual companioning, and healing in the way of Jesus. This holistic ministry is a discipling process in itself in which the Gestalt Pastoral Care Minister works with groups and individuals to heal the brokenness of trauma and life experiences. The spiritual power in this ministry is the capstone of my life of following in the footsteps of Jesus as guided by many individuals. Those who are trained in Gestalt Pastoral Care train others and continue the work through discipling others.

Whether recognized throughout church history as leaders in the Christian faith or not, women were disciples of Jesus (Luke 8:2,3) and directed the faithful in the church from the earliest times (Tabitha in Acts 9:36, Mary with a house church in Acts 12:12, Lydia with a prayer ministry in Acts 16:14, Priscilla teaching in Acts 18:26, and many others). Most people miss the fact that Mary Magdalene was the first member and apostle of the church of Jesus Christ as she recognized Jesus in his resurrected form and told others about it.

Tony's Discipleship Story: Peacing it Together

The life of the compassionate Jesus offers us a clear blueprint for how Christians are to live in this world. His message of good news elevated the poor, the prisoner, the downtrodden, and the dispossessed. His compassionate message was one of liberation and justice for the marginalized.

I learned as a young child that Jesus was an ever-present help in times of trouble. Following Jesus would not only assure the gift of heaven, but it would also make life a much better experience for me if I accepted him into my heart. Learning to follow Jesus is not only derived from reading the Bible, it is reinforced by parents, mentors, and famous courageous people who dared to live exemplary lives. For African Americans, Jesus has also been our balm in Gilead, a place to turn when the storms of life are raging. His suffering made meaningful our suffering, for we knew Jesus understood and cared about our corporate and individual pain. His resurrection gives hope that we too will be free one day.

The first eight years of my life were spent in the Hill District, an African American community in the city of Pittsburgh. It provided a rich and vital cultural heritage for our family, giving us a place to belong and to thrive. It was here where I learned about the resilience of the human spirit, and the idea that God was our refuge. Church life was a central part of our family's routine. Prayer was an essential discipline that we utilized to aid us in our struggles. Prayer time was usually getting on our knees and praying fervently for God to walk with us in our struggles. Thanking God for standing with us was also an important part of our prayers. We understood that we were to have the compassion of Christ in our hearts and open ourselves to loving our misinformed enemies.

When I was eight years old my parents bought a farmhouse on ten acres of land in a rural setting outside the city. The owner of the farm did not like his neighbors, so he sold his property to us to spite them. My parents wanted to give their children a better educational experience, so we moved to a white rural setting where the quality of education was significantly better. This move was made possible in the aftermath of the 1954 Brown vs Board of Education Supreme Court decision, which made it unlawful to segregate public schools.

I remember clearly the day my sister, brother, and I walked down the lane to catch the school bus. When we arrived at the end of the lane, the lady in the house by the lane raised her window and begin yelling at us. We knew we had done nothing to cause such a fury. Our parents told us to say nothing to this lady. We were told that she was misguided and was a victim of her own life circumstances. All human beings are basically the same, but this lady thought of herself as qualitatively better than us. The idea of the superiority of those of European descent is a social construction. Its roots run very deep in our country. Even now white supremist groups are on the rise as the gradual demographic shifts in the nation predict that by 2050 those of European descent will be in the minority.

My mother made it clear to us that we were not inferior to anyone. We know now through the wonders of modern science that aside from the few genes that determine the extent of melanin in our skin, the rest are genetically identical. We were in a country where we were not valued, and it was emotionally costly for all of us. My mother told us to be respectful and to recite Psalm Twenty-Three as we waited for the bus.

My mother began raising money for various charities and went to houses in the community to solicit funds. She always stopped at the home where the yelling lady lived, and the lady would always make a donation. I watched my mother over the years relate to this lady around the various charities she was supporting. My mother had the mind of Christ and sought to find common ground using charities to connect to this white lady. Human contact with my mother gave this white lady an opportunity to have a corrective experience. Eventually the family was invited to have dinner in our home and the white lady would have tea with my mother from time to time. I witnessed a slow transformation of this white woman, brought on by a mother who had love and compassion for her enemies. My mother understood the words of Jesus when he said "Love your neighbor as yourself."

It was not always easy for me in the new school environment. I was a third grader now in school with kids of Irish, German, Polish, Italian, and French extraction. I was the only African American student in the class. On the first day of class I entered the classroom after all of the students were seated at their desks. I remember well what happened when I walked into the classroom. The students were surprised to see me and giggled nervously, using the N-word to describe me. It was a statement not so much about the young impressionable students, but about the larger environment they were living in. This way of thinking starts early and can perpetuate hate for a lifetime.

Weeks later the superintendent of the school district entered our classroom, had a few words with the teacher, and then approached my desk. He asked me to go with him. I was terrified, thinking I had done something wrong. Once outside of the classroom, he got down on one knee, looked me in the eyes, and said "I hear you can sing! How about we go to the other classes and you sing a song for the students?" He had heard from the music teacher that I had musical talent. Since I could not refuse the superintendent of the school district, I went with him, was introduced by him to other students, and proceeded to sing. It was a powerful moment as the students seemingly humanized me and were impressed that the superintendent had brought me to their classroom.

This was a transformative moment for the teachers and students that day. It helped me on the playground as I was easily included by my peers in their games. I later learned that the superintendent was a devout Christian. His Christian faith had motivated him to reach out to me, and I felt affirmed and safe. It was a teachable moment for us all.

One act of compassion can have a profound rippling effect on a community. It is now our time to be compassionate members of our communities, to be motivated by the heart of Christ to transform lives. I knew as a young child that my life mattered and that I was here on earth to make a difference in the world. My mother used to remind me that when she was pregnant with me, she would lay her hands on her belly and pray that this child would be a church minister.

Even though I didn't meet the expectations of my family, I found a way to use God-given gifts to further that sense of call through music and story. In partial fulfillment of her dream for my life, during my junior and senior years I attended Central Christian High School in Ohio as a boarding student. It was a Mennonite school, and while there I learned about Mennonite theology and culture, including the concept of "the centrality of Jesus." The beatitudes in Jesus' Sermon on the Mount also helped clarify what it meant to follow Jesus, and they set a high standard.

While at that school, the music teacher, Mr. Ewing, came to me with a proposal: "I have a study hall at the same time that you do. How about we meet weekly, and I will teach you vocal technique?" I agreed, and the results changed my life. Mr. Ewing entered me into vocal competitions, which I won. From then on, music would be an essential part of my life. In addition, Mr. Ewing became my mentor and later my friend.

I studied at Mennonite colleges during my undergraduate years. I had mentors who were peacemakers and who were adamant in the belief that Jesus came to bring a new order and to build God's kingdom here on earth. In the beatitudes, Jesus explicitly tells us what we are to become when we choose to follow him. We are to be meek, merciful, peacemakers, seek righteousness, and be willing to be persecuted for righteousness' sake. This is God's message to us through Jesus.

While in college I requested Selective Service conscientious objector status, seeking to serve my country through alternative service, for I stood in opposition to the Vietnam war. It did not seem to me that killing my Vietnamese brothers and sisters displayed the mind of Christ. I was denied conscientious objector status, but because I received a high lottery number, I was not obligated to participate in the U.S. war machine. Committed to loving my enemies, I would have been ready to go to prison for my faith.

I now find that I love to connect with people of different perspectives and walks of life. My goal is to find places of intersection where we can connect across our differences. Becoming a professional psychotherapist and college professor, teaching social sciences and serving as artist in residence, I continued to study music and sing across the United States. Eventually I traveled to global conflict areas, using music and the spoken word to bring people together across divides that had torn them apart. Despite the divides of race, culture, nationality, and religion, we are one humanity. I believe we have far more in common than many accept, and that we must find common places where we can meet each other as part of this great human family.

In 2007 I created a foundation titled Peacing It Together. The foundation uses music and storytelling to bring people together in areas of conflict. My travels have taken me to many areas of conflict, including Northern Ireland, Bosnia, Ethiopia, Uganda, Colombia, Thailand, Philippines. China, and Vietnam. While there, I have had the opportunity to speak to government officials, educators, religious leaders, paramilitary groups, and young people.

I have a concern for the United States as well, and am committed to the serious challenges that face my country. I think the true test of one's faith is not to travel far away to tend to the concerns of others, but in facing the challenges at home. For those willing to declare Jesus as Lord, there is a great deal of work to be done here in the United States. I offer my time and energy to work toward dismantling racism, sexism, homophobia, nationalism, and gun violence.

The following words attributed to sixteenth century Spanish saint Teresa of Ávila are words of wisdom for us all: "Christ has no body now but yours. No hands, no feet on earth but yours. Yours are the eyes through which he looks compassion on this world. Yours are the feet with which he walks to do good. Yours are the hands through which he blesses all the world. Yours are the hands, yours are the feet, yours are the eyes, you are his body. Christ has no body now on earth but yours."

In my efforts to further God's kingdom in the United States, I am intentional about relating to others across the current political divide. While making friends on the far left and the far right, I seek ways beyond politics. I have learned that when we are respectful and able to get beyond dogma and fear, we all have the same interests, hopes, and dreams. A weekly pancake breakfast with men on the political right has taught me that when we get beyond politics there is a fertile field for building God's beloved community. Former President John Kennedy said it well when he stated, "God's work here on earth must truly be our own." Discipleship is doing God's work together!

Sara's Discipleship Story: Character before Career

Becoming a disciple of Jesus begins with a decision—a choice to believe in him, accept him into your heart, and follow him. The decision can be made in an instant. Discipleship itself is the intentional, lifelong discipline of following Jesus.

When we accept Jesus and the gift of salvation, the Holy Spirit dwells in us and begins the lifelong process of sanctification, or making us more like Jesus. Discipleship involves growing in relationship with Jesus through disciplines like prayer, Bible study, worship, and meditation. Further, discipleship involves making disciples of others and encouraging them in their faith. However, Christian discipleship does not stop there: "faith by itself, if it has no works, is dead" (Jas 2:17). This is not to say that our action is a means to salvation. It is not. Rather, our faith is meant to produce good works that bring glory to God and benefit to others. We are called to love God and others above ourselves. We are called to live out our faith—to care for orphans and widows, give to those in need, do good, seek justice, and correct oppression.

My discipleship story began as a young child and continues today. You could even say it started before I was born. As the grandchild of Baptist missionaries and child of Presbyterian pastors, I accepted Jesus into my heart as a young child. I grew up in the church. I loved God, simply and sincerely. My grandparents and parents—through their profession of ministry and their personal lives—discipled me in my faith and modeled for me what it meant to be a Christian. Thus, beginning in childhood, I sought to know God and to honor him with how I lived my life. I prayed, read the Bible, and attended church regularly.

Starting in high school, I earnestly desired God's will and purpose for my life. Like most students, I looked to fulfill my purpose through the pursuit of a certain career. Given my family's calling into ministry, I grappled with whether to pursue a career in ministry or one outside of a traditional ministry vocation. After high school, I attended Mount Holyoke College—a diverse, all-women's college—where I made friends from all over the world, including from cultural and religious backgrounds different from my own. Some of them remain my dearest friends today. During college, I participated in InterVarsity Christian Fellowship, where I was further discipled in my faith and later encouraged others in theirs by leading Bible study groups. During several summers, I worked at a Christian camp, helping youth to encounter Christ. At this time, my desire focused on developing character, and I discovered that character is built on faith in God and results in caring for others.

It was at Mount Holyoke that I began to study international development (which involves addressing poverty and injustice in developing countries) and environmental studies—two areas that sparked a God-given passion in me. God calls us to help those in need, and to care for what he has entrusted to us. I began to understand that being a disciple of Jesus influenced how I interacted not only with others, but also with the social and natural environment within the United States and around the world. For me, pursuing an advanced degree in public policy with a specialization in international development, and a career in international development, was my way of fulfilling my purpose.

For a decade, I worked at RTI International, furthering its mission to improve the human condition in developing countries. For me, it was a means to an end—a way of helping people who were suffering and in poverty around the world. This work became my calling. It also felt like an extension of the work that my grandparents began in developing countries decades before—sharing the love of Jesus and helping those in need. During this time, I got married. Two years later, I gave birth to my son and then my daughter after that. When I became a mother, my focus naturally shifted to my children.

In this new season of life, I have found my calling in loving and caring for my children. Discipleship has involved raising my children to love God and others. Not working outside of the home has enabled me to fully embrace this season of my life and my calling as a mother. It has also afforded me the opportunity to grow deeper in my faith and serve in my church community. In doing so, I have sought to encourage other women, mothers, and children in their faith through serving in women's Bible study, Mothers of Preschoolers (MOPS), and children's ministry. Further, being a disciple has meant staying informed and engaged in what is going on the world, and doing my part to advocate for the needs of others. By teaching my children about Jesus and living out my faith in these ways, I hope to instill in my children the same love for Christ and others that my grandparents and parents did in me.

My experience as a disciple has taught me that in different seasons of life, God's calling may look different, but God uses and equips those who are willing and obedient—no matter their background, education, or vocation—for it is God's Spirit working in and through us that produces every good work.

Further, it has taught me that remaining in Christ, and prioritizing him above all else, is central to being a disciple. Throughout my life, I have strived to do my best in everything I do, but I have often been reminded that striving in my own effort—without remaining connected to God—is in vain. It is only through abiding in Christ that my life can bear fruit (John 15:4). There are many priorities and responsibilities pulling

Christians in different directions, but for me to be right with others, I must first be right with God. Discipleship begins with God. When we remain in Christ and prioritize him first, discipleship follows naturally, and everything else falls into place. If we focus on God, prioritizing the teachings of Christ, all other priorities and responsibilities will remain on target.

As I look back on my life, I am grateful for my grandparents and parents, who have discipled me in my faith and have modeled what it means to live out the Christian faith. I am ever grateful to God for his incredible love and grace, and for his Spirit working in and through me to accomplish what I could not on my own.

Marybeth's Discipleship Story: Always Questioning

When asked to describe radical/authentic discipleship in the twenty-first century, I thought of the dictionary definition: a disciple is a student or learner in training, one in pursuit of knowledge and following a specific discipline. For Christianity, a disciple is a person in the process of being more like Jesus.

Of course, this is not a new concern, for it began with the first disciples, but as a twenty-first-century disciple, I wonder if Christianity has not lost the authenticity of the discipline taught by Jesus. By making the Christian life complicated, Christianity has created division rather than unity. Much can be said about the evolution of intelligence and consciousness in humans over time, as well as the effects of power, materialism, and social inequities that influence the church, but can we simply get back to the basics of being more like Jesus? My hope and prayer is that I am part of that process.

I am an inquisitive person, and I find I always learn best through reflection and by asking questions. As I reflect on my life, I realize that being a disciple involves a series of stages, a journey I'm still on, one guided by many questions I have asked over the years, many of them never fully answered, each question simply nudging me forward to the next.

I believe that authentic discipleship only happens by the grace of God and by the power (or what I call "energy") of the Holy Spirit, given to us by Jesus and manifest in his followers throughout the world. Discipleship begins with our openness to this possibility, and works through our acceptance of the Spirit, a gift from God. Is it possible to live daily in this Reality? If so, our thoughts, words, and actions humbly convey Jesus' good news to those around us. It's not about recruitment, but about awakening! Such awareness is radical discipleship, simply because it is the opposite of the ego-based, self-centered, self-referential human nature into which we are all born.

I was reared in a Catholic family, and I received a foundation of faith in a Catholic school. While I still love my church and have a healthy respect for its history and tradition, I have nothing against other faiths. I believe that how people practice faith is up to them, as long as God is central in their lives, for we are all one in God's eyes.

As a child, I asked many questions about Jesus, for in my innocence, I wanted to know more about his human side. When I asked the nun who taught my second-grade class whether Jesus had any brothers or sisters, her response was that we didn't know for sure. Soon after, at the funeral of my five-year-old cousin Maureen, I asked whether she was now an angel. Even then, the thought of death did not frighten me, for somehow I knew and trusted that there was something better beyond this life.

As a fourth and fifth grader, I wondered why people acted differently in church than away from church, and later, as a teenager, I became aware that the rules of the Catholic Church sometimes changed. So I started questioning religious rules. Do they come from God, or are they made by human beings to control or punish? I knew the rule about divorce caused my mother much shame, and yet I realized that we were all better off without the verbal, emotional, and even occasional physical abuse previously present in our home. I still question certain religious rules, and I hope my church can return to simpler times. By this I mean, to focus more on the "Golden Rules" of Jesus, such as loving God and your neighbor as yourself. Perhaps ongoing questioning is part of God's grace in my pursuit of discipleship.

These early questions about Jesus, my church, and the behavior of others were followed by a period of self-searching. Some of my later questioning was influenced by the dysfunction in my childhood, such as, will I ever find true love, if my own father doesn't love me? I knew my mother loved me, and my grandmother always made me feel special. I also knew that God loved me, but he was omnipotent and "up there in heaven." He was busy taking care of the whole world. However, when I look back now, it was my grandmother who was my saving grace, the face of God in my life at that time. Most of my adolescent questions, however, were similar to those asked by most teens and young adults. Would I be successful and self-sufficient? Do I belong? Why do I feel different? Although I did well academically and athletically, I was socially backward, perhaps too guarded and serious. Trust in relationships had always been a struggle, surely rooted in the double-edged sword of feeling unlovable and being fearful that others might take advantage of me.

After college, I became a nurse, eventually promoted to a coordinator position in a large hospital. Serving and caring for others was rewarding, and I felt I had found my niche, while gaining job security. Throughout my life, I had always related to Saint Francis and his love and care for others. His lifestyle and service to others made him one of the most respected and beloved disciples of all times, and his famous prayer informs my discipleship.

Self-searching turned into soul-searching as my questions sought greater spiritual knowledge and practice. My questioning began with belief regarding God, Jesus, and the Holy Spirit, but it evolved into an affirmation of the personal presence of God in my life. Despite ongoing questioning, I discovered that the source of the unconditional and infinite love I had always longed for is God. This awareness gave me assurance that I didn't need to know all the answers, and that I would never be alone again, and that no matter what happened, I would be okay. I had moved from belief to experience.

As a result, I felt more comfortable in relationships, and this led to a twenty-year-long marriage to the love of my life, until his death from end-stage liver cancer. I still miss him every day, but I know he is in a better place. A part of him will always be in my heart, and I believe that one day our hearts will be together again. God was with me every step of that great loss, as well as in the sudden loss of my closest sister seven months later. Practicing daily meditation, journaling, and experiencing God's everlasting love got me through those difficult times. I became more God-centered and less self-centered, more in touch with my True Self. If discipleship is about learning, it has to be about growth and change, about letting go and accepting things we cannot understand or control.

As my spiritual journey continues, current questions have shifted from my own insecurity to my love for and relationship with God. How can I trust in God's goodness every moment? How can I help my church? How can we spread Christ's love and service? Now, I am trying to get myself out of the way, as I realize more fully God's work in my life. I am learning to be the mirror as well as the reflection of God's love.

Now it is spiritual guides such as Thomas Merton and Richard Rohr as well as my daily practice of reading scripture, books with spiritual content, and audio and video presentations relating to my spiritual journey that feed my spirit. Through these, the energy of the Holy Spirit is alive in me. In addition, I have joined a book discussion of people from multiple faith backgrounds. I joined initially to learn more about the Bible, and reading books by Dr. Vande Kappelle gave me knowledge and insight not only into the Bible, including its historical and literary context, but also how we can use the Bible to explore lifelong spiritual growth.

Our questions are endless, but so is the mystery of God. I now trust that God's Spirit is alive and forever at work in this world. Through questioning, I have discovered that the closer I get to God, the less I need to know, for as the Bible indicates, God alone is good, and that is sufficient answer for me.

Questions for Discussion and Reflection

1. Briefly describe your understanding of radical discipleship in the twenty-first century, and if possible, illustrate your understanding of discipleship from your spiritual journey.

2. Susan's story discusses how discipleship involves being mentored by others, in her case, by her parents, Sunday School teachers, church youth leaders, and others. If possible, identify the primary individuals who mentored you in your faith journey.

3. Susan's story indicates how opportunities arose in her adult life and career to serve Christ by volunteering with local nonprofit organizations. If possible, identify similar opportunities for service in your adult life.

4. Tony's story discusses how his early life was marked by racist experiences. Are there times when you have exhibited racist behavior? If so, have such attitudes and behavior changed over time? If not, why not?

5. Have there been times when you have experienced racist, sexist, or classist prejudice? If so, how did you feel? In your estimation, what can you and our society do to end prejudicial attitudes and behavior?

6. Can you provide an example from your life of observing someone intervene on behalf of another, like the superintendent of Tony's school district did with him, in a way that empowered a victimized member of society and that changed his or her life profoundly? Explain your answer.

7. Like Tony during the Vietnam war, have you been in a situation when you had to take an unpopular stand, when to do so came with a heavy price? Explain your answer.

8. Assess the merits of Sara's statement that being disciples of Jesus influences how we interact with our social as well as the natural environment.

9. Assess the merits of Sara's view that to be right with others, we must first be right with God.

10. Assess the merits of Marybeth's view that radical discipleship involves awakening from ego-based self-centeredness to other-based God-centeredness.

11. Marybeth's spiritual growth took place through questioning, progressing from self-searching to soul-searching, and by discovering that specific answers to faith questions are not always necessary. Do you agree? Explain your answer.

Chapter 11

Radical Discipleship Illustrated, Part III

WHY DON'T PEOPLE CARE for one another? That's the question Matt asked his aunt Georgia repeatedly while he was AWOL from the army. He had wanted to serve his country, and had enlisted at the earliest age possible. After boot camp, he was deployed to Afghanistan, where he tried his best to adjust; he performed admirably, but he found himself ill-suited to the task at hand. Despondent, he tried to leave the army, but unable to do so, he did the only thing he knew to do, which was to put a bad situation behind him.

We all know people who are deeply compassionate, and have heard of people who put the needs of others before their own. However, such examples are rare, even when they involve family members or close friends. The topic of compassion reminds me of the statue in London's Piccadilly Circus celebrating the life of Lord Shaftsbury, the Victorian politician, philanthropist, and social reformer. Popularly misnamed the Eros statue, the iconic sculpture actually represents Anteros, Eros's twin brother, the ancient Greek symbol of selfless love. In 1886, sculptor Alfred Gilbert was commissioned to create a memorial to Anthony Ashley-Cooper, the seventh Earl of Shaftsbury.

Gilbert spent a long time considering how to celebrate the life of Shaftsbury, who had campaigned vigorously against many social injustices, introducing parliamentary legislation against such abuses as child labor, women's labor conditions, and cruelty to the insane, while advocating for religious freedom for Jews and for basic education for everyone in England. Gilbert eventually decided on a fountain, topped with the winged figure of Anteros, whom he described as portraying "reflective and mature love, as opposed to Eros or Cupid," the god of sensual love.

The monument was unveiled in 1893 to mixed response. Some thought the monument should be renamed as The Statue of Christian Charity, giving the figure a Christian approximation, preferring selfless divine agape love over pagan sentiment.

Are people naturally self-centered and inclined to place their needs above those of others? If so, it is easy to blame biology, for we all have the need for survival. Setting biological needs aside, however, another answer is sociological. As adolescents and young adults mature, they acquire independence, and that means they must learn to be responsible and self-sufficient, prioritizing their needs above those of others. To be self-sufficient requires education and training suitable for employment, and these take time and resources. In many cases, young adults get married and begin families of their own, and these responsibilities keep people in debt and quite busy, giving them the sense that in order to survive and live comfortably they need all the resources they can accumulate. Such obligations leave little or no time, energy, and resources for needy people.

A third reason involves collapsed idealism. When people are young, many believe they can go forth and change the world. But then things get complicated. Perhaps they got burned, or ran into "users," and the lack of boundaries becomes a source of irritation, more a burden than a joy. Sometimes people also discover that if their motive is to feel good, then they can easily become discouraged, or bitter. A fourth reason often given for self-centeredness is theological. Many belief systems emphasize the doctrine of original sin, with its teaching that only the grace of God can transform inherently selfish people into compassionate ones.

While other persuasive arguments might be given in answer to Matt's question, this chapter focuses on two individuals, my friend Georgia and my son Peter, who have been profoundly altered by following Jesus, so much so that it is evident to those around them that as adults, they are driven by compassion and by a deep desire to share who they are, what they know, and what they have with others. Having acquired the "mind of Christ," their biological nature has been altered from selfishness to selflessness, their delight being to serve rather than to be served. In addition, both individuals have learned to live responsibly and maturely, caring for their own needs equally with those of others, loving neighbor as themselves. Their stories are given in response to my question, "How does following Jesus make you more compassionate?"

Georgia, co-owner with her husband Jim of a small business in western Pennsylvania and the convener of a discussion group dedicated to reading and studying my books on second-half-of-life spirituality, tells a compelling story of discipleship, which in her case demonstrates the triumph of love over adversity.

My son Peter, a practicing pediatric cardiologist and father of four children, two boys and two girls, grew up active in sports, primarily soccer but also basketball and running cross-country. However, his greatest sports accomplishments occurred in tennis, at which he became proficient, his love of tennis resulting in building a backyard court for himself and his family. Once set in his career, he immediately found a church home, where he led small-group Bible studies. As his father, I am inspired by his love of God, devotion to his family, and his service of others. Like Georgia, faithful discipleship is his greatest passion.

Georgia's Discipleship Story: Serving Smarter, Not Harder

Like many of us, I survived childhood, but only through the grace of God. Had it not been for my twin sister Helen and my grandparents, with whom Helen and I lived during some of our early years, I would likely not have thrived.

Helen and I lived with our mother for the first three and a half years. There was no question she loved us, but as we grew up, she was suffering from postpartum depression and trauma disorder, and because she didn't get immediate help, she experienced psychosis. She sent us to Sunday School and tried to meet our physical, emotional, and spiritual needs, but her inability to care for us, coupled with fear that she was unable to keep us safe or prevent us from running into the road, led to extreme punishments. Around that time, she became increasingly sick, and her growing mental illness led to further abuse. When my parents' marriage failed and she and my father separated, she was institutionalized and Helen and I went to live with our paternal grandparents and other relatives. Living with them was like living in a nature conservancy. Flowers were everywhere, and Helen and I had a pony to ride and enjoy.

As a preschooler, I felt a strong bond with animals and all living creatures. Whenever an animal suffered or was abused by someone, I suffered as well. During this formative period, I shared everything with my identical twin. We did everything together, and functioned as each other's half. Missing our mother, we often went into the woods together, looking for God. At this time I trusted God fully, viewing God as a living force in the universe, more like a spirit being than a human person.

The relationship I had with God, both then and now, is similar to the experience of bummer lambs, that is, of newborn lambs that for reasons of neglect or loss of the mother sheep, are known to be taken by shepherds into their homes, where they are bottle-fed, held, and kept warm by the family hearth. When the lamb is strong enough, it is taken back to the flock, but in the morning, when the shepherd calls the sheep, the first to run to the shepherd are the bummer lambs, who know the shepherd's voice. Does the shepherd love the bummer lambs more than the others? Not really, but they experienced the shepherd's love and care when they were vulnerable and broken, and that grace bonds the lambs to the shepherd for life.

I believe all people have a "bummer lamb" experience with God, whether it be when a parent dies, when divorce occurs, or through feelings of neglect, rejection, or abuse by others in our lives, and even later in life, by failed marriages, bad jobs, or rejection by friends or coworkers.

While living with our grandmother, Helen and I prayed for our mother every day. One day, about a year later, she returned, and we saw her appearance as an answer to prayer, and it strengthened our faith. However, due to shock therapy, she had changed, and was but a shell of herself. However, her drive to be with her family helped her overcome her mental illness, and she went on to overcome many obstacles, becoming a loving and successful single mother. Around the age of nine, we were reunited and lived together, this time with our maternal grandparents.

During my childhood years, my desire to please God was deep. Initially, that desire was directed toward stray animals, but as I got older, my passion became directed toward suffering people. I believe God has always blessed me with the gift of service, but it is a gift I have not always handled wisely, maturely, or in a healthy manner. At times I neglected my own needs, or placed too much care for others on my own shoulders, instead of allowing God supremacy.

In retrospect, I realize that I believed in God throughout my childhood, but not so much in Jesus. By the time I was thirty-two, I had fallen into addictive patterns of my own, using alcohol as a refuge instead of God. Through the help of a Catholic priest, I experienced a release from my addictive "worship disorder," and it was then that I came to understand the saving work of Jesus. That experience initiated my longing for a relationship with Jesus, a relationship I had not known to be possible. I also acquired a love for scripture, and it became my goal to read the Bible from cover to cover, something I have now done eight times. On one occasion, I was led to draw about forty illustrations of scenes in the Bible, including my favorite of Jacob wrestling with God. Relying on Jesus and on scripture made life much easier to navigate, though I found I still took on too much responsibility when serving others.

In 2000 God blessed me with marriage to my husband Jim. I found him to be even more passionate about serving others than I. Having been reared a Methodist, he surrendered to the lordship of Jesus through the ministry of Kenneth Copland. After coming to Christ, he underwent training to become a Methodist lay minister. Prior to our marriage, he started a youth ministry, and after our marriage, he joined my Gladden Presbyterian church where he served as a Sunday School teacher and later as a ruling elder. Together, we began a ministry to shut-ins, in addition to mentoring others in the faith. As a couple, we also support one other in our own privately run small business. With Jim, I have learned the value of a sense of humor and that healthy relationships are the key to happiness; being equally yoked is an added blessing!

One of my greatest blessings is helping someone receive Jesus. I have witnessed such conversions on several occasions. The first time, it didn't know what to expect, but it went better than I had expected. I am humbled to know that Jesus lets us share in such transformative experiences.

In 2008 my nephew Matt was "killed by action" (KBA) in Afghanistan. At that time the United States was going through a heroin crisis and many young people were dying; soldiers were completing suicide at the rate of twenty-two per day. Emotionally involved with Matt at this time, I felt a deep desire to help, and I can honestly say that without Jesus, scripture, and my husband, I would not have survived my grief.

In the fall of 2016 I reunited with Dr. Vande Kappelle, my college religion professor, whom students called "Dr. Van." He had written a number of books and I immediately began reading *Securing Life*, his overview of the Bible, finding it to be a treasure. Reading this book taught me a great deal about the Bible, not only about its content and how it was written, but also about biblical interpretation. I found the book's content practical, and I was able to apply what I learned to my work at church and with grief and support groups. A turning point came later, in my group study of *Grace Revealed*, Dr. Van's commentary on Romans, which taught me I didn't have to work so hard to be an effective disciple of Jesus.

It became Jim's and my ministry to convene a small group to study Dr. Van's books, a group we later named "Body in Spirit." This group has been in continuous existence since the spring of 2017 and it has been a source of great personal joy. The members differ in religious background and in points of view, but we are united in service to God and the community. Thus far we have studied twelve of Dr. Van's books. Our common goal is to grow in our spiritual journey. In addition to my own growth spiritually, I've seen every member grow as well.

A few years ago, my friend Lester tried to get me to quit smoking. I turned to food and cigarettes for comfort, and that merely displaced my worship disorder. Lester encouraged me to attend a service led by faith healer Billy Burke. Lester's persistence, together with my husband's support, resulted in a group of us attending a "World Outreach" healing service. Being naïve about healing services. I thought I could only ask for one healing, so I picked to quit smoking, something I had tried repeatedly and failed, for, like trying to stop diarrhea, I discovered it involved more than willpower.

At that time I was experiencing many physical problems, including blood in my urine, COPD symptoms, weak knees, diabetes, high blood pressure, high cholesterol, and I was being tested for lung cancer. I believe Jesus led me to attend the healing service, for I found Pastor Billy Burke and his staff to be joyful and humble. When Pastor Burke asked, "Who has blood in the urine?" I went forward. Once I was up front, I began speaking privately with God, asking, "What have I done? I'm going to screw this up. Am I going to embarrass myself and everyone with me?" Then I saw a bright light, and immediately fell down. Jim told me later that I had been laughing on the floor. When I awoke, I got to my feet and cried. I had experienced grace! I felt a new surrender to the grace of the Holy Spirit, and I was amazed, for I had previously neglected this part of the Trinity.

Since this healing, I have become a new person. The diabetes is gone, my COPD has cleared, I have new knees, I have no cancer, and have lost seventy pounds. In addition, I feel thirty years old! As a result, I follow Billy Burke World Outreach ministries and have learned to surrender completely to the triune God. Discipleship requires less effort now and produces far greater joy.

"Letting go and letting God"—that is the answer, for I have come to understand that discipleship involves total surrender to God. While helping others is beneficial emotionally to both givers and receivers, since such activity is known to release endorphins and to make everyone involved happier, I have come to learn the importance of caring for myself while putting others first. The secret of healthy compassion, I've discovered, starts with God's love.

Peter's Discipleship Story: Living with Eternal Purpose

I believe God has placed a sense of eternity in every human being, and with it, the obligation to know and do God's will. For me, discipleship is to know and love God, and to do God's will by leading others to a saving knowledge of God's atoning work in Christ. My greatest joy is doing God's will as I know it, primarily in bringing others to Christ. Were it not for Christ in my life, I would be obsessed with my own priorities and concerns, and much more selfish. Even now, I feel I do so little for God and others, and what good occurs through me is not my doing, but God's.

Working on self was primary during my early years. Temperamentally an introvert, a good deal of my maturation required personal growth and learning with a predominantly inward focus. During my formative years, I was driven by sports and education to excel in all I did. My parents sacrificed for me, driving me to practice and tournaments, as well as encouraging me to pursue my interests in a multitude of sports. As a high school student, I spent countless hours working on my tennis strokes in practice and matches. My primary goal was to improve my skills in order to defeat others. I played tennis for my high school and college teams, which brought comraderie, but also the realization that tennis is primarily an individual sport. As an introvert, I never had difficulty spending hours hitting tennis balls from a ball machine.

Although sports continue to be a healthy outlet, my primary course in life shifted to my career and ongoing training in medicine. The discipline of learning to be a physician has served me well, providing a continuing framework by which I focused on the next class, the next year, and the next task toward my goal to become a doctor. Altruism was a component of choosing a career in medicine, but it began with self-awareness. In order to succeed in medicine, I focused on training my brain with memorization, my muscle memory for procedures, and my eyes to detect abnormal patient findings. Medicine has a prescribed path for schooling and training that encompassed the majority of my waking hours for several decades. To succeed, I spent much time studying alone in the library.

Throughout my life tough existential questions have arisen, such as "What is the purpose of life?" and "Why am I here?" Through God, I have found the answers for these questions, or better yet, I have discovered God to be the answer to all my existential questions. Through worship, study, and scripture, I have discovered God's plan for my life and for all life. In actuality, it is God who has pursued me and shown me that my purpose and greatest joy in life is to be other-centered. God has given me identity as an adopted child and my mindset has been changed from what I could do to better myself to how I could use the skills and talents he had given me to further his will and kingdom. I believe God is my creator and sustainer. If he gives me life, then I owe my life to him. Through studying the Bible, I have learned God's purpose for creation to be that all his creatures be in right relationship with him, recognizing our indebtedness to him for all we have and our debt of allegiance and obedience. Through scripture, my eyes have been opened to love God with my whole heart and love others as well.

Jesus demonstrated in the gospels how his everyday tasks—healing the sick, bringing sight to the blind, and making the lame to walk—glorified God. My desire is to follow in his footsteps, glorifying God through interactions with patients and families at work. It is a joy to know that I can glorify God through my daily activities as a doctor.

My journey with God has shown me how I depend on him every day. Like Jesus, who showed his personal relationship with God through habitual prayer, I also demonstrate my dependance on God through prayer. Prayer places my mindset on building a relationship with God, and that relationship enables me to be other-centered. God has showed me that he has placed me where I am to do his work here on earth. My disposition has changed from what I can do for myself to what I can do for others. Previously, serving others was a chore, a tedious task that brought relief only when done. Now, I ask God for opportunities to serve others, and I find that doing so is exhilarating. Service is not a one-and-done task. Like discipleship, it is a process, a lifelong journey of bringing others hope and a sense of eternal worth by connecting them to their Lord and Maker.

I find that God has softened my heart to respond to the relationships he places in my path. When I fail consistently to depend on God, I begin to look to myself and do things that are more inward or self-serving by nature. The truth is that there are endless opportunities to serve others in our lives, and a multitude of people that surround us each day. Through my work as a physician, I find ongoing opportunities to serve others, discussing ways to physically improve the quality of my patients' lives, but these can become chores or service for pay unless my attitude is adjusted by humbly submitting to God and recognizing that my work is for God's glory. Everyone has pain and hardship in life. Sometimes uplifting words of encouragement or the hope I have in God can go a long way.

At church I am surrounded by like-minded Christians who have a love for serving others. I am grateful God has placed me where I am and has surrounded me with wonderful examples of how he has given others a similar desire to help those in need. Habitual Bible study, prayer, and church attendance keeps my priorities straight, helping maintain my desire to serve others lovingly and unconditionally. In addition, Bible study at church and interacting with others for spiritual growth helps all of us grow together in our faith and love for God. By participating in weekly Bible study with others, we proclaim God as our source of love for others. As the scriptures remind us, we love because God first loved us.

As I see it, I am a vessel for God to use to promote his kingdom on earth. Growing in relationship with God changes one's priorities. Worship creates in me a longing to be present for others. Worshipping regularly with others, listening to one another's concerns, and encouraging one another with the hope we have from God, and simply being present in relationship with others is helpful. When needs arise, I volunteer to help others with my talents. In addition to serving as a Bible study teacher, I also serve my church as a member of safety teams during Sunday services, where I am on call for medical emergencies that may arise. I have also gone on medical mission trips to several countries to provide medical care to families in need.

God uses all relationships to bring glory to himself. While on earth, Jesus demonstrated how to live life in loving, peaceful, patient relationship with his disciples. As a follower of Jesus and through his example, I find that God continues to shape my heart and desires for others. In addition to being in relationship with others, God's desire is for us to be in relationship with family members. He has given me a loving wife and children to live with each day. As a family, we are a team, focused on how we can use the talents God has given us to enhance each situation placed before us. Marriage to Erin is another relationship that God has used to shepherd my heart for service. Each day I have choices to give of my time and effort in my relationship with my wife. God's love is demonstrated when I choose to spend quality time with her. We enjoy spending time together at meals, taking the kids to their events, and talking with one another when the kids are asleep.

Erin is a perfect example of dedicating her life to serving God through partnering with me in marriage as well as in parenting our children. Our desire is to model how Christian relationships work by giving of ourselves to others and by leading through example, praying that each of our children will also be in loving relationship with God and others.

Serving others requires giving of one's time. In this world there is always something vying for my time. With a full-time job, often requiring that I be on-call on weekends, I sometimes have difficulty finding spare time. In the past I watched television or listened to music habitually, but God has changed my desires and shown me I can find more time for others by allowing my television cable subscription to be discontinued. In addition, not having constant background radio noise while driving frees up more time for prayer. As a disciple of Christ, my desire is to dedicate my waking hours to serving others. Though my children tend to soak up much of that time, praying and reading the Bible habitually keep me open to opportunities to serve others. Being present for my children and giving them my time and energy every day is also a joy. Taking care of a child's every need is the ultimate service driven by love. Spending time with others is energizing in the moment and tiring after a long day, but as long as the Lord gives me the ability to work for his kingdom, I am grateful to reciprocate his love to others. I am thankful to rest my head at night after a long day of living for God. Habitual reading of the Bible helps me understand God's love for me and others, and I pray daily for God to use me to be the hands and feet for his kingdom on earth. Each day is a new occasion to serve God and to say yes to opportunities that arise to serve others. As disciples are in relationship with others, so we are in relationship with God, for serving others is serving God. My days here are numbered, and I don't want to waste any day the Lord gives me to be used to further his work on earth.

As a disciple, nothing gives me greater joy than living with eternal purpose. In this respect, we must be careful that we don't take credit for what we do. Being a disciple is more than being a good person; it is working with God to make an eternal difference in peoples' lives.

Questions for Discussion and Reflection

1. How would you answer Matt's question, "Why don't people care for one another?"
2. We all know people who are truly compassionate, some out of religious motivation but others for purely humanitarian reasons. In your estimation, is supernatural love superior to natural (or secular) love? Explain your answer.
3. Georgia's story discusses her early bond with animals and all living creatures. In your estimation, should compassionate love of other human beings also include compassionate love of animals? Explain your answer.
4. Explain and assess Georgia's example of bummer lambs as an explanation of human attraction and need for God.
5. Explain the Christian perspective that views compassionate service to others as a gift of God's Spirit (see 1 Cor 12:4–7).
6. Explain and assess Georgia's view that at times people of faith serve others in compulsive, immature, or unhealthy ways.
7. Assess Georgia's view that a sense of humor, like healthy relationships, is a key to happiness.
8. Explain and assess Georgia's experience with faith healing.
9. Do you agree with Peter's view that God has placed a sense of eternity in every human being? Explain your answer.
10. Have your ever been instrumental in leading another person to Christ? If so, describe that experience. If not, why not?
11. Can you agree with Peter that you have found God to be the answer to life's existential questions? If so, what role have worship, prayer, and scripture study had in that process? Explain your answer.
12. Can you agree with Peter that you can glorify God through your life's daily activities? Explain your answer.
13. What role do personal prayer and Bible reading have in your current spirituality?

14. Do you find, like Peter, that your church experience is a vital aspect of your spiritual life and a stimulus to serving people in need? Explain your answer.

15. Like Peter, are there habits in your life you need to control or eliminate for the sake of those you need to love and serve? Explain your answer.

Chapter 12

Following Jesus: Then and Now

As a first-century Palestinian Jew, Jesus belonged to a world where religion (theology) and politics went hand in hand. The theology was Jewish monotheism, a doctrine forged through centuries of subjugation and persecution, going back to the Babylonian exile. First-century Jews held their monotheism passionately. Theirs was not an abstract theory about the existence of one God. They believed their God, Yahweh, was the only God, and that all others were idols. A corollary of monotheism was "election," the belief that the Jews had been chosen by this one God, making what happened to Israel of universal significance. Many Jews of Jesus' day believed that God was about to vindicate them, understanding this act as having global implications, as the means of divine judgment and/or mercy upon the rest of the world.

First-century Jewish monotheists, who believed in one God and in their status as God's elect people while currently suffering oppression, also believed the present state of affairs temporary. Monotheism and election thus gave birth to eschatology, a perspective that views history as purposeful and therefore as moving toward a climactic resolution or restoration, at which time everything would be made right. First-century Jewish eschatology claimed that Yahweh would soon act within history to vindicate his people and to establish permanent justice and peace. This belief included the great promises of forgiveness articulated by biblical prophets, notably Isaiah, Jeremiah, and Ezekiel. The so-called post-exilic writings spoke of a forthcoming restoration, a liberation they described as a new exodus.

In keeping with this understanding, it follows that Jesus of Nazareth might have viewed his mission as prophetic, announcing, like John the Baptist before him, God's coming kingdom. But Jesus, it seems, went beyond John's verbal role, embodying in his person and his ministry the presence of that kingdom. For Jesus, the all-encompassing rule of God was near. When it came in its fullness, God would restore Israel's role as "light to the nations" and challenge evil in all its manifestations, political, social, and economic. The coming kingdom of God was not a new sort of religion, a new moral code, or a new soteriology (a doctrine about how one might go to heaven after death). Nor was it a new sociological analysis, critique, or agenda. It was about Israel's story reaching its climax, about Israel's history moving toward its decisive moment.[1]

E. P. Sanders, in his classic text *Jesus and Judaism*, maintains that before the outbreak of the War of the Jews against Rome in 66 CE, "common Judaism" held the following hopes for the future: the restoration of the tribes of Israel; the conversion, destruction, or subjugation of the Gentiles; the renewal of Jerusalem, including a new or rebuilt temple; and the purification of God's people and their worship.[2] Whatever one makes of his idea of a common Judaism, surely the beliefs Sanders highlights were widespread among Jesus' contemporaries, as was apocalyptic eschatology in general. According to Sanders, Jesus was an apocalyptic prophet standing in the tradition of Jewish restoration theology. He shared the beliefs common in Judaism, together with this prevailing understanding of Israel's story and hope. Having established the essential Jewishness of Jesus on this topic, Sanders found primitive Christianity to be a movement in continuity with Jesus' hopes and expectations: "The most certain fact of all is that early Christianity was an eschatological movement."[3]

Biblical support for that contention can be found in the well-known fact that, with the exception of Philemon, 2 John, and 3 John (all three of which are brief and nearly devoid of theology), apocalyptic eschatology or some obvious trace of it appears in all first-century Christian documents. For instance, 1 Thessalonians, the earliest extant Christian writing, is full of apocalyptic expectation. As biblical scholar A. T. Robinson recognized, this letter is a "challenge" for anyone who denies that Christianity began amid apocalyptic enthusiasm.[4] Since Jesus was the point of origination for what became Christianity, one might reasonably infer that he was an

---

1. Borg and Wright, *Meaning of Jesus*, 31–35.
2. Sanders, *Jesus and Judaism*, 279–303.
3. Sanders, "Jesus: His Religious Type," 6.
4. Robinson, *Jesus and His Coming*, 104–17.

apocalyptic figure. If within a year or two of Jesus' death Paul persecuted the followers of Jesus because of their eschatological proclamation, that leaves precious little time in which the followers of a noneschatological Jesus could have developed an entirely new eschatological perspective without a precedent in the preaching and actions of Jesus. The conclusion seems obvious: Eschatology was pervasive at the beginning of the Christian movement because it was central to Jesus and his mission.

This understanding of Jesus as "eschatological Jewish prophet" announcing the inbreaking of God's culminating kingdom is controversial in current biblical scholarship in part because of a debate on the meaning of the term "eschatology," typically defined as "the study of last things." In addition to the idea of "the end of the world," much emphasized by current evangelical Christians but essentially a non-Jewish view,[5] at least three biblical possibilities can be maintained:[6]

1. An *apocalyptic* meaning, in which eschatology truly signifies a time in the future when the course of history will be changed to such an extent that one can speak of an entirely new state of reality; it concerns a cosmic cataclysm and a new age followed by utopian bliss. This view is generally associated with "end-time" events such as the coming of a messianic age, the vindication of Israel or the elect, and sometimes a last judgment and resurrection of the dead. This is not what I believe Jesus had in mind, though biblical memory suggests that he seemed to envision the occurrence of something cataclysmic.

2. An *historical/political* meaning, in keeping with the spirit of the Old Testament pre-exilic prophets, who spoke of the "Day of the Lord" (a day of judgment) as referring to an event or a cluster of events within history, such as the military conquest of Israel or Judah by a foreign empire. Here "end" means "an end of statehood" and newness "a restoration of statehood."

3. A *teleological* meaning, understanding the concept of eschatology in the sense that the "end" it envisions is associated with ultimate

---

5. Jewish eschatologies did not typically involve "the end of the world." The disappearance of the material world is not part of the expectation. The exception may be 2 Peter 3:10–12.

6. G. B. Caird, in *Language and Imagery of the Bible*, 243–71, examines the variety of uses given to the concept of "eschatology" by modern scholars and discovers seven different senses in which the term is used.

purpose, hope, or an ideal vision. This view seems to capture what Jesus meant when he came proclaiming the good news of God, saying, "The time is fulfilled, and the kingdom of God has come near; repent, and believe in the good news" (Mark 1:15).

What adds to the biblical confusion is that various understandings of eschatology lie superimposed one upon another in the New Testament. There were some within the early church who clearly expected the "end of the world" in their generation, including the resurrection of the dead, the last judgment, and the "new heavens and new earth." Where did this expectation arise? Was it grounded in Jesus' own expectation or should the church's expectation of the "last things" be understood as a post-Easter development, a deduction based upon the Easter event itself?

As is well-known, "resurrection" in Judaism was an event expected at the end of time. To some within the early church, the fact that Jesus' resurrection had occurred was an indicator that the general resurrection must be near: Christ was the "first fruits" of those to be raised from the dead (1 Cor 15:23). Moreover, first-century Christians did not think about the imminent coming of the kingdom or talk about the end of the world in a general way. Rather, they spoke of the imminent end of the world only in connection with the return of Jesus. It is important not to exaggerate the extent to which the early church was an "end-time" community. Despite the explicit statements affirming an imminent end, it is not clear that this was an essential expectation (except, perhaps, in the book of Revelation). Though the letters of Paul and the gospel of John contain explicit references to the end, clearly the emphasis of both authors is on the present rather than on the future, acknowledging the present as the time when the reality of God can be known in a decisive way.

The belief in two ages, a characteristic of Jewish eschatology, is found in the thought of the apostle Paul. In his writings, the present evil age is giving way to the coming age of justice and peace, so that the end of the one is the beginning of the other. It is not altogether clear to which of the three categories of biblical meaning this view belongs. Defining and cataloguing such a concept involves a mixture of subjective and objective evaluation. How, for instance, do we understand Isaiah's vision in Isaiah 35:1–10? Read literally, it describes a complete reversal of nature, a final kingdom of justice and peace such as envisioned in the first meaning of "eschatology" above. Read contextually, however, the vision applies to the restoration of Zion (the kingdom of Judah) and can be viewed as an example of the second meaning of eschatology above. Such an understanding, read through Paul's "two-age" understanding of eschatology, applies in the present and can refer to the third meaning of eschatology, namely to the spiritual newness Christian believers are experiencing as the result of the death and resurrection of Christ. We recall the well-known reference in 2 Corinthians 5:17, where, according to Paul, the Christ-event itself signifies the passing of the old age and the inception of the new: "everything old has passed away; see, everything has become new!"

Some scholars, particularly church-based theologians concerned to extricate Jesus from error and from the troubling possibility that his expectations were disappointed, have toned down or reinterpreted many of the eschatological prophecies in the gospels and thereby disassociated Jesus from failure as a prophet. The British scholar C. H. Dodd ingeniously read the Synoptic texts so that they give us "realized eschatology," meaning that we should view the kingdom as having already come in Jesus' ministry. Roman Catholic biblical scholar John Dominic Crossan dissociates Jesus from a large number of biblical traditions about him and from the violent expectations of John the Baptist, occasioned by the last judgment. Crossan's Jesus hopes instead for a utopian future of justice and egalitarianism, a future inaugurated not by the last judgment but by social renewal. Conservative British theologian N. T. Wright passionately promotes a Jesus who used eschatological metaphors to prophesy what actually came to pass in the first century: his own resurrection, the coming of the church, and Jerusalem's violent demise.

Dale Allison, formerly at Pittsburgh Theological Seminary and currently professor of New Testament at Princeton Theological Seminary, disagrees, arguing persuasively that Jesus placed himself as the central figure in the eschatological end-time drama. For Allison, the historical Jesus was not a poet speaking metaphorically about judgment; rather he lived and thought apocalyptically. Citing profusely from the gospels, Allison concludes that Jesus envisaged, as did many other Jews in his time and place, "the advent, after suffering and persecution, of a great judgment, and after that a supernatural utopia, the kingdom of God, inhabited by the dead come back to life, to enjoy a world forever rid of evil and wholly ruled by God. Further, he thought that the night was far gone, the day at hand."[7] The belief of early Christians in the imminence of the

---

7. Allison, *The Historical Christ*, 95.

end, according to Allison, originated not from the church's post-Easter expectations, but with Jesus himself.

This is not to say that Jesus was an apocalyptic extremist, or that he had only eschatology on his mind. Part of the reason that Jesus so fascinates and inspires is that he embodied in his own person the extremes of human experience. On the one hand, Jesus announced and made real the eschatological presence of the God of Israel: Satan has fallen like lightning from heaven and the demons are being routed; the lame walk and the blind see; lepers are cleansed and those in poverty are cheered with good news. The long-awaited kingdom of God has arrived; the bridegroom is here. The old world is gone; the new world has come.

That, however, is only half of the story. Paradoxically, the joyful Jesus is familiar with sorrows and acquainted with grief. He has nowhere to lay his head; respected leaders assail his teachings and behavior; John the Baptist, whom he hails as more than a prophet, is arrested and beheaded; his own companions misunderstand him, betray him, and abandon him. Pagan soldiers whip him, mock him, and nail him to a cross of execution. His end is physical torment and mental anguish, loss of life and loss of meaning. So the tradition gives us a Jesus who "knows how to laugh loudly and to wail miserably, a Jesus who knows the presence of God and the absence of God."[8]

If Jesus had pretended to know only the blessings of the future age, we should turn our backs on him, for we would know his faith to be a hopeless flight from the pain of living. And if he had focused exclusively on the tribulation to come, we would dismiss his hope as inconsequential, the distance between him and God as too great. But by announcing not only tribulation present and future but also salvation present and future and then by living into both, Jesus commends himself to us.

American biblical scholar Marcus Borg represents a growing number of modern scholars who challenge this understanding of Jesus, envisioning instead a non-eschatological Jesus, whose role, if interpreted prophetically, should be limited to that of a social prophet engaged in radical social criticism. According to this model, Jesus was a countercultural revolutionary who opposed the domination systems of his day both in person and through an alternative community of disciples, chosen to represent the New Israel of God. In Borg's view the kingdom of God represents a this-worldly social vision—a vision that empowers

---

8. Allison, *The Historical Christ*, 117.

Christians and defines the church's ongoing role in society—rather than an other-worldly eschatological vision imposed from above and occasioned by a church raptured from this earth, an interpretation popular in many American fundamentalist and evangelical circles today.

Viewing Jesus as a deeply Jewish but non-eschatological figure, Borg challenges another vital element in the popular image of Jesus, namely that Jesus understood himself to be the messiah. According to Borg, the pre-Easter Jesus consistently pointed away from himself to God; his message was theocentric, not christocentric, meaning that he was centered in God and not in messianic pronouncements about himself. On the basis of these two denials of popular but what he considers erroneous images of Jesus, Borg suggests five models in the Jewish tradition that accurately portray the self-understanding of the historical (pre-Easter) Jesus:[9]

1. Jesus as *mystic*. Like Moses, Elijah, and the prophets, Jesus was a "Spirit person," a "mediator of the sacred."

2. Jesus as *healer and exorcist*. The evidence that Jesus performed paranormal healings is very strong; in fact, more healing stories are told about him than about any other figure in the Jewish tradition. While admitting that psychosomatic factors may sometimes have been involved, Borg avoids usage of the term "miracle" in connection with Jesus, since the latter requires accepting a supernatural interventionist model of God. "Interventions, no. Marvels, yes."[10]

3. Jesus as *wisdom teacher*. Using provocative saying and memorable parables, Jesus taught a subversive and alternative wisdom. Conventional Jewish wisdom was based upon the dynamics of retribution, that is, rewards and punishments. Unlike conventional wisdom teachers, who pass on and sometimes elaborate the received traditions or conventions of a community or group, Jesus invited hearers into a different way of seeing—God, themselves, and life itself. His wisdom teaching invited people to live in the Spirit, to walk a path of transformation centered in the Spirit.

4. Jesus as *social prophet*. Like the social prophets of the Hebrew Bible (Amos, Micah, Jeremiah), Jesus criticized the economic, political, and religious elites of his time. Advocating an alternative social

---

9. Borg, *God We Never Knew*, 89–90. A fuller discussion is found in Borg and Wright, *Meaning of Jesus*, 60–76.

10. Borg and Wright, *Meaning of Jesus*, 67.

vision grounded in the compassion of God, he was often in conflict with authorities. In speaking of the kingdom of God, he used a political metaphor that contrasted existing kingdoms: the kingdom of God is what life would be like on earth if God were king, rather than Herod and Caesar.

5. Jesus as *movement founder*. Jesus brought into being a Jewish renewal or revitalization movement that challenged and shattered the social boundaries of his day, a movement that eventually became the early Christian church. Although his public activity was very brief, Jesus formed an embryonic group whose inclusiveness and egalitarian practice embodied his alternative social vision.

It is not pedagogically acceptable to commingle eschatological and noneschatological perspectives of Jesus. Either his mindset was eschatological or it was not, and for that reason modern scholarship does not allow fence-sitting on the matter. There is no question in my mind that Jesus was clearly driven by current Jewish eschatological expectations and that he organized his ministry around those conceptions. As an eschatological prophet, however, he brought the entire package of prophecy to bear on his task, meaning that through his work and ministry he believed he was inaugurating and embodying the works of the kingdom.

The kingdom need not be seen as a strictly "end-time" phenomenon, however, for in a spiritual sense the kingdom is found in whole nowhere, but in part everywhere. Jesus' first sermon, as recorded in Luke 4:18–21, singles out the marks of the kingdom. In that passage Jesus takes the scroll of the prophet Isaiah and finds the place where it is written: "The Spirit of the Lord is upon me, because he has anointed me to bring good news to the poor. He has sent me to proclaim release to the captives and recovery of sight to the blind, to let the oppressed go free, to proclaim the year of the Lord's favor." After reading he said, "Today this scripture has been fulfilled in your hearing." This passage reveals the manifesto of Jesus, who understood himself as embodying the hopes of the long-awaited Jubilee, which decreed the emancipation of land, slaves, and debts at the end of the seventh sabbatical, an appropriate image of what current Judaism envisioned as the coming reign of God. According to Luke's gospel the kingdom Jesus envisioned is already here, "within us" or "in our midst" (Luke 17:21). While the kingdom was embryonically present in Jesus, it cannot be said to have been fully present in him. As Jesus made clear in his parables, the kingdom is an expanding (unfolding) phenomenon. Like yeast in dough, the kingdom must grow continuously until all is leavened (Matt 13:33; Luke 13:21). Every age must announce its coming and commit fully to its hopeful vision. In every age, all who seek the kingdom are its citizens and every messenger is holy.

Once we understand the Jewishness of Jesus, as well as the Jewishness of Mary his mother, of the apostles, of Paul, and even the Jewishness of all the biblical heroes of the Bible, the next step is to study the Bible—not only the Hebrew scriptures (Old Testament) but the Bible in its entirety—from a Jewish perspective, since every author in the entire Bible was Jewish by birth, and the sole exception, Luke, was a Gentile proselyte to Judaism.

The starting point for this understanding of scripture requires knowing how the Jewish people wrote sacred narratives. That information will help us understand how to interpret the narratives found in the Christian gospels and in the book of Acts. If these Christian writings are primarily Jewish works, then they cannot be understood apart from the Jewish context, the Jewish mindset, the Jewish frame of reference, the Jewish vocabulary, and even the Jewish history that shaped and formed those writers.

In recent times a small group of biblical scholars, spearheaded by the British New Testament scholar Michael D. Goulder and popularized in America by Anglican Bishop John Shelby Spong, have argued that the gospels need to be read as *haggadah*—as edifying fiction—in the midrashic style of the Jewish sacred storyteller, and not as objective descriptions of literal events.

The exegetical methodology termed midrash can be traced back to the return of the Israelite people from their exile in Babylon under the favorable rule of the Persians, beginning with the reign of Cyrus in 539 BCE. Since the context in which the Torah had been written was much different from that of the postexilic period, and because there were so many variations of the Israelite religion due to external cultural influence during this period, the religious authorities felt a need for ongoing adaptation and explanation so that the observance of the Torah could be ensured. There developed two basic types of midrashic literature, *halakhic* and *haggadic*. While the former elucidated the Torah in legal terms, the latter was concerned with homiletic and narrative commentary. With the fall of the temple in 70 CE, the rabbinical scribes took these oral traditions and began transferring them into writing, a process that culminated in the Talmudic writings. Building on this tradition, Jewish exegetes continued to produce a vast and rich written and oral reinterpretation of the Hebrew scriptures.

Thus, in the extensive history of Jewish life and literature, there developed a need for commentary and reinterpretation of traditional texts in light of the ever-changing present situations. Midrash, therefore, is the hermeneutical act of rereading and expanding a text in the form of a new narrative to update the existential meaning. Midrash is both a literary genre and a hermeneutical method, used to explain the deeper meaning of a biblical text. In this sense, midrash performs the function of recontextualizing an already existing text so as to enlarge and enhance its significance in and for the currently existing situational context. Such an approach is not concerned with historic accuracy but with meaning and understanding.

By way of example, consider the biblical notion that God parts the waters to rescue his people. At the Red Sea, parting the waters was the sign that God was with Moses (Exodus 14). Later, when Jewish writers of antiquity interpreted God's presence to be with Joshua after the death of Moses, they repeated the parting of the waters (Joshua 3). As Bishop Spong notes,

> When Joshua was said to have parted the waters of the Jordan River, it was not recounted as a literal event of history; rather it was the *midrashic* attempt to relate Joshua to Moses and thus demonstrate the presence of God with his successor. The same pattern operated later when both Elijah (2 Kings 2:8) and Elisha (2 Kings 2:14) were said to have parted the waters of the Jordan River and to have walked across on dry land. When the story of Jesus' baptism was told, the gospel writers asserted that Jesus parted not the Jordan River, but the heavens. This Moses theme was thus being struck yet again (Mark 1:9–10), and indeed, for a similar purpose. The heavens, according to the Jewish creation story, were nothing but the firmament that separated the waters above from the waters below (Genesis 1:6–8). To portray Jesus as splitting the heavenly waters was a Jewish way of suggesting that the holy God encountered in Jesus went even beyond the God presence that had been met in Moses, Joshua, Elijah, and Elisha. That is the way the *midrashic* principle worked. Stories about heroes of the Jewish past were heightened and retold again and again about heroes of the present moment, not because those same events actually occurred, but because the reality of God

revealed in those moments was like the reality of God known in the past.[11]

According to Spong, we are not reading history when we read the scriptures. "We are listening to the experience of Jewish people, processing in a Jewish way what they believed was a new experience with the God of Israel. Jews filtered every new experience through the corporate remembered history of their people, as that history had been recorded in the Hebrew scriptures of the past."[12]

The same holds true for the gospels. Scholars as far apart on the ideological spectrum as Marcus Borg, John Dominic Crossan, and Robert Gundry agree that many of the narratives in the gospels should be read metaphorically, that is, as symbolic narratives created to illustrate a particular meaning. Starting with the birth narratives in Matthew and Luke and extending to narratives such as the wedding feast at Cana (John 2:1–11) and Peter walking on the water (Matt 14:28–31), all should be viewed as parables rather than as recorded history. From one point of view, these scholars are not telling us anything new, for Christians have always allegorized scripture, finding meaning in texts they no longer viewed as historical. But Borg and like-minded scholars are saying something more. They are not claiming that we must, for modern reasons, reinterpret the old texts in new ways, against their authors' original intentions. Instead they contend that the texts were never intended to be understood literally in the first place. As Crossan notes: "When I looked at the so-called nature miracles of Jesus . . . those stories screamed parable at me, not history, not miracle, but parable. They shouted at me: 'It's a parable, dummy.'"[13]

Roger David Aus, urging that the gospels contain large tracts of *haggadah*, which their Jewish-Christian authors knew to be true only in a less-than-literal sense, has written to similar effect: "It is one of the tragedies of the Christian church that the number of its Palestinian Jewish members dwindled so rapidly after the very successful missionizing of the Gentiles. The latter soon made the former into small sects such as the Palestinian Ebionites. Early Palestinian and later even Hellenistic Jewish Christians, however, could have conveyed to Gentile Christians the nature of Jewish *haggadah*, and the centuries-old Gentile Christian debate

11. Spong, *Liberating the Gospels*, 36–37.
12. Spong, *Liberating the Gospels*, 37.
13. Crossan, *A Long Way*, 167–68.

about the 'historicity' or 'facticity' of *haggadic* sayings or narratives [in the canonical gospels] would have been basically unnecessary."[14]

The first generation of Christians, the vast majority of whom were Jewish, undoubtedly saw *haggadah* at work in the gospel tradition, recognizing certain Jewish antecedents present therein and noting that the authors were filtering their experience of Jesus through the corporate remembered history that had been recorded in the Hebrew scriptures of the past. The confusion of tongues at Babel (Gen 11:1–9) is surely related to the overcoming of that confusion of tongues at Pentecost (Acts 2). The story of Pharaoh seeking to kill the Jewish boy babies in Egypt (Exod 1:22) is surely connected to the story of Herod seeking to kill the Jewish boy babies in Bethlehem (Matt 2:16–18). The story of Moses, who, after meeting God on the mountain, had his face shine so brightly that it had to be covered (Exod 34:29–35), is surely related to the story of Jesus being transfigured so that he too shone with an unearthly radiance (Mark 9:2–8). The account of the Palm Sunday procession (Mark 11:2–10) is surely related to the story in Zechariah (9:9–11) where the king came to Jerusalem, lowly and riding on a donkey.[15]

"As long as the Gospels were read and interpreted only by gentile people," Spong notes wryly, "either these ancient Hebrew connections were unknown or it was assumed that these were nothing but Old Testament foreshadowings of the life of Christ. To believe that these texts are actual anticipations of Jesus meant that Christians had to believe that these verses had been placed into the texts of antiquity by the holy God so that hundreds of years later people would see in Jesus' literal fulfillment of these expectations proof of his divine nature."[16] This distorting, anti-Jewish way of reading the gospels continued unchallenged for centuries. The price that Christians paid for this unquestioning prejudice was "the loss of the essential meaning of the Gospels. For the truth found in the Gospels could be revealed only by reading these texts through a Jewish lens."[17]

The second and third generations of Christians, who tended to be Gentiles, read these Jewish antecedents in the gospel story with a deeply prejudiced anti-Jewish bias that distorted the message of these books.

---

14. Aus, *Death, Burial, and Resurrection*, 291.
15. Spong, *Liberating the Gospels*, 33–34.
16. Spong, *Liberating the Gospels*, 34.
17. Spong, *Liberating the Gospels*, 35.

The reasons for this developing bias are cultural and political. The Jewish War against Rome from 66 to 70 CE, resulting in the fall of Jerusalem, with its destruction of the temple and the priesthood, raised the price of an uneasy accommodation between Jewish and Gentile Christians and resulted, over the next twenty years, in a separation so total and hostile that the Jewish Christians were finally expelled from the synagogues.

Prior to the fateful year 70, Judaism tolerated varieties of opinions within its fold, pluralism always being a byproduct of security. Between years 30 and 70, Jewish followers of Jesus continued worshiping in the synagogues. These people, not yet called Christians, were called the "followers of the way" (Acts 9:2; 19:9, 23; 24:22; cf. 11:26). Before the fall of Jerusalem, it was quite clear that Jesus was being incorporated by Jewish people into their faith story. During that period, within the synagogues, Jewish Christians were at best an enriching new tradition and at worst a minor irritation. But when the survival of this faith tradition was at stake, their level of toleration dissipated perceptibly. Acrimony grew between Jews committed to Jesus and traditional Jews who claimed orthodoxy for their convictions, tying their claims to the belief that the God they worshiped could be found only in the unchanging completeness of the Torah. This shift into a survival mentality set the stage for heightened negativity to develop. After the fall of Jerusalem, many followers of Jesus, both Jewish and Gentile, began to interpret the Roman defeat of the Jews and the loss of the temple as God's punishment of traditional Jews for their rejection of Jesus. Thus the stage was set for hostility. Echoes of this rising hostility can be found overtly in the gospels, particularly in Matthew (21:43; 23:31–38; 27:25). As rhetoric heightened, the lines around what Jews could tolerate within Judaism tightened considerably so that Jewish Christians, offended by this increasing hostility, began to move more and more into Gentile circles.

From that point on, fewer Christians wished to identify with the rigidly orthodox survival mentality that began to characterize Judaism, while fewer Jews wanted to see any aspect of the Jesus tradition left within their faith traditions. The final break occurred in the late 80s, when orthodox Jewish leaders revised their regular worship traditions to include "anathemas" against all who deviated from strict orthodox standards. This revision resulted in the excommunication of Jewish Christians from synagogue life and ultimately from Judaism. Because the gospel of Matthew was written during the expulsion and the gospel of John shortly thereafter, the fourth gospel's blatant negativity toward orthodox Jews

(John 8:44) and its descriptions of exclusion from the synagogues reflect that final fracture (John 9:22; 12:42). By the start of the second century the expelled Jewish Christians faded into increasingly Hellenized and Gentile circles, and thereafter Jewish Christians ceased even to think of themselves as Jews, while those who claimed Jewish identity became more firmly entrenched in their tradition. "The common ground between Jews and Christians, once so powerful, became nonexistent. This hostile negativity toward Jews and all things Jewish has remained dominant in Christianity to this day."[18]

The Gentile reading of the gospels was challenged less and less, until the new way of reading the Hebrew scriptures became viewed as orthodoxy. That created finally the long historical period during which the gospels were cut away from their essential Jewishness. Ignorance joined with prejudice first to distort truth and understanding and then finally to lose altogether the original meaning of the gospels. This ignorance imposed on the gospel texts a non-Jewish literalness that their Jewish authors would never have understood or appreciated. Somewhere around the year 140 CE, the status of the gospels as Jewish descended so low that a man named Marcion actually sought to remove the Hebrew God, every gospel except Luke, and anything else Jewish from Christianity. He failed officially, but succeeded, far more than Christians would recognize, unofficially. As a result of that unofficial success, the gospels were for centuries covered with a negativity to all things Jewish.

An example of this Christian negativity toward things Jewish is the way Christians use the Old Testament even to this day. The primary value the Hebrew sacred story has for most Christians lies in the assumption that the meaning of the Old Testament is exhausted once its task of pointing to and being fulfilled by the New Testament has been accomplished. The prophets were thought to be similar to fortunetellers who served as divine predictors of future events, primarily concerning the life and mission of Jesus.

In the early years of the Christian church, as Christianity spread westward, a spirit of anti-Jewish hatred developed and became so pervasive that the very idea of the gospels as the products of Jewish authors and as a Jewish gift to the world seemed both incomprehensible and even revolting. The Christian church locked itself into certain basic assumptions by which it lived and to which it admitted no challenge. Among these assumptions was that the Bible, especially the gospels, were objectively

18. Spong, *Liberating the Gospels*, 53.

true, that they described events of literal history, and that one could confidently assert that all they contained did in fact happen just as written. This mentality produced a comfortable feeling of security enduring for centuries, until the Enlightenment, which gave birth to rationalism and modern science.

The fact we must acknowledge is that Christianity was not born as a Western religion. A Western mentality has been imposed on this Middle Eastern understanding of the Bible. This mentality, concentrating on an external world, is rooted in time, space, and objectivity. It always seeks to answer historical questions, such as "Is this real?" "Is this objectively true?" Guided by these questions, the Western mind has rarely embraced the truth found in myth, legend, intuition, or poetry. Western questions always require a "yes" or "no" answer. Only begrudgingly will Western mentality admit hesitantly to something. A hesitant "yes" answer is a compromise with both honesty and courage that only postpones the inevitable, while a "no" answer removes spirit, mystery, and meaning from any objective consideration. Thus in the post-Christian contemporary world the "yes" answer produces the passion of the religious right; the hesitant "yes" answer nudges conservatives toward liberalism; and the "no" answer produces the secular humanists, who want to be free of all things religious. We need a better alternative, for there is little hope and little future for the Christian faith in any of these.[19]

If we read the gospels through Western eyes, we end up with Western questions: "Did it really happen?" or "Is it true?" Jewish people, on the other hand, did not relate to sacred history as if it were an objective description of literal events. Instead of asking whether something actually happened, they asked, "What does it mean?" "Why was this image chosen to convey this insight?" Modern readers of the gospels, if they wish to remain true to the intentions of the Jewish originators of that tradition, need to abandon their Western concern about facts while focusing instead on entering the experience lying behind the description in the biblical text.

Compassion, Not Empathy Only

While each of us has different beliefs, experiences, and responses to those around us, as disciples of Jesus, it is important that we start from a place

---

19. Spong, *Liberating the Gospels*, 18–19.

of self-awareness, taking the time to reflect on our own individual life, thinking about our needs, desires, and priorities. As we do this, we also need to reach out to those who come across our path. Soon we discover that we cannot respond to everyone we meet and that we have to start small, with one person we believe God is calling us to help or befriend. Later, we may feel led to join a group or commit to a cause. For the time being, we need to consider the motto Frank Laubach (1884–1970) used when he embarked on his crusade of universal literacy: "Each one teach one," modifying it to "Each one help one."

To begin, we modern disciples may wish to respond with compassion to situations that reflect our own experience, beliefs, and values. As we do, we must be aware that when faced with someone's grief or difficulty, it is often natural to react from our own pain, discomfort, fears, and anxieties. Even though our intention is rarely to hurt someone who is struggling or in pain, we often say and do things that can cause harm. Then, instead of being helpful or making a positive difference, we end up centering on our own needs rather than on the needs of those coming to us for support. In such cases, we need to consider times when we were in pain and someone offered unhelpful advice or platitudes. What did we feel like? What would have been helpful?

As a practice, compassion is not the same as agreement with someone's beliefs, decisions, or even full understanding of their situation. Compassion is making room for someone else's experience to be held with love and acceptance, regardless of our ability to relate to or identify with it. When the impulse to judge or criticize comes up, let us see this as an opportunity to strengthen our compassion muscles by shifting our focus back to the person we need to befriend. Instead of offering advice, we should ask thoughtful questions and listen for understanding. The goal of radical discipleship is not to be right but to remain open and to find ways to be helpful.

If you decide to join a group or local organization in your area already engaged in a cause, ask how you can partner with them and what support would be most helpful. Aim to collaborate, not to recreate what is already in place. If no such group exists, issue an invitation for others to join you. As you continue to grow in compassion, you will grow in your capacity to hold space for the mystical experiences people have, and find ways to meet people in need with love and acceptance. Each time you offer compassion, you move closer to being the kind of person God calls you to be, a radical disciple.

No two life stories, no two life experiences, are alike. We don't need to experience something personally to care for those who do. I may never understand fully what it is like to be a victim of racism, sexism, or classism, but I can choose to respond with compassion when those in need share their stories with me.

When we talk about compassion, we need to be careful not to conflate it with empathy. While empathy involves feeling someone else's experience as our own, which can be overwhelming and even numbing, compassion is a process. Unlike empathy, which often remains passive, compassion is active. All of us can learn to be more compassionate, but doing so requires conviction, self-awareness, reflection, and regular practice.

When someone we don't know tells us of their pain, whether it be mental, emotional, physical, or spiritual, it is easy to say words of comfort and assurance, and even to respond with concern or a hug. But imagine if someone you loved told you their story of suffering due to prejudice, abuse, or injustice. How do you think you would respond? How might you feel, and what might you wish to do to alleviate their pain or rectify their loss?

While talking about being compassionate and getting involved in situations of need might make us uncomfortable, we need to understand that radical discipleship calls us to be imitators of Jesus by taking action, initiating purposeful steps toward cocreating with God a world we long to inhabit, one that supports the human flourishing of all people.

When Jesus declared in John 10:10 that his mission was to bring human beings life, and to ensure that they had life in abundance, what do you suppose he meant? While some might limit the statement to the spiritual life or the afterlife, commonly called "eternal life," let us be clear that the context in John's narrative is that of a shepherd assuring the safety and well-being of his flock. As John 10:9 makes clear, the salvation the shepherd guarantees includes security from predators, freedom of movement, and adequate pasture for grazing, all of these encompassing this-worldly mental, emotional, and physical needs. According to the Bible, humans are created with eternity in mind, but for Jesus, eternal life begins now (see John 3:36 and 6:47). And living fully now involves more than mere survival. Abundant life is joy-filled and fear-free, full of opportunity and hope, and such abundance is as much about the well-being of our neighborhoods, societies, nations, and planet as it is about the state of our individual lives. All are intertwined. If Jesus were to speak as our contemporary about discipleship, he would emphasize that our focus and priorities should be on creating and maintaining societies that ensure for all human beings their fundamental rights to life, liberty, and the pursuit of happiness, conditions necessary for thriving as individuals, families, communities, societies, and nations.

Ultimately, what radical discipleship requires for twenty-first century believers is their response to the question, "If you are called to radical discipleship, how will you respond to those conditions that interfere with a person's or a group's ability to experience abundant life?" In her book, *Mary Magdalene Revealed*, Meggan Watterson writes about "the Christianity we haven't tried yet." Like Jesus, radical disciples are motivated by the possibility of a world guided by compassion and unconditional love and care for others, particularly for those in need (see 1 John 4:19–21). Together, such disciples can embody a radical, collective love they know is within their reach. To those many who feel desperate, alone, ignored, and unloved, radical disciples are God's answer to their prayers. May you and I be the ones for whom the world has been waiting!

Questions for Discussion and Reflection

1. Explain and assess E. P. Sanders's view that Jesus was an apocalyptic prophet standing in the tradition of Jewish restoration theology.

2. If Jesus believed God's eschatological rule or kingdom was imminent, was he also convinced that God's coming rule would end evil on earth and, as a result, bring Israel's story to its climax and human history to its consummation? Explain your answer.

3. If Jesus was an apocalypticist (an eschatological Jewish prophet), can we infer that early Christianity was essentially a continuation of his perspective? Explain your answer.

4. Without belief in Jesus' resurrection from the dead, it is safe to say that Christianity would have been just another failed messianic movement. What role did belief in the general resurrection of humanity from the dead play in apocalyptic theology?

5. In your estimation, are we living in the "last days"? Explain your answer.

6. Explain and assess C. H. Dodd's concept of "realized eschatology."

7. Explain and assess Marcus Borg's and John Dominic Crossan's portrayal of Jesus as a social prophet and compassionate healer rather than as an apocalyptic figure.

8. Modern scholarship is divided regarding Jesus' self-understanding. Some scholars view Jesus to be an apocalyptic prophet, whereas others envision a non-apocalyptic Jesus. Scholars such as Marcus Borg suggests alternative models said to accurately portray Jesus' self-understanding: mystic, healer, wisdom teacher, and social critic. It has become all too easy to see Jesus in one's own image. Some see him as a wandering Cynic, others as a feminist, and still others as social or political liberator. How do you view Jesus, apocalyptically or non-apocalyptically? Explain your answer.

9. In your estimation, what do Christians mean by the phrase "the kingdom of God"? How do popular notions of God's kingdom differ from what Jesus taught and believed about God's kingdom?

10. Explain and assess the view that the gospels need to be read as *haggadah*—as Jewish edifying fiction—and not as objective descriptions of literal events.

11. Explain and assess the views of Goulder, Spong, Aus, and others who argue that Gentile Christianity changed the meaning of Jesus and of how the Christian scriptures should be interpreted and understood.

12. Explain the difference between the Western question regarding the gospels, "What really happened?" or "Are these accounts true"? to the Jewish question, "What do these accounts mean?"

13. Explain the difference between empathy for others and compassion for others and their needs.

14. If Jesus were to appear in our midst today, what would he want us to know about his nature and his mission?

Appendix

Called to Discipleship: A Sermon

Exodus 3:1-14; 13:17-22; Philippians 4:4-7

Today, I want to ask you two questions, both applicable to you individually and to your spiritual community or congregation of worship:

1. "Do you believe God has a purpose for your life?"
2. "If so, are you fulfilling that purpose?"

Let me tell you the faith story of a disciple named Jim Seluta. The beginning of the story is simple and quite common in our society. However, something happened to him that was surprising and altogether uncommon. It is the story of a person who was living comfortably and successfully. He had a happy life with his wife and children, living in a pleasant suburb of Boston, with a secure job as a salesman. But if you asked him the questions I just asked you, he would have given you a perplexed look, for he wouldn't have known what you were talking about. You see, he hadn't received his call to discipleship.

One day, Jim and his wife were invited to a church service, and he reluctantly agreed to attend. Nothing much got his attention there, except for one verse from scripture that he heard. And he couldn't get it out of his head. The verse contained an intriguing idea, for it talked about having peace that "surpasses all understanding." It was a concept that gripped him like a vice, because even though on the whole things were fine in his life, he knew he didn't have this kind of peace.

Since he was a salesperson, one night he was on the road and was staying in a motel. That's when he felt God speaking to him, and he thought again about that church service and about that elusive yet compelling peace "that surpasses understanding."

"Where did that verse come from in the Bible," he wondered? He instinctively reached into the drawer on the nightstand by his bed and there he found a Gideon's Bible. He found a marker in the Bible, so when he opened the Bible the marker indicated that he was in the fourth chapter of the book of Philippians. But more surprising was the fact that someone had underlined one of the verses on that page, Philippians 4:7, and he began to read: "And the peace of God, which surpasses all understanding, will guard your hears and your minds in Christ Jesus."

That was the moment when Jim Seluta knew that God had a purpose for his life. And after hearing that call to discipleship, everything changed in his life. Jim trained to become a minister and later moved to southeastern Pennsylvania, where he became the chaplain at a nursing home and retirement center where my father was living at the time. In fact, Jim was the person who performed my father's funeral some years back.

I believe that God's call upon Jim's life was similar to the call Moses received in the wilderness near Mount Sinai. In both cases, God took the initiative, both individuals were in hiding (Moses from the Pharaoh, certainly, but also from God), and both had an encounter with God that resulted in a change of perspective, where suddenly everything was different. For Moses, the rocky red soil became "holy ground"; a common bush became afire with God; and a humble shepherd's staff was changed to the "rod of God," with which he confronted the Pharaoh, parted the seas, won battles, and drew water from a rock.

The lesson Moses learned by that burning bush and that Jim Seluta learned in that motel room was a simple yet thoroughly profound lesson: that in order to discover our purpose in life, we must encounter God, hear God's voice, and say "yes" to that voice, say "yes" to God's voice and will.

There are many similarities between where Christians are today, individually and corporately, and the story of Moses and the Israelites who left Egypt and embarked on a great adventure, moving toward the Promised Land.

The truth, it seems to me, is that either we have had an encounter with God, or we are in hiding—from God, certainly, but in a profound sense, from our true calling and destiny. However that may be, once we have that encounter with God, once we have assurance that God has called us to discipleship, there are two principles we can follow in order to be sure that the decisions we make along life's way are in accordance with God's will.

1. The first and most important principle in discerning God's will, whether for our lives or in a particular situation, is to *get our initial leading right*. Getting this initial leading right is often not easy. The first thing to do when discerning God's will is to give it time, that is, not to make the decision hastily, and secondly, not allow our instincts to pressure us into making a wrong decision. Our impulses can get us into deep trouble because they are the voice of our own spirit speaking. I'm not referring to the conscience, but rather to the ego, that part of us that wants to assert its independence and pride, that wants its own way.

There's a difference between persuasion and demand. Our own ego demands, circumstances demand, even institutional religion demands. But God persuades. God draws us, like a magnet, in the right direction. In our decision-making, God wants us to be relaxed, not coerced. When making important spiritual decisions, it is important that we slow down and refrain from acting until by prayer, meditation, and through the advice of discerning friends, God gives us a clear direction. Then, once we get our bearings, we must not doubt God's leading.

We read in Exodus that when God's people were delivered out of Egypt, there was a shortcut they could have taken to get to the Promised Land. That shortcut, however, was by way of the land belonging to the Philistines. Undoubtedly Moses knew the geometric axiom about "the shortest distance between two points being a straight line." But God knew that if the Israelites went that way, their first battle would be the hardest of their entire trip. And they wouldn't be ready for it. God knew they would become so frightened that they would follow their impulses and flee, returning to Egypt. Before fighting pitched battles, they had to be hardened by desert travel. In addition, they had to overcome lesser enemies, but most importantly, they had to learn to trust God. And it took them forty years of wandering in the wilderness before they learned their first lesson in discipleship.

2. Thus, it is important first to get our initial leading right, to get on the right road. And then, once we get on the way, we must *stay on the way*, we must *keep the course*.

You might recall John Bunyan's classic story of *The Pilgrim's Progress*. There, it is important for the main character—appropriately called Christian—to traverse strange lands and overcome awesome obstacles.

And his sole means of reaching the goal to his long journey was basically quite simple: to stay on the right road. Of course, in practice that was not always easy.

We are all familiar with the story of *The Wizard of Oz*. In many ways, this is a secular parallel to *Pilgrim's Progress*. As Dorothy and her strange party head for the land of the wizard, they know that they will get there, but only if they "follow the yellow-brick road."

At the beginning of Jesus' ministry, we are told that Satan came to test him, to try to confuse and mislead him. However, Jesus overcame the forces of evil because he was sure of his initial leading, and did not doubt it.

The Israelites, once on the right road, were given certain signs in order that they might stay on the way. The account indicates that a pillar of cloud led them along the way by day, and by night a pillar of fire to give them light, in order that they might be able to travel either by day or by night. And we are told that these signposts never departed from before the people as they traveled through the wilderness.

A story comes to us from the Second World War of a secluded and secure harbor where Allied ships could go to seek shelter. But there was a secret to this harbor. There was only one point of entry that would allow a ship to enter all the way to port in safety. Around this point of entry and along the entire channel were rocks and shoals. And only certain captains knew the secret of guiding their vessels to the innermost safety of that harbor. The secret was three lights or beacons that shone from onshore. The captain had to guide his vessel until all three lights were aligned, and then, when all blended into one beam of light, the captain knew he was on course.

Likewise, God has given us three lights to guide us as we make the important decisions of our lives, and to keep us on course.

1. The first principle, the first light, is *scripture*. No leading from God is ever out of harmony with that which is clear in the scriptures. Our decisions are right when they are in harmony with clear principles in scripture. Some things are obviously wrong, and we should avoid them. If we know something is right, such as loving and serving those in need, forgiving others, and worshipping God, we don't need to pray about these or delay in doing them.

2. The second principle, the second light, is *God's Holy Spirit* within us. Before Jesus was crucified, he told his followers that he would

leave them with a Comforter, with one who would lead them into all truth. It is this Spirit that we must consult for guidance. Our own spirit, our ego, can cause us to act impulsively and unreasonably, but when the Spirit leads us, we receive the peace that "surpasses all understanding," and are led to do that which is ultimately right and reasonable.

3. The third principle, the third beacon of guidance, is *circumstances*. God has the ability to work all things together for good. And God's timing is always impeccable! Those who follow Jesus and the leading of God will discover that the right door opens at the right time. Furthermore, God never give us a burden for something we cannot do, or asks us to pursue something we are not intended to accomplish. Disciples are asked to knock and wait, and God will open the door at the right time.

As we remember these principles, let us remember that they work together in harmony. If we are guided only by circumstances, then, like Jonah, we may discover that we are on the wrong boat. If we are guided only by the Spirit, it is possible that we might be led by the wrong spirit. And if we use as our guide and compass only the scriptures, we may have nothing more than dry literalism and dead orthodoxy. However, when our decisions are supported by these three factors, working together in unity, then we will be in the light. Through the inner process of discipleship, led by the Spirit and guided by the life and teachings of Jesus, we find we are on the road marked "Right," and on that road we experience, with Moses and Reverend Seluta, the peace that "surpasses all understanding."

Bibliography

Allen, Diogenes. *Christian Belief in a Postmodern World: The Full Wealth of Conviction.* Louisville, KY: Westminster John Knox, 1989.
Allison, Dale C., Jr. *Constructing Jesus.* Grand Rapids, MI: Baker, 2010.
———. *The Historical Christ and the Theological Jesus.* Grand Rapids, MI: Eerdmans, 2009.
———. *Jesus of Nazareth: Millenarian Prophet.* Minneapolis, MN: Fortress, 1998.
Aus, Roger David. *The Death, Burial, and Resurrection of Jesus, and the Death, Burial, and Translation of Moses in Judaic Tradition.* Lantham MD: University Press of America, 2008.
Baillie, Donald M. *God Was in Christ.* New York: Charles Scribner's Sons, 1948.
Bass, Diana Butler. *Freeing Jesus: Rediscovering Jesus as Friend, Teacher, Savior, Lord, Way, and Presence.* New York: HarperOne, 2021.
Bass, Diana Butler, and Brian McLaren. "Christianity Is Many Things." In *Learning How to See* (May 20, 2022). No pages. Online: cac.org/podcast/Christianity-is-many-things/.
Bergsma, John. *Jesus and the Dead Sea Scrolls: Revealing the Jewish Roots of Christianity.* New York: Image, 2019.
Borg, Marcus J. *The God We Never Knew.* San Francisco: HarperSanFrancisco, 1998.
———. *The Heart of Christianity: Rediscovering a Life of Faith.* San Francisco: HarperSanFrancisco, 2003.
———. *Meeting Jesus Again for the First Time.* San Francisco: HarperSanFrancisco, 1995.
———. *Reading the Bible Again for the First Time.* San Francisco: HarperSanFrancisco, 2002.
Borg, Marcus J., and N. T. Wright. *The Meaning of Jesus: Two Visions.* San Francisco: HarperSanFrancisco, 2000.
Caird, G. B. *The Language and Imagery of the Bible.* Philadelphia: Westminster, 1980.
Campbell, Joseph. *The Power of Myth: with Bill Moyers.* New York: Doubleday, 1988.
Conzelmann, Hans. *The Theology of St. Luke.* 2nd ed. Translated by Geoffrey Buswell. Philadelphia: Fortress, 1982.
Craddock, Fred B. *Luke.* Interpretation: A Bible Commentary for Teaching and Preaching. Louisville: John Knox, 1990.
Creed, John M. *The Divinity of Jesus Christ.* Fontana ed. London: Collins, 1964 [1938].
Cronon, William, "Only Connect . . ." *The American Scholar* 67, No. 4 (1998) 73–80.

Crossan, John Dominic. *The Birth of Christianity.* San Francisco: HarperSanFrancisco, 1998.

———. *A Long Way from Tipperary: A Memoir.* San Francisco: HarperSanFrancisco, 2000.

Crossan, John Dominic, and Richard G. Watts. *Who Is Jesus? Answers to Your Questions About the Historical Jesus.* Louisville, KY: Westminster John Knox, 1996.

Ehrman, Bart D. *Jesus: Apocalyptic Prophet of the New Millennium.* New York: Oxford University Press, 1999.

Haberer, Jack. *Godviews: The Convictions that Drive Us and Divide Us.* Louisville: Westminster John Knox, 2001.

Hauerwas, Stanley, and William H. Willimon. *Resident Aliens: Life in the Christian Colony.* Nashville: Abingdon, 1989.

Haught, John F. *Deeper Than Darwin: The Prospect for Religion in the Age of Evolution.* Boulder, CO: Westview, 2003.

———. *God After Darwin: A Theology of Evolution.* Boulder, CO: Westview, 2000.

———. *Responses to 101 Questions on God and Evolution.* Mahwah, NJ: Paulist, 2001.

———. *Science and Religion: From Conflict to Conversation.* Mahwah, NJ: Paulist, 1995.

Hawking, Stephen, and Leonard Mlodinow. *The Grand Design.* New York: Bantam, 2010.

Holmes, Urban T. *The History of Christian Spirituality.* New York: Seabury, 1980.

Jung, Carl G. *AION: Researches into the Phenomenology of the Self.* In *Collected Works*, 9:2. New York: Pantheon, 1953.

Keirsey, David, and Marilyn Bates. *Please Understand Me: Character & Temperament Types.* Del Mar, CA: Prometheus Nemesis, 1978.

McKibben, Bill. *Falter: Has the Human Game Begun to Play Itself Out?* New York: Holt, 2019.

McLaren, Brian. *Faith After Doubt: Why Your Beliefs Stopped Working and What to Do About It.* New York: St. Martin's, 2021.

McLaren, Brian, and Gareth Higgins. *The Seventh Story: Us, Them, and the End of Violence.* Cleveland, TN: Porch, 2018

Neill, Stephen, *The Interpretation of the New Testament.* New York: Oxford University Press, 1966.

Palmer, Helen. *The Enneagram: Understanding Yourself and the Others in Your Life.* San Francisco: HarperSanFrancisco, 1991.

Purves, Andrew. *Reconstructing Pastoral Theology: A Christological Foundation.* Louisville, KY: Westminster John Knox, 2004.

Ray, Roger L. *Progressive Conversations: Essays on Matters of Social Justice for Critical Thinkers.* Eugene, OR: Resource, 2016.

———. *Progressive Faith and Practice: Thou Shalt Not Stand Idly By.* Eugene, OR: Wipf & Stock, 2014.

Richardson, Peter Tufts. *Four Spiritualities.* Palo Alto, CA: Davies-Black, 1996.

Robinson, John A. T. *Jesus and His Coming.* 2nd ed. Philadelphia: Westminster, 1979.

Rohr, Richard. *Eager to Love: The Alternative Way of Francis of Assisi.* Cincinnati, OH: Franciscan Media, 2014.

———. *Falling Upward: A Spirituality for the Two Halves of Life.* San Francisco: Jossey-Bass, 2011.

———. *The Good News According to Luke.* New York: Crossroad, 1997.

———. *Immortal Diamond: The Search for Our True Self*. San Francisco: Jossey-Bass, 2013.
———. *The Naked Now: Learning to See as the Mystics See*. New York: Crossroad, 2009.
———. *The Universal Christ*. New York: Convergent, 2019.
Sagan, Carl. *The Demon-Haunted World: Science as a Candle in the Dark*. New York: Random House, 1995.
Sanders, E. P. *Jesus and Judaism*. Philadelphia: Fortress, 1985.
———. "Jesus: His Religious Type," *Reflections* 87 (1992) 4–12.
Schneider, Robert J. "Science and Faith: Perspectives on Christianity and Science." No pages. Online: http://community.berea.edu/scienceandfaith/default.asp.
Smith, Huston. *Forgotten Truth: The Common Vision of the World's Religions*. San Francisco: HarperSanFrancisco, 1992 (1976).
———. *The World's Religions*. Rev. 2nd ed. San Francisco: HarperSanFrancisco, 1991.
Spong, John Shelby. *Liberating the Gospels: Reading the Bible with Jewish Eyes*. San Francisco: HarperSanFrancisco, 1996.
———. *This Hebrew Lord: A Bishop's Search for the Authentic Jesus*. New York: HarperOne, 1993.
———. *Why Christianity Must Change or Die: A Bishop Speaks to Believers in Exile*. New York: HarperOne, 1999.
Tailor, Monalisa, and Stillman, Michael. "Dead Man Walking." *New England Journal of Medicine* (November 14, 2013) 1880–81.
Thurmond, Howard. *Jesus and the Disinherited*. Boston: Beacon, 1996.
Vande Kappelle, Robert P. *Beyond Belief: Faith, Science, and the Value of Unknowing*. Eugene, OR: Wipf & Stock, 2012.
———. *Dark Splendor: Spiritual Fitness for the Second Half of Life*. Eugene, OR: Resource, 2015.
———. *In the Potter's Workshop: Experiencing the Divine Presence in Everyday Life*. Eugene, OR: Wipf & Stock, 2019.
———. *Into Thin Places: One Man's Search for the Center*. Eugene, OR: Resource, 2010.
———. *Power Revealed: The Message of Luke–Acts, Then and Now*. Eugene, OR: Wipf & Stock, 2019.
———. *The Scandal of Divine Love: A Study on Biblical Christology for Skeptics, Seekers, and Survivors*. Eugene, OR: Wipf & Stock, 2017.
———. *Securing Life: The Enduring Message of the Bible*. Eugene, OR: Wipf & Stock, 2016.
———. *Walking on Water: Living into a New Way of Thinking*. Eugene, OR: Wipf & Stock, 2020.
Watterson, Meggan. *Mary Magdalene Revealed: The First Apostle, Her Feminist Gospel, and the Christianity We Haven't Tried Yet*. Carlsbad, CA: Hay House, 2019.
Whitehead, Alfred North. *Science and the Modern World*. New York: Free Press, 1967.
Witherington, Ben, III. *The Acts of the Apostles: A Socio-Rhetorical Commentary*. Grand Rapids, MI: Eerdmans, 1998.
———. *Jesus the Sage: The Pilgrimage of Wisdom*. Minneapolis: Fortress, 1994.
Yoder, John Howard. *The Politics of Jesus*. Grand Rapids, MI: Eerdmans, 1972.

Index

afterlife, 2
Allison, Dale, 171, 172
Aquinas, Thomas, 5, 92
Aristotle, 22, 33
Armstrong, Karen, 133
Augustine, 5, 77, 89, 92
Aus, Roger David, 177

Bacon, Francis, 4, 5
Barth, Karl, 92, 101
Basil of Caesarea, 23
Bass, Diana Butler, 43
belief, 3, 90, 125–26
Bible. *See* scripture
Blake, William, 105
Bonhoeffer, Dietrich, 16, 113, 132, 133
Borg, Marcus, 94, 95, 133, 172–73, 177
Brunner, Emil, 100
Buber, Martin, 97
Buechner, Frederick, 97
Bultmann, Rudolph, 132, 133
Bunyan, John, 189
Burke, Billy, 160

Calvin, John, 5
Campbell, Joseph, 85
Carey, William, 23
Castro, Fidel, 129
Chabad-Lubavitch, 83–84
Chalcedon, 4, 15, 16
Christendom, xi, 12, 14, 17
Christian(s), ix, x, xi, 1, 7, 90, 96, 98, 124–25, 126, 178–80
  life, 2, 150
  as transforming agents, x
Christianity, x, 1, 2, 14, 15, 21, 75, 85, 87, 92, 98, 103, 105, 124, 125, 134, 150, 180, 181
  as "The Way," 85
Christology, 14, 15, 16, 19, 55
  definition of, 14–15
church, 126
  definition of, 126
civil rights, 112–13
climate change, 118–21
compassion, 23, 103, 109, 116, 155, 156, 161, 181–83, 184
Constantine, 14
conversion, 106
Conzelmann, Hans, 45–46
Cook, Robert, 56, 130
Copland, Kenneth, 159
Creed, J. M., 16
Cronon, William, 6
Crossan, John Dominic, 133, 171, 177

D'Arcy, Paula, 97
Darwin, Charles, 3, 17
Dawkins, Richard, 131, 133
Day, Dorothy, 113
democracy, 8, 10–11, 22, 25, 108, 115, 117
Dickens, Charles, 1
disciple, discipleship, ix, 103, 127, 138, 147, 148, 149, 157, 160, 164, 184
  communal, ix
  definition of, ix, 103, 124, 140, 150

disciple, discipleship (*continued*)
    as divine calling, 127
    examples of, 124–64
    as imitation, 39, 70
    in Luke–Acts, 44–53, 56–62
    modern, 181–84
    and New Testament usage, 41
    as participation, 39, 70
    and personality, 25–37
    radical, ix, xi, 62, 72, 81, 98, 124, 126, 127, 150, 182, 184
    in scripture, 37, 39–62
Dodd, C. H., 171
dualism, x, 106, 137n3

elegance, 11–12
Enlightenment, 2, 19, 88, 181
Enneagram, the, 35–37, 129, 140
    definition of, 36
environmental care, 117–22, 148–49
eschatology, 167
    apocalyptic, 84n1
    definition of, 169
    Jewish, 167–71
    realized, 171
Essenes, 84, 85
Eusebius, 14
experimentation, 9–10

faith, 2, 76, 81, 87–90, 136, 148
    and belief, 2, 76, 87–88, 89
    as faithfulness, 88
    healing, 160
    journey of, 131–38, 150
    leap of, 90
    as trust, 88, 89
    as vision, 89
False Self, x, 69, 70–76, 80
    definition of, 69
first half of life, 31, 72, 123, 125, 126, 127, 137
Francis of Assisi, x, 152

Galen, 32, 33
Galileo Galilei, 4, 5
Gandhi, Mohandas, 8, 113
Gestalt Pastoral Care (GPC), 141, 142–43

Gilbert, Alfred, 155
God, 14, 40, 74–75, 90–98, 102, 132, 149–50, 152, 153, 158, 160, 161, 187–91
    as Abba, 97
    belief in, 3, 90, 91, 158, 167
    as creator, 3, 91, 95
    existence of, 91
    glorifying, 148, 162
    as Ground of Being, 96
    image of, 22, 39–40, 107
    living for, 161–64
    loving, 41, 148, 152, 157
    as loving Presence, 87, 97, 98, 151
    as Monarch, 94, 95, 98
    as personal, 91–92, 97, 98, 134
    as Persuasive Lover, 93
    as Spirit, 94–96
    as Totally Other, 92
    as transpersonal, 98
Good Samaritan, parable of, 23, 58
Goodell, Jeff, 120
Great Commandment, the, 23, 41, 58, 86, 102, 116, 126, 145, 151
gun violence, 111
Gundry, Robert, 177
Gurdjieff, George, 35–36

Haberer, Jack, 27
Hansen, James, 120
Hasidic Judaism, Hasidism, 83
healthcare, 23, 113–14, 115–16
Hick, John, 133
Hillel, Rabbi, 102
Hindu, Hinduism, 27–28, 105, 129
Hippocrates, 32, 33
Hodge, Charles, 5
Holmes, Urban, 26
Holy Spirit, 5, 40, 41, 55, 70, 71, 75, 76, 91, 94–96, 103, 141, 142, 148, 150, 152, 153, 160, 174, 191–92
humility, 9

imagination, 7
incarnation, the, 76–79

first, 77
second, 77
third, 77
intuition, 7

James, William, 99–100
Jesus, ix, 1, 14, 15, 72, 105, 116, 125, 143, 149, 158, 172, 183–84
    as apocalyptic prophet, 64–66, 67, 168–72, 174–75
    as archetype of the self, 69–81
    ascension of, 78
    and caring for the environment, 107, 117–22
    and current political issues, 105, 107, 108
    death and resurrection of, 70–76
    and discipleship, 39, 40, 41, 42
    divinity of, 12, 15, 17, 67
    and evil, 51–52
    following, xi, 39, 48, 76, 103, 146, 147
    as healer, 173
    historical, x, 12, 55, 86, 101, 108, 124, 127, 167–75
    humanity of, 12, 17–19, 20–21, 67, 74, 151
    imitating, xi, 183
    incarnation of, 76, 77
    influence of, 21–23
    and John the Baptist, 84, 85
    as mentor, 12, 125, 143, 162, 163
    as Messiah, 52
    and nondualism, x, 107
    as our contemporary, 83, 85, 86, 97, 107, 108, 112, 116, 121, 183–84
    as prophet, 47, 173–74
    relationship with, 148, 149, 158
    as Savior, 44–46, 75
    as Servant of God, 50–51
    as shepherd, 183
    and social justice, 107, 112–17
    as Son of God, 44, 55, 74
    as Son of Man, 44, 65n5, 66
    as Spirit person, 99, 173
    as teacher, 173
    titles for, 15
    two natures of, 16
    understanding of, 43
    and walking on water, 20–21
John, gospel of, xi, 12, 19, 42, 44, 63, 69, 70, 74, 75, 77, 80
John the Baptist, 41, 59, 72, 84, 85, 171
Jung, Carl, 25, 27, 28, 30, 31, 75

Keirsey, David, 33, 34, 129
Kierkegaard, Søren, 14, 90
King, Jr., Martin Luther, 8, 23, 113
kingdom of God, 51, 55, 56, 57–58, 59, 60, 62–66, 106, 126, 146, 163, 168, 169–71, 172, 174, 175
    definition of, 63
Kuhn, Thomas, 11

Laubach, Frank, 182
lobbying legislators, 111, 114
Loftus, John W., 131
Luke-Acts, books of
    discipleship in, 44–53, 56–62
    servanthood in, 49–50
    table fellowship in, 49, 61
Luther, Martin, 41

Mandela, Nelson, 113
Marcion, 180
Mary and Martha account, 58–59
Mary Magdalene, 73, 80, 143, 184
McKibben, Bill, 117, 118
McLaren, Brian, xi, 63–64, 133
Merton, Thomas, 153
Metzger, Bruce, 130
midrash, 175–78
military roles and spending, 109–10, 115
mindfulness, 105
minimum wage, 116
Mother Teresa, 23
Myers-Briggs Type Inventory (MBTI), 28–32, 33, 34, 129
myth, mythology, 20, 21, 73, 132, 138

Neil, Stephen, 19

Nicene Creed, 15
Niles, D. T., 140
Norberg, Tilda, 142
nuclear weapons, 110

original sin, doctrine of, 156
Otto, Rudolph, 73

Palmer, Helen, 37
panentheism, 92, 93, 94, 100, 132, 134–35, 138
    definition of, 93, 134–35
Pascal, Blaise, 90
Paul (apostle), 16, 18, 41, 45, 46, 60, 61, 74, 78, 100, 102, 107, 126, 169, 170, 171
Paulus, Heinrich, 19, 20
peacemaking, 81, 109
Pence, Mike, 138
personality. *See* discipleship and personality
Plato, 22, 33
Plotkin, Bill, 137
Postcritical Paradigm, 2–3, 98, 99
poverty, 116–17
Precritical Paradigm, 1–2, 3, 98
Prejean, Helen, 113
Purves, Andrew, 70

racism, xi, 2, 22, 107, 108, 113, 147, 183
Ray, Roger, 108n1, 113
religion, 7, 75, 85–86, 96, 125, 151
    definition of, 74, 85–86
    healthy, 86–87
    junk, 86
    role of, 85
    and science, 1, 3–12, 125
Resurrection, 74, 75, 76, 79, 81
    general, 170
revelation
    general, 100
    special, 100
    verbal, 101
reverence/awe, 8, 121
Richardson, Peter Tufts, 31–32
Robinson, John A. T., 132, 168
Rohr, Richard, 153

Romero, Oscar, 113

Sagan, Carl, 6
salvation, 44–46, 73, 125
Sanders, E. P., 168
Satan, 69, 75, 172
Schneerson, Menachem Mendel, 83–84
science, 3, 6–7
    and religion, 1, 3–12, 125, 134
scripture, 2, 4, 21, 43, 57, 98–103, 138, 153, 159, 163, 164, 174, 190, 191
    discipleship in, 37, 39–62
    as fallible, 101
    as historical product, 98–99
    inspiration of, 10
    interpretation of, 4, 43, 125, 134, 159, 175, 180–81
    as means of revelation, 100–101
    as metaphor, 99
    as midrash, 175–78
    as sacrament, 99
    as sacred, 98, 99
    and story theology, 102–3
    as Word of God, 101
second half of life, 31, 124, 126, 136–38
self-criticism, 7–8
Sermon on the Mount, 50, 51, 65, 146
Shaftsbury, Lord, 23, 155
Sheldon, Charles, 67
"sign" of Jonah, 59, 72
sin, xi, 74, 95, 96
Singh, Kathleen Dowling, 73
Smith, Huston, 27
soul, 138
spirit, 8, 86
spirituality, xi, 8, 85, 105, 138
    and personality, 26–28
Spong, John Shelby, 96, 133, 175, 176, 177, 178
Strauss, David Friedrich, 19–21

Teilhard de Chardin, Pierre, 16
temperament, 26, 32–35
Teresa of Ávila, 147

Tertullian, 4
Thoreau, Henry David, 121
Tillich, Paul, 96, 132, 133
Trinity, 14, 16, 17, 96, 160
True Self, x, 69, 70–76, 79, 80, 81, 100, 152
    definition of, 69
Two Books, 4–6

Watterson, Meggan, 184
White, Andrew Dickson, 3
Whitehead, Alfred North, 4, 92, 93
Wilberforce, William, 23
Wood, Robert W., 10
Wright, N. T., 171

www.ingramcontent.com/pod-product-compliance
Lightning Source LLC
Chambersburg PA
CBHW060609230426
43670CB00011B/2035